Strategies of Multinational Corporations and Social Regulations

Xavier Richet • Violaine Delteil •
Patrick Dieuaide
Editors

Strategies of Multinational Corporations and Social Regulations

European and Asian Perspectives

Editors
Xavier Richet
Violaine Delteil
Patrick Dieuaide
Département des Etudes Européennes
Université Sorbonne Nouvelle-Paris 3
  Institut d'Etudes Européennes
Paris
France

ISBN 978-3-642-41368-1   ISBN 978-3-642-41369-8 (eBook)
DOI 10.1007/978-3-642-41369-8
Springer Heidelberg New York Dordrecht London

Library of Congress Control Number: 2014934296

© Springer-Verlag Berlin Heidelberg 2014

This work is subject to copyright. All rights are reserved by the Publisher, whether the whole or part of the material is concerned, specifically the rights of translation, reprinting, reuse of illustrations, recitation, broadcasting, reproduction on microfilms or in any other physical way, and transmission or information storage and retrieval, electronic adaptation, computer software, or by similar or dissimilar methodology now known or hereafter developed. Exempted from this legal reservation are brief excerpts in connection with reviews or scholarly analysis or material supplied specifically for the purpose of being entered and executed on a computer system, for exclusive use by the purchaser of the work. Duplication of this publication or parts thereof is permitted only under the provisions of the Copyright Law of the Publisher's location, in its current version, and permission for use must always be obtained from Springer. Permissions for use may be obtained through RightsLink at the Copyright Clearance Center. Violations are liable to prosecution under the respective Copyright Law.

The use of general descriptive names, registered names, trademarks, service marks, etc. in this publication does not imply, even in the absence of a specific statement, that such names are exempt from the relevant protective laws and regulations and therefore free for general use.

While the advice and information in this book are believed to be true and accurate at the date of publication, neither the authors nor the editors nor the publisher can accept any legal responsibility for any errors or omissions that may be made. The publisher makes no warranty, express or implied, with respect to the material contained herein.

Printed on acid-free paper

Springer is part of Springer Science+Business Media (www.springer.com)

Contents

1 Introduction 1
  Violaine Delteil, Patrick Dieuaide, and Xavier Richet

Part I FDI Flows and Institutional Dynamics in Europe and Asia

2 Catching-Up and Integration in New and Future EU
  Member States Through FDI 19
  Srdjan Redzepagic and Xavier Richet

3 The Internationalisation of Chinese Firms: Growth,
  Motivations and Strategies 37
  Xavier Richet

**Part II Redesigning of Public Policies to Meet Competitiveness
and Attractiveness Challenges, While Dealing with
Business Lobbying**

4 From Dirigisme to Realism: Chinese Industrial Policy
  in the Era of Globalisation 57
  Jean-François Huchet

5 Indian Firms in World Production: The State, Markets,
  and Innovation 77
  Joël Ruet

6 Joint Ventures, Technology Acquisition and Emerging
  Multinationals: The Case of the Chinese Automotive
  Industry 93
  Giovanni Balcet

7 Multinational Corporations, Sub-national Governance
  and Human Resources: A Cross-national Comparison
  for Europe 107
  Phil Almond, Anthony Ferner, Maria Gonzalez Menendez,
  Jonathan Lavelle, David Luque Balbona, and Sinead Monaghan

Part III   Multinational Companies Across Home and Host Countries: Transfer, Hybridization, Adaptation of Business Model and Labour Relations ?

8   Internationalisation Process, HRM Strategy and Transfer in Chinese MNCs' Subsidiaries in the UK 125
    Miao Zhang, Christine Edwards, and Jiaying Ma

9   Between Europe and Asia: Labour Relations in German Companies in Russia and China 137
    Martin Krzywdzinski

10 The Revival of State Interventionism and European Industrial Relations: Some Lessons from a Survey 155
    Patrick Dieuaide

Part IV   Reshaping Industrial Relations and Labour Activism in Multinational Companies

11 Guangdong Economic Rebalancing and Its Implication for the Labor Market 175
    Stéphane Cieniewski

12 New Social Conflicts in the Guangdong Province: Historical and Sociological Perspectives 193
    Jean Ruffier

13 The Dynamics and Dilemma of Workplace Trade Union Reform in China: The Case of Honda Workers' Strike 203
    Chris King-Chi Chan and Elaine Sio-Ieng Hui

14 Domestic Labor Regulation and Foreign Business Influence: The Case of the Guangdong "Transnational Capitalism" 219
    Violaine Delteil

Introduction

Violaine Delteil, Patrick Dieuaide, and Xavier Richet

This book examines the place and the role of multinational corporations (MNCs) in the growth and development of the economies of the EU and emerging countries (China, India and the CEECs). It covers both European MNCs investing in Asia, as well as American and Asian firms operating in Europe. Location choices, motivations and strategies are discussed, by considering their impact on the transformation and adaptation of these economies, on new specialisations, their consequences for social relations and the local environment.

1.1 FDI as a Vector of Modernisation and Up-grading

Foreign Direct Investment (FDI) is both a factor and a result of globalisation. Its growth has followed directly from the liberalisation of capital movements and the opening of economies to foreign firms. At the same time, FDI has shaped the characteristics of globalisation, which henceforth concerns trade as much as production. FDI is a leading factor in this process, via investment strategies by MNCs which shift capital to new areas. They do so in search of markets, and to benefit from more abundant physical and human resources, at lower costs, in order to take advantage of more permissive institutional systems, or to overcome trade barriers. FDI thus facilitates the emergence of new specialisations and contributes to the internationalisation of the value chain.

In transition and emerging economies, FDI brings with it a new organisational model within firms (the OLI paradigm). It does so by rapidly raising local standards of MNC affiliates (or greenfield establishments) to those prevailing in the MNCs' home countries (the organisation of production, product quality, catching-up and up-grading, the training of labour). Positive externalities are numerous, including

---

V. Delteil (✉) • P. Dieuaide • X. Richet
Department for European Studies, Université Sorbonne Nouvelle-Paris 3, Research Center on Integration and Cooperation in the European Area, (ICEE), 13 Rue Santeuil, 75005 Paris, France
e-mail: viodelteil@hotmail.com; patrick.dieuaide@univ-paris3.fr; xrichet@gmail.com

spin-offs, the development of subcontracting, the in-depth transformation of local industry, the impact on the labour market (turnover, and pay policy), and the development of foreign trade favouring higher value-added exports. These effects explain why host economies pursue proactive policies to attract FDI.

The presence of MNCs also generates negative externalities when it leads to dualism between companies with foreign (or mixed) capital and domestic firms; creates pressures in local labour markets (wages tend to be higher than in domestic firms, but work intensity is also greater); and puts pressure on public finances associated with "friendly" yet costly policies to attract investments (tax rebates on production, on the repatriation of profits and on wages).[1] The presence of abundant labour which is little constrained (absence or low levels of unionisation, low levels of regulation and taxation on payrolls) is also an important factor in the choice of locating activity abroad.

As part of this study, we have focused on economic areas that have experienced significant developments in recent decades: the post-socialist economies of Central and Eastern Europe on the one hand, and the two emerging economies of Asia – China and India – on the other hand.

To differing degrees, foreign direct investment has played a non-negligible role in the adjustment and modernisation strategies of industry, in the development of new business models, and lastly in relations between companies, governments and social partners.

1.2 Eastern Europe, China and India: A Variety of Business Models

FDI has played a non-negligible role in the modernisation and adjustment of East European economies during the last quarter-century. These economies had been administered and autarkic, oriented towards the former Soviet Union. They were transformed into market economies in scarcely 15 years for the most part, and entered the European Union. Apart from micro- and macroeconomic adjustments, these economies have undertaken profound institutional change (democratisation, the spread of the rule of law, as well as changes in institutional and social systems). Within this framework, FDI and MNCs played an important role in transforming their productive apparatus, in parallel to measures privatising companies. MNCs were able to enter a number of sectors, either by buying up and restructuring existing assets or through greenfield investments. In both cases, FDI was undertaken to achieve several objectives: market growth, integration into regional value chains via the relocation of operations (the car industry), the development of low-cost activities to meet the specific needs of local markets or accede to other

---

[1] This occurs not only in emerging countries of the South. See Richard Brooks (2013), *The Great Tax Robbery: How Britain Became a Tax Haven for Fat Cats and Big Business*, Oneworld Publications.

similar markets (Renault-Dacia). Several consequences follow from this massive presence of FDI: the reshaping of the regional, industrial and social landscape: strong hierarchical links with West European (EU-15) companies: the weakness of national controls on foreign capital operating in these countries.

Within a few years, Eastern Europe thus shifted from a quasi-autarkic model (the "bloc autarky" of the Soviet era) to a model with semi-dependent economies while the share of foreign capital in gross fixed capital formation (GFCF), and in exports is significant. The dependence of local industries on large Western firms from the EU-15 is manifest. New industrial belts developed around Warsaw, Krakow-Katowice, Bratislava, Budapest-Györ, the product of massive foreign investment in the region. This dependency is even clearer in the banking sector, in which 80 % of capital (the regional average) came under foreign ownership.

"National accumulation" is focused around a few formal monopolies setup during the socialist era, and which have escaped privatisation. They include energy, electricity and telephony. At the same time, sectors with high value-added are at present largely controlled by foreign firms. The sustained contraction of growth in the EU-28, and especially the euro area could have negative and durable effects on employment, notably in sectors like the car industry and finance.

In emerging Asian countries, in particular China and India, FDI has played a very different role. It is notable in China, but much more modest in India.

In China, even if its share of GFCF has been remained modest, FDI has played a decisive role in the modernisation and upgrading of sectors deemed to be priorities by central government, especially during the 1990s. These sectors include the car industry, electronics and some capital equipment industries. FDI has induced strong spin-offs within China's industrial fabric, in and around industries (cluster effects). This has favoured the emergence of new domestic firms and the appropriation of technological and managerial know-how. The resulting technology transfer has been facilitated by various government support policies that fit in with a coherent industrial project, including: the selection of industries, the required levels of investments demanded of foreign firms in research & development, as well as the location of investment in regions chosen by central government. Another factor which contributes to this success has been the competitive environment, including: the multitude of property types (state, private and foreign firms), and low entry barriers in several industries.

It may be asked whether FDI is still the main driver of the modernisation of the Chinese industry. There is indeed a reassessment of FDI in China today, which considers that MNCs limit the transfer of more-easily protected technology, since China has joined the WTO. For western companies, advanced cooperation with Chinese firms has led to a degree of knowledge whereby they have emerged as a risk in the long run.[2]

---

[2] See Françoise Hay, Christian Milleli, Yunnan Shi (2013), *Faut-il encore investir en Chine? Opportunités, risques et logiques économiques*, L'Harmattan, Questions contemporaines.

India has seen a somewhat different business model develop. It is equally characterised by the internationalisation of firms, especially in high technology sectors. In contrast to China, India has been more reticent about the entry of FDI. Indian firms are autonomous *vis-à-vis* the State, compared to Chinese companies. Yet, with the opening of the Indian economy during the 1990s, and with active support by the State, Indian firms have cooperated with MNCs on a give-and-take basis. Large Indian companies, especially in the car industry, have cooperated with large foreign firms allowing the latter to access a vast market and giving them the opportunity to experiment in low-cost products. In exchange, MNCs have provided technologies that Indian firms were lacking in high value-added segments of production.

1.3 In Contrast with the CEECs, State-Industry Relations Are Ever-Present in China and India

In the CEECs, economic liberalism was advocated by the international institutions at the beginning of the transition. Subsequently, the demands of the EU also weighed with substantial force on challenging the role of the State in the economy. Sweeping away socialist interventionism, the political elites which had converted to liberalism (either profoundly or superficially) clearly worked towards a marked process of state disintermediation. This occurred against the backdrop of deficits in natural resources, and vast privatization programmes that were open to foreign investors. While some countries did proceed more gradually in order to protect national capital (the Czech Republic along with Slovenia, and to a lesser extent Poland), state ownership was progressively reduced to a minimum. Given EU policy constraints, spearheaded by competition policy, CEEC governments lost significant powers to intervene directly to support modernisation and the up-market shift of their companies. These tasks were largely delegated to foreign investors. Closely linked to the objective of attracting FDI, States chose instead to shape the permissive institutional environment as of the mid-1990s. On top of competitive tax reduction policies (strong cuts in corporate and income tax rates, tax exemptions, etc.) policies to control the cost of labour and raise job market flexibility were implemented to varying degrees. During the 2000s, East European States sought to strengthen their territorial competitiveness, following the example of West European States. Supported by structural funds, cluster policies have only affected a limited number of areas and have only produced significant effects in the most dynamic regions in which FDI has been important. The crisis in 2008 seems to have strengthened the desire by certain States to adopt more interventionist strategies (aid or tax exemptions in the car industry, targeted especially on green technologies). Such proactive policies have nevertheless run up against two obstacles, namely EU opposition to State aid, and the growing opposition in civil society with respect to State interventionism favouring sectors that are in the hands of foreigners.

This sharp decline in State intervention in Eastern Europe has led to the emergence of neoliberal States with limited resources, and contrasts strongly with the adjustment and redefinition of the role of the State in China and India.[3] By turning their backs on the "Washington Consensus", these emerging countries are contributing to re-legitimising the notion of a Strategic or Developmental State.

The rise of State capitalism in China has not been accompanied by the withdrawal of the public authorities in the direct and indirect control of companies. The State's policy has primarily been characterised by its strategic vision, the search for effective governance comprising specific regulations, adjustments to the business cycle, the enhanced financial situation of firms, and lastly the sharing out of tasks between companies (State-owned enterprises, as well as private and foreign firms) in terms of strategy, innovation and market shares. The adoption of targeted industrial policies based on goals to ensure mastery of certain technologies, and the spread of technology throughout China's industrial fabric have played an important role in China's catching-up and up-grading strategy, in parallel to the role played by multinational firms.

China's openness strategy beginning in the early 1980s, and notably the welcoming of FDI, led to three interesting phenomena within a few years. The first concerns the policy of the endogenisation of technical progress, research & development and the implementation of clear policies of reverse engineering. This led the government to reconsider the attractiveness of FDI. Foreign FDI was thus more and more concentrated on high value-added activities, and the participation of foreign firms in the development of priority projects with numerous spin-offs in terms of employment, new products and exports. The second phenomenon stems from the macroeconomic and financial impact of the success of the Chinese model. This has led to a rise in China's financial and monetary reserves. The appreciation of China's currency (the renminbi, or RMB) makes exports more expensive, and reduces exporters' margins, including those of multinational firms. Recently, numerous industrial and social disputes have broken out, especially in the south of the country, leading to strong pressure on wages. These have risen by about 20 % in the last 2 years. The industrial and social disputes have affected large MNCs as well as Chinese companies (State-owned or private). As a result, companies with labour-intensive production are relocating to countries where wages are lower (Vietnam, Cambodia and North Korea). This is something quite new. Multinational Asian firms, which are worried about nationalist outbreaks in China, are also investing in higher value-added sectors in the new emerging economies of the region (Vietnam). The third notable phenomenon is the internationalisation of Chinese firms. They are looking for new markets and raw materials, but also technologies that are difficult to acquire from foreign MNCs operating in China.

---

[3] An exception to this has been the change in policy adopted by the conservative Hungarian government which challenges a large number of contracts signed with multinational firms. It has also adopted a nationalist discourse against foreign capital and Brussels.

India – Asia's other giant – has followed a different path in terms of its transformation since independence, but shows some similarities relating to the (late) opening of its economy, the role and intervention of the State, as well as the development of large firms and their internationalisation. State interventionism, to the extent that it developed in India, was limited and measured (the so-called "License Raj"). It did not take place at the expense of private companies, especially India's large conglomerates. In these firms, diversification occurred as companies which dominated one sector (Tata in steel) entered into other sectors, drawing on technical and managerial competencies acquired in the initial sector to enter the new sectors better (IT, finance, etc.). Furthermore, the national innovation system, along with India's quality education system have allowed Indian companies to specialise very much upstream in the R&D cycle, and so contribute to important technological breakthroughs in sectors which are highly competitive worldwide, like IT, pharmaceuticals and biotechnologies.

Compared to China, the rise of Indian firms took place before economic opening. India's large conglomerates have tended more to seek out participation with foreign companies rather than be receptacles of agreements signed between central government and State enterprises on the one hand, and MNCs on the other hand.

1.4 The Social and Political Sustainability of Business Models in Host Countries

In East European countries, as in China, the strong contribution of MNCs to growth has been accompanied by profound imbalances and strong tensions between institutions, the State and civil society. The rise of nationalism, coloured by populism in the CEECs, and the occurrence of repeated industrial disputes in China, all raise questions about the social and political sustainability of their different business models.

The economies of Eastern Europe (including Russia) have experienced three successive shocks during the last quarter century: the shock of the collapse of the socialist model, the shock of adjusting to the new market environment, and lastly the institutional shock of joining the European Union. The latter has entailed the adoption of minimal economic and social standards prevailing in the EU, within a context of economic reconstruction and the development of new social practices. If institutional compliance has favoured the integration of East European economies into the single market, these two processes have not been enough to ensure convergence of the new member states on the development level of existing EU countries. Apart from some regional capitals which have overtaken average EU GDP per capita, regional cohesion remains a problem. In many respects, Central and Eastern Europe continue to be the backyard of the EU-15, a new hinterland for German firms, and to a lesser extent for the other major economies present in the region. Social trends in the East are both at the origin and result of this "peripheral" Europe, which is "dependent" on the economic heartland of old Europe. Despite a certain number of national particularities, the East European countries manifest numerous similarities from a social point of view: the collapse of trade union membership and the weak legitimacy of unions, the development of inter-individual negotiations and informal industrial relations, the development of internal and especially external flexibility, etc. In a general way, the MNCs have profited from the absence of unions and their weakness to impose huge industrial restructuring associated with the important destruction of jobs in brownfield sites, buying off employees when necessary, with "voluntary" redundancy packages and promises of future investments. In greenfield subsidiaries, MNCs have benefited from greater room for manoeuvre to experiment new employment practices. While these adopt slightly higher social standards than those prevailing in host countries, they are nevertheless far below practices in home countries. In exchange, MNCs have not been neutral concerning the institutional framework and public policies of East European States, contributing to their redesign in ways which sometimes contradict the project of institutional convergence at the EU level. As previously emphasised, targeted competitive tax exemptions for foreign firms have nourished national resentment, and led to rising euroscepticism, which is often tainted by populism. These are all trends which challenge the ability of the EU institutions to pilot the integration process of economies within Europe. It may therefore be asked whether EU action for integrating the economic policies of member states should not be reconsidered. This question needs more attention than ever, given the integration of the Western Balkans, whose economic model is one of "dependent capitalism" *par excellence*.

The situation for China is completely different. As can clearly be seen in the region of Guangdong, economic, political and social conditions show without doubt that capitalism in China cannot follow a sustainable path, if two key issues are left aside, namely social progress and the modernisation of institutions. The forced march to industrialization, which was launched at the end of the 1970s and followed by the opening up to foreign capital implemented by Deng Xiaoping in the 1990s, has been accompanied by the explosion of unprecedented social inequalities, the indebtedness of local authorities and pollution. However, the increasingly pressing need for reforms of taxation, the distribution of income, urbanisation, and public health have all run up against democratic centralism and the imperative of growth imposed by the Chinese Communist Party, which has maintained its hold over the state apparatus and strategic goals. As the incessant increase of industrial disputes in the Guangdong region shows, the social and political demands of China's population cannot be left unmet. Some tentative responses have been put forward with a sustained rise in wages in recent years, in regions which have shown much conflict. Social policies have also been adopted to help, with a project for developing social insurance and retirement schemes provided that savings are channelled into domestic demand. But more fundamentally, the democratisation of China's social and political structures is the cornerstone of its economy's future development.

The rise of FDI in the last two decades is without doubt one of the major features of globalisation. This chapter seeks to stimulate analysis of the diversity of this phenomenon, both for the EU and Asia, and its impact on the growth regimes of these zones. FDI flows affect domestic industrial structures, types of specialisation, forms a property, and the terms of trade integration between countries of origin and host countries.

This globalisation is driven by the strategies of MNCs. It raises foremost the question of factors governing location decisions. Globalisation also calls for identification of the different ways in which firms enter host countries, as well as specialisation strategies. Accounting for the forces at work in this dynamic process helps measure the globalisation of territorial spaces and areas of production at various levels. Globalisation is "constructed bottom up" as a consequence of company strategies. At the same time, it is also "constructed by States and sub-State entities" via public policies which shape the attractiveness of territories, especially in terms of access to certain strategic resources for companies, or through the implementation of a level institutional "playing field" (the harmonisation of a certain number of trade, technical and institutional rules).

1.4.1 Part I: FDI Flows and Institutional Dynamics in Europe and Asia

Measuring FDI flows and their consequences can help feed two main debates which have recently opened up concerning the nature of relationships between territories and globalisation. A first debate draws on the "Varieties of Capitalism" (VoC) approach, and focuses on the convergence or differentiation between models of capitalism. Looking into the black box of national capitalisms to examine the models of companies therein tends to support the idea put forward by VoC of a persistent diversity between national models of capitalism. The latter are the fruit of the depth of national histories, industrial strategies and specific public intervention. The second debate seeks to move beyond the comparative approach of VoC, to look at reciprocal and asymmetric dependencies between capitalisms, which are more or less connected and intertwined with each other. This analysis ultimately makes it possible to identify forms of hierarchy between national capitalisms and find amongst these a diversity of "dependent" capitalisms in the zones studied.

It will be understood at this stage that globalisation does not signify convergence in the way territories are integrated into this new dynamics, nor the convergence of national capitalisms. A comparison of the way FDI has strongly impacted on the CEECs, and on Asia illustrates and supports this observation.

The contribution by Srdjan Redzepagic and Xavier Richet is also centred on the EU, but enlarges the geographical area considered by analysing the specific dynamics of the two groups of countries benefiting from FDI. They include the last countries to enter the EU (CEECs) as well as the Western Balkans, which are still due to enter the Union. Taking a historical perspective, the authors recall the key role played by FDI in resolving the dilemma faced by the post-socialist economies, namely how to structure "capitalism without capitalists". Again, from a comparative perspective, the text stresses the impact of FDI on the paths to catch-up and the sectoral specialisation taken by the countries considered. Upstream, the authors point to the determining role played by adjustment in institutional frameworks – correlated with the pace of EU membership – such as public policies favouring attractiveness. Starting by observing the high level of control which FDI has had over host country assets, the authors look at the hierarchy and domination affects which West European MNCs have over companies in host countries (both subsidiaries and local firms). They stress that the former are not ready to lose their "strategic and organisational advantage", despite the relative spread of technology. In view of the new wave of EU enlargement to the Western Balkans, the text also calls for examination of the strong "dependency" of these countries on FDI, which is less supportive of productive integration and trade than it was for the CEECs.

In line with this work on Europe, the text by Xavier Richet looks at the specificities and dynamics of Chinese FDI. It gives special attention to outbound Chinese investments which are studied less than FDI into China. Having been the main beneficiary of FDI, China is henceforth the main investor in emerging countries. But it is also a significant investor in the industrialised world. As the author points out, the dynamics of inward and outward Chinese FDI are far from being independent of each other. In contrast to Japan and South Korea, China opted for a policy of openness to FDI as of the 1980s, and has made FDI a powerful force in the modernisation of its business model, an instrument for acquiring advanced technologies and competencies, as well as for inserting itself into Western trade networks. These are all key factors in the takeoff and rapid growth of the Chinese economy. Linked to the latter, the rising needs of the Chinese economy for raw materials and energy were the initial drivers of growth in outward FDI.

Inward or outward FDI, institutional reforms, industrial policies, economic openness and certain types of liberalisation policies have all played a determining role. Policies fostering the attractiveness of FDI, proactive policies which have progressively become more selective and targeted on FDI with strong and median value-added do indeed correspond to a policy of encouraging and supporting the internationalisation of Chinese firms. The latter has weighed on the assertion of outgoing FDI, which is increasingly geared to buying up strategic assets and entering protected Western markets via mergers & acquisitions, as exemplified by Geely's takeover of Volvo. If Chinese firms have succeeded well in the face of the crisis, the author nevertheless stresses the fragility of the rise of Chinese multinationals in the developed world, as shown by the failure of numerous acquisitions. By reviewing theoretical interpretations of the growth of outward FDI, the author concludes noting how strongly the domestic and exogenous forces pushing for FDI are intertwined.

1.4.2 Part II: Redesigning Public Policies to Meet Competitiveness and Attractiveness Challenges, While Dealing with Business Lobbying

The contributions drawn together in this second part look at the "return of the State" which can be observed over the last 15 years. More generally they examine the new contours of public governance whose renewed forms – far removed from Fordism or Socialist dirigisme – are drawing up new relations between the State and industry in emerging countries. Both governments' preoccupations to reinforce the attractiveness and competitiveness of their economies and the rising practices of firms lobbying public decision-makers bear witness to the gulf which separates the proactive action by the State from a conception of growth and development based on laissez-faire. In Europe, the "return of the State" raises very different issues. It is unfolding in a decentralised context of consolidating "local business systems". Competitiveness and attractiveness are ever more discussed and negotiated via close relationships constructed by multinational firms and their subsidiaries with local and regional public authorities.

The text by Jean-François Huchet looks beyond the teleological reading of the Chinese miracle, to shed light on the successes, the failures and the paradoxes which have accompanied the evolution of industrial policies since openness was initiated in 1978. The policy of linking protection of the domestic market, selective openness to FDI (via joint-ventures) and the progressive introduction of competition played a decisive role in economic take-off and technological catching-up. However, the industrial dirigisme which prevailed until the early 1990s has shown its limits: a significant wastage of natural resources and the difficulty of creating industrial groups capable of meeting international competition. The readjustment of industrial policy which began in the mid-1990s has, in a pragmatic and successful way, drawn on the lessons from early, proactive interventionism. Dirigisme has receded to make way for incentives aimed at improving firms' environment, enlarging the field of industrial policy and new ambitions concerning energy and the environment. Together these bear out a profoundly-renewed proactive approach by the State.

From a similar perspective, the contribution by Joël Ruet focuses on Indian capitalism and its integration into globalisation following the progressive abandonment in the 1980s of import substitution policies, as well as the gradual "liberalisation" initiated in 1991 and the implementation of selective public policies to support the development of the private sector and openness to FDI. Guided by semi-dirigiste state intervention, the transition of a "conglomerate business model" (family-owned) to the internationalisation of Indian firms has gone hand-in-hand with the assertion of new key sectors in the globalised Indian economy, ranging from IT to cars. The author stresses the variety of levers supporting these dynamic developments, beginning with the "reverse brain drain" of Indian IT researchers who had spent time in the United States, to the strategic alliances and technological partnerships of the car industry, and the recent policy of acquiring foreign companies. These have been supported by public policies in R&D, education and the creation of technology parks.

The contribution by Giovanni Balcet illustrates the industrial strategies implemented in the car industry, in China. The sector had a key place in the industrial choices of the Chinese government in the 1980s and 1990s. The rise of the car industry was based on constant links and close cooperation between the State administration and China's major conglomerates. But both the characteristics of the sector and of corporate governance indicate that the industry is still highly fragmented, largely controlled by public capital (both at the national and provincial level) and still organized on the basis of alliances and strategic joint-ventures promoted by public authorities. Internationalisation is still very limited in the industry compared to India, where for example the major conglomerates have – with some historical irony – taken control of "jewels in the crown" like Jaguar. China has developed a more dualist strategy: the acquisition of technology to move up-market in quality domestically (the takeover of Volvo), together with investments in several developing countries (Iran, Algeria, Russia and Ukraine) to create down-market products.

The text by Phil Almond et al. focuses on Europe and draws on the work of new economic geography, public policy and firm policy to analyse the links between public governance and MNC strategies. It takes a "sub-national governance" perspective. This shift from national coordination towards sub-national or local coordination is not fortuitous. Instead it refers to the growing embeddedness of firms in local economic fabrics, and their aim to draw on the benefits provided by territories and areas. These include qualified labour, "tacit knowledge", technological and logistical resources, or advantages of spatial proximity. The meso-economic level is especially pertinent in taking into account the strengths of structuring "local business systems", which are based on narrow interaction and the quasi-permanent negotiation between company managers and local decision-makers. To illustrate the variety of dynamics possible, the authors have decided to look at the issue of human resources, and to study six sub-regions from a comparative point of view where regional development policies have been especially significant (two each in from Ireland, the United Kingdom and Spain). The chief conclusion here is that the establishment of some form of nexus between governance actors and inward investors at sub-national levels is highly contingent on the degree and modalities of the regionalisation of national governance.

1.4.3 Part III: Multinational Companies Across Home and Host Countries: Transfer, Hybridization, Adaptation of Business Model and Labour Relations?

The contributions of Part III are based on detailed, long-term field surveys. Their aim is to examine notions of transfer and hybridisation within a context of cross-investment strategies between Europe and emerging countries (China, Russia and the CEECs). The contributions also give non-negligible space to State policies in pursuing and implementing such strategies.

For about 20 years, several studies have looked at these ideas, straddling the borders between international economics, the sociology of labour relations and management. In a context of rapid FDI growth, this body of research has sought to understand better the choices, motivations and room for manoeuvre which MNCs have, in order to adapt their management and labour relations systems in countries where they operate. Whether the companies are Japanese, German, or North American, several studies stress the mediation role played by institutions in the countries of origin, as well as in host countries in the selection or transformation of management tools and practices transferred from company head offices.

The contributions in Part III extend such analysis. But the context is specific to Europe-Asia. The notions of transfer and hybridisation are discussed, shedding original light on the questioning and research approach taken by different authors.

In the contribution by Miao Zhang, Christine Edwards and Jiaying Ma, transfer and hybridisation are discussed with respect to the dynamics of catching up, which dominates the management choices and practices of subsidiaries of Chinese MNCs operating in Great Britain. The survey indicates primarily the importance of learning and knowledge, as the prime motivations of transfer operations by the parent company when compared to other considerations, relative to the institutions and growth of British markets. For the authors, subsidiaries really function as "knowledge seekers" and are tightly controlled by company headquarters, both in the service sector (finance and commerce) as well as in industry.

For Martin Krzywdzinski, transfer and hybridisation raise different questions about the extent to which institutions and national systems of labour relations in Russia and China favour the adoption of the co-management model of large German MNCs, in the car sector. In Russia, as the corporatist model is drifting into greater authoritarianism, the unique field survey here stresses the problems which parent companies have in imposing a relationship between divided unions and local management, based on cooperation. The situation is noticeably different in China. Despite a persistent deficit in social democracy in terms of union representation, the survey reveals a favourable trend towards social dialogue with management, in a spirit that is closer to German co-management. To conclude, the author rejects the theory put forward concerning the CEECs about the refusal of German MNCs to transfer the co-management model to emerging countries, especially on grounds of costs. In contrast, he explains that its slow spread follows tensions between cultural norms which underpin co-management and the various political obstacles at play in each of these two countries.

Lastly, these contributions converge with the text by Patrick Dieuaide, who stresses the singular role of the State in transfer and hybridisation policies pushed by FDI strategies. This is very clear in the case of Chinese MNCs operating in Great Britain, where the Chinese government is very much in touch with management, the control of management decisions, while also providing significant financial support to the MNCs it owns. The role of the State is also decisive in the CEECs and Russia. In Russia, cooperative relationships between unions and MNCs have to a large extent followed from the initiative, influence or even "power of persuasion" exercised by the Russian government on "social partners". In the light of the survey of French MNCs operating in the CEECs, P. Dieuaide also shows that EU States played an active role in the post-communist transition, helping the reformulation of socio-political compromises, which are sources of social stability within subsidiaries. But by doing so, MNCs in addition have demonstrated their proactive policies, which have been manifest in company rescues and the promotion of real industrial strategies, especially in the car industry.

1.4.4 Part IV: Reshaping Industrial Relations and Labour Activism in Multinational Companies

The Guangdong region has been a showcase of Chinese capitalism for a long-time. But since the mid-2000s it has suffered a number of economic and social difficulties. Bordering Hong Kong, Guangdong is one of the richest and most populated areas of activity in China. Its growth regime and development model have been driven by massive FDI inflows and export sales, yet these are now faltering under pressure from structural and regional imbalances, including urban congestion, environmental degradation and rising inequalities. From a sectoral point of view, the region is subject to slow yet profound changes, with the rise of services and finance, as well as the dynamism of high-tech, high value-added sectors (electronics and IT).

The contributions in Part IV are based on field observations and detailed surveys. They analyse the impact of these trends in terms of employment, wages, working conditions and more broadly speaking, industrial and social conflicts, as well as labour law. The authors share the same view that the region has entered a phase of social and political turbulence, in which the world of work, and more generally civil society are calling for more justice, fairness and democracy.

For Stéphane Cieniewski, Guangdong is suffering from a shortage of skilled workers and needs to change its employment model to deal with this. For many years, the model was based on labour flowing in from poor, up-country regions. Workers were recruited in the private sector. They were underpaid and considered as a second-class of citizens. Income disparities have risen relentlessly between employees in the private sector and the public sector, while the sharing out of productivity gains has mainly benefited companies in the State sector, and to a lesser extent, the export sector. In this context, the arrival in the 1980s of a new generation of workers who were younger and better educated, seeking a better life has contributed to the emergence of industrial disputes within companies. For the author, the new labour law voted in 2008 meets their aspirations and may be considered as a concession. It therefore reflects the willingness of central and regional government to boost a new development model in the region, which is capable of seducing and attracting more skilled labour.

The observation, put forward by Jean Ruffier is similar, though it remains more "optimistic" about the future. According to him, the age of low wages and docile labour in China are over. The province of Guangdong is modernising and along with this civil society is demanding new freedoms and rights of expression. The survey work as well as the gathering and compilation of local information conducted by the Franco-Chinese Centre at the University of Sun Yatsen (to which the author belongs) is categorical. Since the mid-2000s, there has been a turnaround in behaviour and attitudes. The population no longer fears unemployment and insecure work. Instead, it openly demands "to work less and earn more" and its activists, who are ever more numerous, no longer hesitate about striking to push their claims. For J. Ruffier, obstacles to changes are political. The central government is neutralised by clan struggles and local authorities have a tendency to favour company interests to guarantee a certain level of employment as well as tax revenues. For him, Guangdong is at a crossroads. The socio-economic situation holds out the possibility for an intensification of conflicts... leading probably to a "workers' spring".

For Chris King-Chi Chan and Elaine Sio-leng Hui, the rise of local conflicts is inseparable from the issues concerning the transformation of Chinese unionism. Based on a field survey of the "exemplary" strike by workers at the Honda factory in May 2010, the analysis explores the problems encountered by workers at the local level, in imposing the opening of wage negotiations and even more so in obtaining the democratic election of employee representatives. The strength of the conflict reflects the distance which separates the aspiration of a new class of employees and local union structures. The former are better educated and better organised, with a strong sense of justice, while the latter are bureaucratic and tightly integrated into patron-client relationships between global capital and local states. They are little sensitive to the promises of democratisation conceded by the single union at the national level. The strength of local mobilisation, its capacity to strike alliances with civil society, and even to obtain media support are all grounds for a certain level of optimism. However, the authors point to the persistent obstacles which this new working class faces in converting greater political maturity into reform of worker representation on the ground. These obstacles relate to the ambivalent role of local unions as well as to State-Party opposition to independent labour organisation. They illustrate the scale of the democratic deficit which the authorities face.

The text by Violaine Delteil looks at the power of influence of foreign capital, operating through foreign Chambers of Commerce, on the application of new labour legislation and labour relationships. By going back to the issues studied when national labour laws were voted in 2007 and 2008, this analysis questions the influence of foreign Chambers of Commerce in Guangdong on the implementation of two collective bargaining laws: the Collective Consultation Ordinance (Guangdong), and the Democratic Management Regulations (Shenzhen). A field survey of Chambers of Commerce, embassies and foreign consulates was carried out in 2011. It highlights the variety of positions defended by representatives of foreign capital with respect to regional legislation which constitutes a first step in the institutionalisation of worker representation rights within companies, dealing with the new conflictual background to industrial relations in the region. These positions range from the prudence of the European Chamber of Commerce, to strong opposition by trade associations from Hong Kong, via the more qualified opposition of the American Chambers of Commerce. The positions also reflect the variety of social models and types of specialisation of foreign firms. Lobbying capacities are also unequally distributed, favouring Asian Chambers of Commerce (with Hong Kong associations in the lead). The latter can count on greater political connections as well as on stronger powers of economic boycott. The above-mentioned laws were enacted at the height of the crisis, but their application has been delayed. This can only be interpreted as a strong erosion in the autonomy of domestic actors in the face of foreign capital. Political decision-making is thus more a reflection of the convergence of detailed interests between national and foreign business on the one hand, and between the government of Guangdong and China's national government on the other hand.

Part I
FDI Flows and Institutional Dynamics in Europe and Asia

Catching-Up and Integration in New and Future EU Member States Through FDI

Srdjan Redzepagic and Xavier Richet

The experience of the recent enlargement within the European Union is unique if we consider both the number of countries, the population, the level of economic development, the systemic characteristics of most of these countries, the speed and the cost. Those countries have supported in less than 20 years, three major shocks: a systemic shock with the implosion of the socialist system, an economic shock with the adjustment to the new market environment, an institutional shock with the membership to the European Union (EU) for those who have applied to become members. A fourth shock, for some last comers and further EU members has been the violent disintegration of the Former Yugoslavia, which has delayed and hampered negotiations for future membership of the former Republics involved in the conflict (Croatia, Serbia...).

The EU enlargement to 12 new members, of which 10 were communist economies under the control of the Soviet Union, took place in 2004 (10) and in 2007 (2), it has been the outcome of a long transformation process which started right after the fall of the Berlin wall in 1989.

During this process, the leaders of those economies had to handle and manage to reach two main objectives: the transition from a socialist economy to a market economy, on the one hand and the upgrading of these economies in order to allow them to become future members of the EU on the other hand.

Following the June 2003 EU summit in Thessaloniki other candidates are crowding in at the door, all, except Turkey, from the Western Balkans (ex-Yugoslavia States, Albania), some being very close to the requirement to become a member (Croatia will officially join in January 2013), other have been

S. Redzepagic (✉)
Institute of Economic Sciences, Belgrade, Serbia
e-mail: sredzepagic@gmail.com

X. Richet
Université Sorbonne nouvelle, Paris, France
e-mail: xrichet@gmail.com

admitted as "accession States" and are discussing with the European Commission the fulfilment of conditions and the timing to become officially members.

The round of new membership had strong impact on the functioning of the European economy, both in terms of regulation, distribution of resources, place of economic and regional development, catching up policies (converging policies). The structural and regional imbalance among "old" and "new" member states, the need to re-industrialize many regions in order to create new jobs and wealth are real issues. Regional GDP per head among the 271 EU regions (NUTS 2) displays a very high disparity with the poorest region in eastern Bulgaria scoring 27 % against 332 % for Inner London. In the same time, as it can be witnessed in some regions of Central and Eastern Europe (The Bratislava region, Western Hungary, Warsaw region and Southern Poland), there are strong movements of industrial development, relocation of new industries, even in countries and regions which didn't have specific advantages in this field under the socialist system (see the car industry in Slovakia).

This goes along with an important flow of foreign capital pouring in the region where the rate of domestic accumulation is still very low and would never match investment requirements to develop a strong industrial base (Transition Report). This raises the question of the development of "a capitalist economy without capitalists" which has been underlined earlier at the beginning of the transition (Eyal et al. 1998). On the other hand, it highlights the fact that industrial recovery and economic growth are fuelled by foreign investments in the region. FDI has contributed to create a new industrial landscape in the region, it has also created a new economic dependency of these countries: most of them are today the host of big transnational corporations which have a strong impact on domestic industrial structure, specialization, ownership, developing strong links with Western European economies.

Today Eastern European economies appear to be a backyard for Western Economies which, taking advantage of proximity, low costs, qualified labour, have relocated businesses which account, in some countries, for the main parts of fixed capital, added value, exports. These investments have contributed to create strong linkages between western Multinational corporations and their regional subsidiaries. On the one hand, they have taken advantage of existing competencies inherited from the former socialist system (Radosevic 2004). On the other hand, their presence has contributed to the catching up, the development of new specialisations.

In this contribution, our aim is to highlight the transformation of these economies with their linkage through their new specialization, control to EU-15 economies through the strong presence of Western Multinational Corporation (MNC).

Section 2.1 presents the main components of transforming policies conducted in the region; Sect. 2.2 assesses the role of FDI in the region has a driver of sectoral adjustment and catching up. Even for Balkan 'late comers' countries that have lately adjusted, Sect. 2.3 concentrates on the development of a new industrial area illustrating the impact of FDI and the linkage strategy with Western companies which has resulted.

2.1 A Wide Enlargement Strategy

2.1.1 A Difficult Adjustment

Considering the size, the population, history, level of development, the last wave of enlargement, which has taken place in 2004 and 2007, is exceptional if we consider the history of the EU expansion since the foundation of the Common market in the late fifties (Drouet and Richet 2007; Redzepagic and Djukic 2011).

The number of new members entering in one row: up to now, earlier enlargements consisted of the entry of up to three countries, generally of same economic level which had no difficulty to adjust to the new institutional and economic environment as they were already developed market economies (with the notable exception of Spain, Portugal and Greece).

Difference in living standard and income distribution. All the new members, even the most economically advanced (Slovenia, Czech Republic) are still far behind the mean level in the EU-15. With the exception of Cyprus and Malta, the 10 countries from Central and Eastern European countries have a mean GDP per head which is 50 % compared to EU-15 (Fig. 2.1). The collapse of the former socialist industries has created strong regional inequalities and a high level of unemployment.

A systemic dimension. It is the first time that the EU integrates former socialist countries with noticeable differences among them: 3 countries (the Baltic States) were part of the Former Soviet Union, one in the former pro-market Yugoslavia (Slovenia), other belonged the COMECON and had partly specialized their economies in order to serve the Soviet economy and developed an autarkic economies with low specialization and limited exchanges with the world economy. In all cases, those countries had to develop market mechanisms, and then adjust to the standards of the EU to be able to support the competitiveness from the other members' states as stipulated by the EU regulations.

A new geopolitical environment. With this new wave of enlargements, the frontiers of the EU are moving eastward and southward raising new questions: security, political and economic cooperation. The European Commission and the EU leaders have set up a new neighbourhood policy which has to match different aims: assure the integration of the new members without deepening the gap with countries that are not yet members and that will join the EU 1 day (West Balkans countries), set up specific mechanisms to develop economic cooperation with other countries (especially from the South of Europe, Middle East and North Africa countries), fill up the strategic partnership with Russia, securing peaceful development in the region. The opening of official discussions with Turkey illustrates a sharp question discussed in the EU concerning where up to close the frontier of Eastern border of the EU.

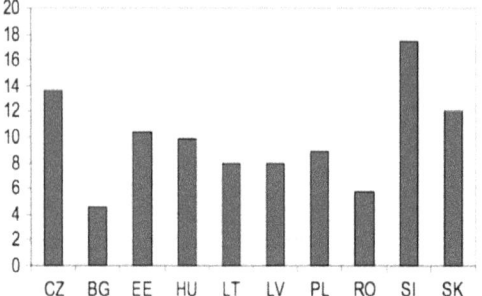

Fig. 2.1 GDP per head (1,000 €), 2010. 70–80 % of EMU average: Slovenia, Czech Republic, Slovakia. 50–60 % of EMU average: Estonia, Hungary, Poland, Lithuania, Latvia. Around 40 % of EMU average: Bulgaria, Romania (Source: Eurostat)

70%-80% of EMU average: Slovenia, Czech Republic, Slovakia
50%-60% of EMU average: Estonia, Hungary, Poland, Lithuania, Latvia,
Around 40% of EMU average: Bulgaria, Romania

2.1.2 Managing the Transition

Integrating the EU is the last step of the long process of transformation. A precedent step has been the transition from non-market to a market economy. This has required from policy makers a set of tools and policies in order to speed up and deepen the process of transformation. Consensus, among decision-makers with the population, has been reached in some countries on the different objectives to match; in other countries, dispenses prevailed and have limited both the scope and the pace of reforms.

In spite of these differences, all former socialist countries shared among them common characteristics concerning the industrial organisation, the control of firms, their financing, their level of technology, their specialisation in basic industries (military, heavy industries), their poor records in intermediary and consumer goods, the total absence of a financial industry, the under-development of services industries. This has shaped what we could call a "bad industrialisation" if we refer to the mode of allocation of resources among sectors in market economies, to the low rate of innovation, to the under-capitalisation of firms, and, finally to the rigidity of the whole economic system. A socialist company has never been considered has an autonomous centre of decision-making, managing its material, and human and financial assets, following a strategy among competitors. On the contrary, the system had low or even inexistent incentives, the State had a paternalist attitude towards companies, providing finance, capital goods, parts, creating a permanent shortage situation, leading large parts of the population either to "live on the beast" or to enter in illegal (but often tolerated) activities of the unofficial economy. Finally, the autarkic organisation of foreign trade, at the level of the former COMECON, has contributed to develop many comparative disadvantages among the economies of the region (Richet 1997, 2004).

Transition is not a *tabula rasa*, although that many industries have been difficult to turn around and to adjust and that many "industrial cemeteries" filled up the landscape in countries which had concentrated their industrial development in sector finally difficult or impossible to adjust.

2.1.3 The Great Transformation

How to go to the market? How to adjust and restructure such economies, how to change the behaviour of workers and consumers confronted with a new environment such as unemployment, strong inequalities, insecurity concerning the future of important fractions of the population? How to create, often from scrape, a market economy? Did privatisations and the right to create new businesses are sufficient to promote entrepreneurship? Is it possible to jump from an administrated economy towards an institutional capitalism, economising on entrepreneurial capitalism which has played a crucial role in the early step of capitalist development in shaping the industry through the growth of big industrial groups? What kind of institutional compromise can be reached in order to control efficiently new private companies? Does a strong financial system is preferable to monopolies, *chaebols* or *keretsu* types of organisation in order to foster growth, fill the technological gap with western developed economies?

The post-socialist transition has focused around four set of policies, each set having specific aims to reach on the one hand, the four set being interlinked, on the other (Richet 1992). Concretely, this means that government which have committed themselves, let say only on two sets leaving apart or paying less attention to the two others (which is the reason in the delay of some countries to join the EU) have failed to adjust rapidly their economies and to create the new market environment necessary to support competition in an open economy.

(a) *Macro stabilisation* for containing deficits and curbing inflation by reducing subsidies, increasing interest rates, introducing competition through liberalisation of foreign trade. Partial convertibility (before total liberalisation) has created a strong incentive to adjust, to relocate resources in more productive sectors with export prospects. Almost all governments have followed strict macro-policies.

(b) *Implementation of market institutions* and adoption of new regulation assuming property right and protection of private investments, establishment, economic laws on companies, for competition, for labour; creation of financial markets, of a two tier banking system.

(c) *Re-entering into the world economy*, lowering tariffs and other entry barriers, promoting the development of new specialisations: in few years, all countries will have switched their exports towards Western markets, beneficiating of price advantage but also of specialization of their exports on higher added value segment in part thanks to re-exporting strategies of MNC towards Western markets.

(d) *Privatisation and restructuring* former state-owned enterprises in order to de-monopolise big industrial groups by breaking them down through direct selling or through mass privatisation (free distribution to the population or to workers of the units concerned) (Fig. 2.2).

Another dimension of the privatisations strategy, privatisations "from below", has been the right to new entrepreneurs to enter the market and to establish their businesses (SME), it has also facilitated the entry of foreign enterprises on these

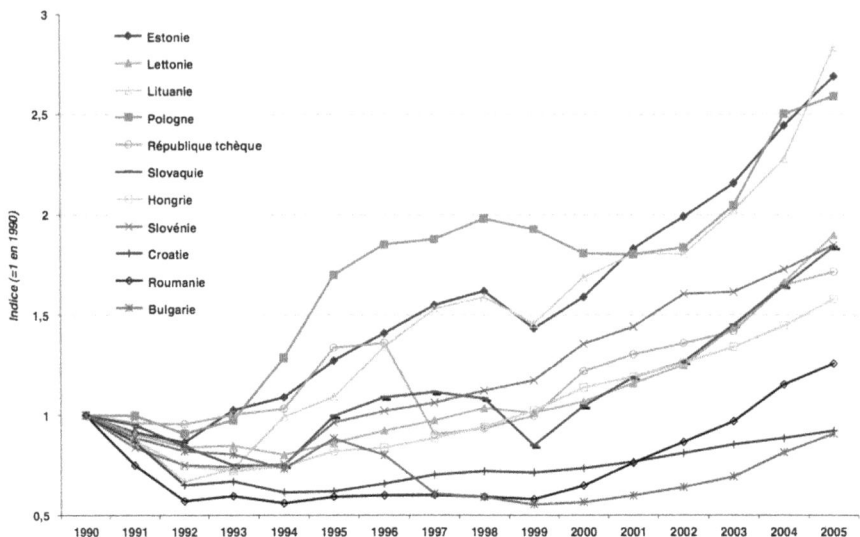

Fig. 2.2 Changes of the manufacturing production in CEES (1990–2005) (Source: adapted from Transition Report 2006)

new markets through majority acquisition (through privatisations), new investments (Greenfield investments) or joint-ventures following opportunities, risks, legal environment.

In all cases, new owners (external, former managers and workers, depending on how privatisation has been implemented) had to reshape very quickly their businesses by investing in order to avoid the loss of value of their new assets or to be stuck by strong insiders opposing the necessary restructuring. Corporate governance has become an important issue in the region, along with the development of competition policies and of financial markets.

2.1.4 Transition and Integration

Besides the building up of a new institutional environment, privatisation, the search of new competitive advantage concentrating on industries and services which could compete with EU-15 has been the main economic policy objective. The task has been made difficult as there were no more central bodies to promote and finance industrial policies at sectoral levels, there were no managing competencies available, the financial and economic environment was not clear. In the same times, the former specialisations of Central European economies have disappeared with the collapse of the Former Soviet Union as exports destinations shrank (Gros and Steinherre 2004).

Price competition, in the first step has played an import role in re-switching exchanges towards Western markets, then, quality effect has taken the lead, mostly

Table 2.1 Foreign trade structure with the EU according to the nature of the specialization, early years of the transition (in %)

	Intra-Industries trade			
	Horizontal	Vertical	Total	Inter industrial
Poland (1998)	6.3	25.5	31.8	68.2
Hungary (1998)	7.4	39.1	46.5	53.5
Czech Rep. (1998)	10.9	47.0	57.9	42.1
Slovakia (1996)	5.7	19.7	25.4	74.6
Spain (1995)	19.5	34.2	53.7	46.3
Portugal (1995)	10.5	22.1	32.6	67.4
Greece (1995)	4.6	9.0	13.6	86.4
EU (1995)	19.2	42.3	61.5	38.5

Source: Conjoncture, BNP, September 2004, no. 8

thank to the role of FDI in the region which have been attracted by market prospects, low labour cost and high quality of human resources, quality of human resources. Restructuring has pushed non-performing companies to leave the market. Market opportunities have attracted foreign companies, leading to a strong connection with EU-15 economies both in inter and intra trade, the latter showing the level of integration with EU economies (Table 2.1).

Concerning labour, new member countries have relied on two advantages: the low cost of labour compared to EU and other developed market economies, on the one hand (Fig. 2.3), and the quality of the work force on the other, which, both have played a major role in attracting foreign investment in the region.

2.2 FDI, an Engine for Economic Growth and Regional Specialisation

The combination of the different measures implemented during the 90s (stabilisation, institutions building, opening to the world economy, privatisation/restructuring of enterprises) has led to a new competitive environment in the region which shows higher rate of growth than in the EU-15.

Besides these measures, FDI has played the role of a real growth engine; bringing in capital, markets access, management know-how; it has also contributed largely to the spreading of new businesses in the region, often upstream, downstream and around the businesses that has been acquired of created through greenfield investments (Guerraoui and Richet 1997).

Although the level of FDI is not so important compared to other destinations (around 6 % of total world FDI) (World Investment Report 2012), nonetheless it accounts for a non-neglectable share of GDP, of exports in some countries. Completing the transformation has began to attract big amount of foreign capital in countries which had been reluctant at the beginning of the transition to welcome foreign investment (Czech Republic, Poland). Countries which had been left behind

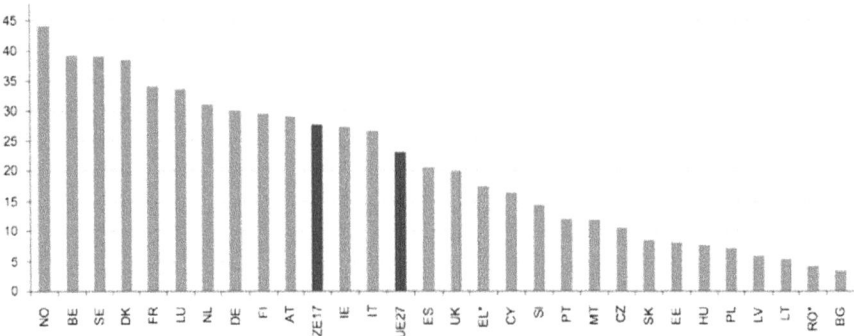

Fig. 2.3 Estimated work force hourly cost in manufacturing in the EU (Source: Eurostat)

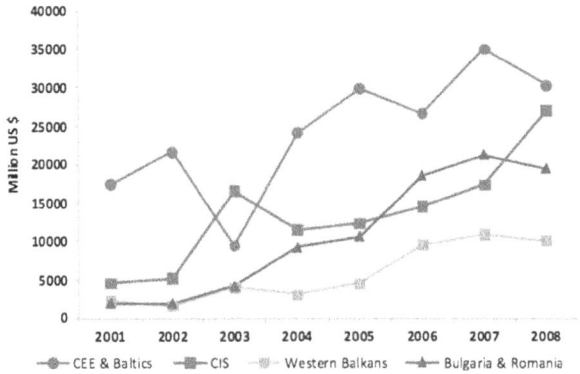

Fig. 2.4 FDI in transition countries (Source: Transition Report 2010)

and had not been able to join the first wave of new membership are getting substantial share of FDI, both Bulgaria and Romania, but also West Balkan countries (Fig. 2.4).

2.2.1 Attractivity Policies: Size, Proximity, Commitment

Among the different reasons which explain attractivity of countries to FDI market access, factor costs, there are specific reasons concerning this particular region.
(a) Proximity: most FDI outflows come from EU-15 companies (European or affiliates of US companies), quite few directly from overseas countries (Japan, South Korea).
(b) Regional integration and division of labour. The proximity factor reduces risks and entry costs, facilitates the development of regional strategies ("linkage") among invested companies in the region. For instance, Skoda-VW, in the Czech Republic assembles its cars and exports parts and components to other assembling units of the group. In the same time, it integrates parts and components

produced in Germany or elsewhere among the group's partners. Another impact of the presence of Western companies is to push suppliers (first and second tier) to invest near the new facilities in host countries in order to produce bigger volumes by reducing cost (economies of scale), take advantage of the new markets. Almost all suppliers of big car assemblers have invested near the newly acquired and invested firms in the region. Thus FDI create positives externalities by upgrading existing companies with strong impacts upstream and downstream the business, creating many spill over through the economy.

(c) Labour cost and qualifications: The low cost of labour plays an important role in attracting FDI especially in manufacturing industries which requires a qualified manpower. With equivalent training and productivity, the gross cost of the work force in the region was around one/fifth of labour cost un Germany at the start of the transformation. Costs are rising but convergence with Western wages level could take a very long time. Taxation is another issue: the flat tax policy applied by many countries in the region makes a big differential with taxation in the EU raising the accusation of a taxation dumping and retaliation measures from the EU commission.

Finally, mixing proximity, labour cost, workforce qualification and productivity, institutional reform and attractivity policies, country size, the distribution of FDI within the region as favoured both "early reformers" countries (Hungary), biggest countries, even last comers (Romania). Very small countries (Estonia) have taken advantage of powerful neighbourhood (Sweden, Finland) to turn around their economies.

Besides wage costs, high qualification in some manufacturing sectors require very qualified workers, technicians and engineers. Some member States are attracting investments requiring high tech manufacturing (electronics), in high added-value sectors. Big companies relocates some of their research facilities in the region. Nokia and Ericsson have R&D facilities in Hungary, Japanese, Korean and Indian companies are investing in clusters in the Czech Republic. As a result, the content of added-value products in export is increasing.

In less than 15 years Central and East European Economies (CEEE) have deeply changed their economic structure, specialisation and have matched the condition to join, for the majority of them, the EU. They have become fully fledged market economies, able to sustain competition among European economies. Some of them have been able to enter the EMU (EU-17) and adopt the euro as their national currency.

In this adjustment process, socially and economically costly, FDI has played an import role, as a kind of "uninvited guest". Some Western companies have acted as first mover and made a strategic move in future markets with growth potential linked to the former specialization. Other has taken advantage of 'discount prices' of assets in the privatisation (Table 2.2).

Programmes across the region. Other, finally, waited for a more safer institutional environment to invest in more secure markets. First movers have been able to negotiate good deal, holiday taxes, even subsidies to control partially or totally strategic assets. Thus they get a strategic advantage, buying market shares, building (temporary) barriers to entry against followers.

Table 2.2 Growth of inward stock and flow of FDI, 2002–2012

Countries	Inward FDI stock, (€ Millions)		Inward FDI stock per capita, €		Inward FDI stock as % of GDP (%)		FDI inflow as % of gross fixed capital formation (%)	
	2002	2010	2002	2010	2002	2010	2002	2010
Bulgaria	3,927	35,901	500	4,784	23.1	99.6	31.5	19.4
C. Republic	36,884	97,191	3,615	9,238	46.1	67.0	41.0	16.8
Estonia	4,035	12,269	2,975	9,156	51.9	84.6	13.3	44.3
Hungary	34,575	68,522	3,409	6,856	48.8	69.6	19.5	6.4
Latvia	2,676	8,250	1,148	3,713	27.0	45.9	11.4	8.2
Lithuania	3,818	10,166	1,103	3,134	25.4	37.1	25.3	10.8
Poland	46,139	138,000	1,207	3,600	22.0	39.0	11.1	10.0
Romania	7,482	52,396	344	2,442	15.4	43.0	11.7	9.7
Slovakia	8,563	37,000	1,592	6,800	33.0	56.1	61.9	3.0
Slovenia	3,948	11,242	1,979	5,492	16.1	31.2	30.4	7.8
NMS-10	152,046	470,938	1,480	4,610	29.8	51.4	23.5	11.0
Albania	–	3,600	–	1,100	–	39.5	7.9	28.5
B&H	799	5,700	209	1,500	11.3	45.2	–	1.6
Croatia	5,794	25,725	1,304	5,800	20.6	56.0	19.1	4.4
Macedonia	1,161	3,300	574	1,600	29.0	47.9	16.9	16.2
Montenegro	81	4,060	131	6,429	6.0	135.3	38.4	70.6
Serbia	776	15,780	104	2,164	4.8	54.1	26.3	14.3
SEE	8,610	58,065	400	2,700	14.0	54.5	21.5	12.4

Source: WIIW Database on 2011 Foreign Direct Investment in Central, East and Southeast Europe

Table 2.3 Investments entry and risk assessment

Action	Strategy	Examples
First Mover	Entry before the setting of reliable market institutions	VW in the Czech Republic
Opportunistic	Privatisation foreign invested firms	Sanofi, Suez, Hungary
Secured	In the framework of a well established institutional market environment	Tesco, Carrefour, all countries

Privatization foreign investments have been a hot issue in some countries (Hungary). In both cases, as market mechanisms were not implemented, foreign companies have generally realized good deals fuelling, in some countries, a national resentment against the process of privatisation (selling the crown jewels.) (Table 2.3).

Levels of risk have been linked to the progress of the economic transformation, to the opening up, to the institutional measures, which have been implemented.

Among the main factors that have accelerated or hampered the entry of FDI, the pace of macro-stabilisation and institutional reforms has played the major role. Except Hungary, all the other countries, at different degrees and for different reasons have hindered policies encouraging FDI entry either frightened by the control of the industry by foreign companies, or willing to keep direct or indirect control on state assets either between the hands of the States, or for possible private appropriation. Countries which have postponed FDI entry have delayed their adjustment but have not closed the door to entry: Bulgaria, Romania, Western Balkan countries are also recipients of FDI which contribute to the up-grading of their economies and to their integration in the new European industrial network. Countries which have the first opened their economies to FDI have beneficiated of a rapid adjustment and regional integration.

Obviously, there is a strong correlation between institutional changes and the growth of FDI in the region as shown in Table 2.2 some countries taking the lion's share as they have advanced in their adjustment but also beneficiated of their size (Poland, Romania) of their proximity (Czech Republic, Hungary, Slovakia).

- The sectorial distribution of FDI illustrates both the weakness of some industrial sectors under the former socialist system and their growth potential in the framework of a market economy. Most of sectorial FDI among NMS-10 have been directed towards specific sectors: manufacturing (28.8 %), trade (13.1 %), financial intermediaries (18.8 %), real estate, business activities (19.4 %) followed by electricity, gas, water (5.8 %), transport, communication (6.8 %). This distribution can be explained both by the 'competitive advantage' (cost, work force qualifications) inherited from the former socialist system which was an asset for investors and by the weak development of other sectors essential for the normal functioning of market economy (trade, finance, transport). FDI distribution among 'late comers' confirms the privileged destination of foreign investors.

Finally, FDI sectoral distribution in the region highlights two interesting points:
- FDI is allocated towards sectors following restructuring or Greenfield investments, are supporting adjustment and up-grading to Western standards to beneficiary companies in order to allow them to integrate industrial networks.
- FDI brings in the flow of capital necessary to develop under-developed or non-existent sectors (trade, consumer, finance).

Proximity is another dimension of the specificity of CEES attractiveness to FDI. Most FDI in the region originate from EU-15 countries with three majors countries: Austria, Germany, and Netherland[1]. Some countries (Italy, France) have a strong presence thanks to big investment in one sector (car industry) or in the financial sector (Austria). Proximity effect can be seen from the case of Austria massively present in neighbour courtiers as Sweden, or Germany. Major investments in specific industries (car, real estate, trade) result in the development of new industrial rings (Western Hungary, Bratislava region, Warsaw, Southern Poland) with cluster effects and strong spin off.

---

[1] Netherland is a special case: many European headquarters are located in the Netherland for taxation purpose.

2.3 Delocalisation, Specialization and Control: Central and Eastern European Economies as the Backyard of Western Economies?

2.3.1 Up-grading and the Role of Foreign Companies

Proximity, as it has been under lined has been a factor which has accelerated the pace of FDI entry in the region. Once institutional barriers have been remove and that transition has neared its completion, FDI has spread in different sectors of host economies even among late EU comers and even, now, the last applicants to become members. Institutional reforms have paved the way and broaden attractivity to foreign companies to invest. Investments, as we have pointed out, have been directed in two directions: sectors where they were an obvious need to fill up the gap with the requirements of a standard market economy, particularly to supply new needs (consumer, financial services), to up-grade underdeveloped infrastructures (communication, trade).

Besides, FDI have been directed towards sectors which presented potential competitive advantages linked to proximity, to a growing domestic demand, to the qualification and the low cost of the domestic work force. It has been quiet easy for Western managers, once they have taken the control of former socialists companies to turn them around and make them work rapidly on the same standards than in the West.

Case studies have shown that adjustment of those companies have been realized very quickly, often in less than 1 year, often at a high cost when Western companies have been obliged to post numerous managers in the new facilities to build up the management and organisational system, both inside and outside de firm (networking building). 'Friendly policies' towards foreign investors have helped "holiday taxes", weak protection of labour. Growth potential of domestic markets, on the one hand, economic stagnation and high wages in Western economies, on the other have contributed to the rapid development of FDI and fuelled, in some countries, relocation of capital in these economies.[2]

Another driver for the development of FDI in the region has been opportunity for Western MNC to realise both horizontal and vertical investments. Horizontal investments, through investments in new facilities to gain market shares (answering local and regional demand), vertical (vertically disintegrated) by transferring parts of the value chain of the process in different locations in the area. As a consequence, the whole productive organization at the European level has been deeply modified with some positive impacts (job creation in host countries) and negative (job losses in original countries).

The outcome of these strategies by European MNC has been the reshaping of the industrial landscape by realizing huge investments in some industries consuming

---

[2] In the reality the frontier is not always clear between new investments and relocation: in the first case, there is a net investment when it doesn't have impact on local jobs (country origin).

Table 2.4 Largest foreign investors in CE – 2010

Company	Sector	Origin
1. Volkswagen	Car	Germany
2. E.ON	Energy	Germany
3. Metro	Distribution	Germany
4. RWE	Energy, Water	Germany
5. OMV	Energy	Austria
6. Samsung Electronics	Electronics	South Korea
7. Lukoil	Oil and Gas	Russia
8. Tesco	Distribution	UK
9. Deutsche Telekom	Communication	Germany
10. Arcelor Mittal	Steel	UK-Luxemburg
11. Foxconn	Communication	Taiwan
12. Nokia	Telecommunication	Finland
13. France Telecom	Telecommunication	France
14. Renault	Car	France
15. Fiat	Car	Italy
16. REWE	Distribution	Germany
17. Kaufland	Distribution	Germany
18. BP	Oil	UK
19. British American Tobacco	Tobacco	UK
20. Philips	Electronics	Netherland
21. Eni	Oil	Italy
22. Shell	Oil	UK-Netherland
23. U.S. Steel	Steel	US
24. Carrefour	Distribution	France
25. Lidl	Distribution	Germany

Source: Deloitte 2011

capital and labour (automobile). Table 2.4 shows the relocation movement in the region. The bulk of FDI comes from Western Europe 81 %, the remaining parts from North America and Asia (Japan, South Korea). Three sub areas have come up from this movement of relocation: a first one in the Baltic with FDI from Nordic States, the biggest one eastward of Germany with Poland, the Czech Republic, Hungary, a third one with Balkan countries.

The reshaping of the Central and East European economies in the framework of enlargement policies had three consequences: a linkage effect, a hierarchical effect and domination effect.

2.3.2 A Linkage Effect

The linkage effect is highlighted by the car industry. Almost inexistent under the former socialist system (only Czechoslovakia had an original and historic car

Table 2.5 Total inward FDI in Central and East Europe 2011

Total inward FDI in 2010	443662 mios US$
Of which	
USA	4 %
EU-15	77 %
Japan	0.8 %

Source: WIIW Database 2011 on Foreign Direct Investment in Central, East and southeast Europe

industry; East Germany tried to develop an ersatz of the historic VW, the Trabant), other countries (with the exception of Bulgaria and Hungary barred from the URSS to develop their own industry) mainly Romania and Poland have relied of industrial cooperation and FDI (Fiat, Renault) in to develop cars which never matched the standards both in production (quality, volumes) of Western makers. Hungary was specialized in assembling buses; Slovakia has no car industry at all.

In few years, almost all the biggest European car makers have entered the market, either through acquisition, revamping all facilities (Skoda) either by Greenfield, often both, with the exceptionally growth of the sector (Table 2.5). General Motors came in through its German partner Opel; Asian countries (Japan, South Korea) have also invested in the framework of a larger strategy encompassing other countries (Russia, Central Asia countries).

Western producers have linked these new facilities to parent companies in different way, by designating specific functions, or specializing specifics tasks. For instance, Renault develops its low cost car in Romania, where different functions, even R&D have been relocated. It's from the Romanian headquarter that the regional strategy is set up, to enter new markets, to monitor new investments. The Clio car made in Slovenia by Renault is distributed in Southern Europe, Italy, and the South of France. VW has set up a regional division of labour with some companies producing and assembling whole cars (Skoda), other making motors (Györ, in Hungary), gearboxes (Slovakia), develop jointly a new product (PSA and Toyota making light trucks in the Czech Republic). Skoda produces components for the other group's facilities, in the same time, the company has access to other companies' products. Thus complementarities and economy of scales are two dimensions to the integration with the group. In the same time, first and second tier component suppliers (almost 15 by car makers have located in the area) have set up around the new facilities in order to supply local assembly companies by reducing cost. R&D facilities are developing locally or regionally. Component makers produce for all assemblers in the region. Finally, competition among enlarged car maker group lead to develop best practices. As a result, better equipped, better managed, many of these companies show a better efficiency and competitiveness (Table 2.6).

Today, according to the latest data, the production in the region of light vehicle (including Russia, the biggest market) account for 576352 units, nearly half of Western European (12 179938) itself equals to the US (12280019), but far behind Asia (34210699). Almost from scratch, FDI has contributed to the development of

Table 2.6 Largest foreign car maker's investors in CE

Rank	Top 500 rank	Company name	Country
1	4	Skoda	Czech Republic
2	7	Fiat	Poland
3	14	Audi Hungaria	Hungary
4	28	Volkswagen Slovakia	Slovakia
5	48	Automobile Dacia	Romania
6	55	Toyota Peugeot Citroën Automobile Czech	Czech Republic
7	59	PCA Slovakia	Slovakia
8	62	Volkswagen	Poland
9	71	Kia Motors Slovakia	Slovakia
10	82	Magyar Suzuki	Hungary

Source: Deloitte 2011

the automobile industry in the region. There are fears, of course that the present economic crisis will have negative impact on the growth of the sector. Competition from Russian (a much bigger market for which Western maker show a big appetite) and Asia are real and could lead to a durable stagnation even a decline of this sector.

2.3.3 Hierarchical and Domination Effects

All governments, international institutions support the role of FDI as a tool for modernizing, catching up and linking backward economies. Removing barriers, setting up attractivity policies have been set up and have contributed to the adjustment of Central and Eastern economies. The presence of FDI, with the benefits of integration, has contributed to sustain economic growth in the region. Even late comers countries (Bulgaria, Romania) have beneficiated from entry of FDI, showing that there was still room, and opportunities in the region to welcome foreign capital.

Although it is not a frequent question, an issue with the massive presence of FDI in the region concerns the hierarchical and domination effect. In other worlds, CE economies have moved from a domestic accumulation of capital strategy (under the socialist system) to a model of international control of domestic assets by foreign investors. Opening up policies and privatizing public assets had to consequence in terms of control of domestic assets. First, big domestic monopolies (energy production and distribution, telecommunication network, some insurance and banking) have been kept under the hand of local governments. In other sectors (car, distribution, telecommunication, technology), big foreign companies have build up a dominant position (ranking, market shares) with the exception of former national monopolies (telecommunication, energy distribution) which were not offered for sale during the round of privatization of State property (Table 2.7).

Hierarchy control can be considered from two views point. First, through the linkage effect which analysed above Western companies have both a strategic and

Table 2.7 Foreign companies, by country among the 500 first companies in Central Europe

Status 2010	Non CE private sector	CE private sector	State owned	Total
Bosnia and Herzegovina	/	/	1	1
Bulgaria	11	1	2	14
Croatia	3	7	7	17
Czech Republic	48	14	11	73
Estonia	5	/	1	6
Hungary	50	8	5	63
Latvia	4	2	/	6
Lithuania	1	6	2	9
Poland	97	42	41	180
Republic of Macedonia	1	/	/	1
Romania	26	1	5	32
Serbia	6	2	4	12
Slovakia	17	5	7	29
Slovenia	5	11	2	18
Ukraine	12	19	8	39
Total	285	116	96	500

Source: Deloitte (2011)

organizational advantage (OLI) which is not eroded over the time. Does local companies, either by their initial level of technology, by the learning curve, by the relocation of R&D facilities, can become equal players with Western MNC and compete with them? Secondly, through the control effect (capital control, property rights, protection of intellectual property rights) do host country companies further autonomy appear difficult to get. Case studies in different countries of the region (Stephan 2012) have concluded to interesting conclusions: embeddedness of technologies in acquired companies, the supply of qualified workforce (intermediate level, university graduates) in certain sectors are source of local technology diffusion and autonomy and constitute a comparative advantage.

Finally, there is a wide consensus on the positive role of FDI in the region both in terms of growth, of catching up, integration. But the question which remains is to which extent the positive externalities created by the presence of FDI can expend? How local companies, subcontractors, SME can beneficiate of the positive impact of FDI in the region (Table 2.8)?

Conclusion

In this paper we have discussed three important points which make CEECs integration and up grading a particular case.

First, the magnitude of the last rounds of enlargement and integration to which the EU has faced and the importance of the institutional shocks to which new comers have been confronted. Speed (less than 15 years for the most advanced countries) and deepness of changes that have occurred (economic adjustment, opening up, development of market mechanisms) at a relatively

Table 2.8 Sectorial breakdown by ownership

Status 2010	Non CE private sector	CE private sector	State owned	Total
Consumer Business and Transportation	91	46	20	157
Energy and Resources	63	31	54	149
Life Sciences and Health Care	15	9	–	23
Manufacturing	79	28	10	116
Public Sector	–	–	5	5
Real Estate	9	2	–	11
Technology, Media and Telecommunications	30	4	5	39
Total	287	119	97	500

Source: Deloitte (2011)

low cost (for the EU budget) have been the main characteristics of this round of enlargement.

The process of enlargement and integration has been almost continuous with further integration of 'late comers' (Bulgaria, Romania), and further acceding countries from Western Balkans.

The role of FDI has played an important role in the region to transform, adjust, specialized industries, creating jobs, increase exports of higher added value products, and reconstruct an industrial network linking industries of the region with Western companies and markets.

Mostly, the driver to enter these countries has been opportunities for market growth, for competitive advantages (getting good and cheap domestic assets). It has been also an opportunity to deeply reshaping the European industry, introducing a new division of labour through specialisation along the regional value chain.

Entry of Western Balkan still has a positive impact on regional growth both in term of economic adjustment of new specialization. Although the linkage factor in less evident, FDI is pouring in the region, and, at a lesser pace, contribute to the economic transformation of the region.

References

Deloitte (2011) Top 500 Central Europe 2011. www.deloitte.com/cetop500
Drouet M, Richet X (eds) (2007) Vers l'élargissement de l'Union européenne à l'Europe de l'Est. PUR, Rennes
Eyal G, Szelényi I, Townsley E (1998) Making capitalism without capitalists. The new ruling elites in Eastern Europe. Verso, London
Gros D, Steinherr A (2004) Economic transition in Central and Eastern Europe. Cambridge University, Cambridge
Guerraoui D, Richet X (1997) Les investissements directs étrangers. Facteurs d' attractivité. Les Editions Toubkal/Casablanca/l' Harmattan, Paris

Guerraoui D, Richet X (2001) Economies émergentes: politiques de promotion de la PME. Expériences comparées. L'Harmattan, Paris

Radocevic S (2004) The emerging industrial structure of the wider Europe. Done, Routledge

Redzepagic S, Djukic M (2011) Contemporary issues in the integration processes of Western Balkan countries in the European Union. In: Serbian place in the process of globalization toward the European integration. International Center for Promotion of Enterprises, Ljubljana

Richet X (1992) Les économies socialistes européennes. Crise et transition. Armand Colin, Paris

Richet X (1997) Firm adjustment and barriers to restructuring in transition economies (with Hare P). Cuadernos del Este 20:155–164

Richet X (2004) Transforming economies, technology transfer and multinational corporations strategies. Zagreb Int Rev Econ Bus 17(1):1–22

Stephan J (2012) The technological role of inward manufacturing foreign direct investment in Central Est Europe – an investigation into the condition of technology transfer and diffusion. Habilitationsschrift, T.U. Bergakademie, Freiberg, 240 p

Transition report 2013, EBRD, London

World Investment Report (2012) UNCTAD. United Nations, Geneva

The Internationalisation of Chinese Firms: Growth, Motivations and Strategies

Xavier Richet

Globalisation has led to a new phenomenon which attracts the attention of scholars, namely the internationalisation of firms from emerging countries such as China. These firms are still limited in number and the volume of capital invested. But they are entering different markets in the North and the South, in search for production factors (material resources, technology and human capital), as well as sales outlets. The accumulation of financial resources, along with technical and managerial know-how through industrial cooperation with foreign companies operating in these emerging countries and the spin-offs this creates, all favour the investment in greenfield sites, as well as the acquisition abroad of assets that are sometimes prestigious (see for example the purchase of Volvo by the Chinese car producer Geely).

The mainstream press views these trends as a threat. Western firms are seeking to protect their technology, and governments are putting into place rules limiting the entry of foreign capital (the United States). According to the 2011 BCG *New Global Challengers* inventory, there are no less than 43 Chinese firms among the top 100 companies from the most dynamic emerging countries, which are operating in several sectors, running from energy to information technology and financial services. These firms are directly or indirectly controlled by States, and some are associated with inter-governmental contracts, especially in Africa which helps their entry into markets.

The internationalisation of Chinese firms and the development of their operations in various continents is a new phenomenon which has arisen during the last two decades. The literature on this subject is already abundant, analysing its causes, motivations, as well as its sustained and regular growth (Alon and McIntyre 2008, Alon et al. 2010, 2012; Chen 2011; Pearse 2011). This rapid progress is linked to the strong GDP growth recorded by China over several decades, and which has followed its economic reforms and opening. Having been

---

X. Richet (✉)
Département Sciences Économiques, University Sorbonne nouvelle, Paris, France
e-mail: xrichet@gmail.com

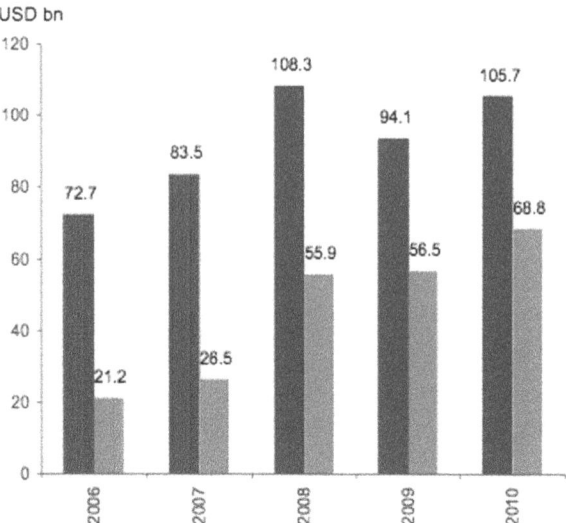

Graph 3.1 Chinese inward and outward FDI flows (in $ billions) (Source: BBVA 2012)

the main recipient of FDI, China is today one of the main new sources of FDI in the South (UNCTAD 2012). Outward FDI (OFDI) growth rates from China in recent years have converged on rates of inward FDI (IFDI): see Graph 3.1. In 2010, Chinese IFDI stood at $105.7 billion, while OFDI was $68.8 billion (BBVA 2011).

It must be stressed that this move to internationalisation is not unique to China. The BIRCs, which are among the main emerging market economies, have a certain number of companies that are spreading internationally, both into the developed economies (South-North), as well as into the developing economies (South-South), via greenfield investments and acquisitions. Most of the Chinese firms are "national champions" (BCG 2012). They have expanded thanks to a number of factors: innovation, and specialisation in protected markets, the development of internal competencies, market size, favoured access to finance from banks that have monopoly positions, the nature of regulation, the exchange rate, specific industrial policies that target certain sectors, research and development (R&D) policies. Furthermore, the continued appreciation of the Chinese Yuan – the Renminbi (RMB) – in recent years, against the US dollar and the euro, has cut the costs of buying up western companies, just as it raises domestic costs which today push Chinese firms that are labour intensive to locate to offshore production (e.g., to Vietnam, and Cambodia).

To be sure, in terms of the numbers of companies and volumes of flows, FDI from emerging countries, including China, are still modest (UNCTAD 2012). But China accounts for the lion's share today, and outperforms other emerging nations both in the number of new (greenfield investments) and acquisitions: this is true for the sectoral distribution of FDI as well as its location across the five world continents. The *Fortune Global 500* ranking for 2011 of major global companies includes 61 Chinese firms (including 4 from Hong Kong), 8 Indian companies, as well as 7 firms from Russia and Brazil. The Chinese firms, of which nearly 80 % are state enterprises, belong to nearly all sectors, ranging from mining and oil extraction to banking, passing via electronics, capital equipment and transport.

How is this strong growth to be explained? Is there a link to the massive inflow of FDI into China, which played a vital role in technological catch-up and the appropriation of know-how, followed by the rise of Chinese outward FDI? What are the specificities of China's industrial model that favoured this expansion, and which allowed the emergence of such a large number of companies capable of competing in certain niches with the major multinationals from the developed world? What are the specificities of these countries in comparison with their counterparts in the developed market economies?

A few Chinese companies today hold dominating market shares in developed world markets (Haier, Huawei). Others are undertaking technological breakthroughs via acquisition strategies, which allow them both to obtain technology and to position themselves in new, competitive market segments that are more profitable, including within China itself (Geely). Other firms, however, have failed or have run into difficulties integrating their acquisitions or greenfield investments within their global strategies.

Section 3.1 looks at the role of inward FDI into China and its contribution to industrial catch-up. The second section presents the growth and sectoral as well as geographic distribution of Chinese outward FDI. Section 3.3 outlines the motivations of Chinese firms seeking to internationalise, while the last section examines some theoretical interpretations of the internationalisation process of these companies.

3.1 FDI in China as a Vector of Modernisation

China's hosting of FDI has played a role in accelerating its economic development, even if it has at times been viewed negatively by certain observers (Huang 2003). In contrast to Eastern Europe, FDI into China has been strongly regulated (in terms of volume, ownership and the control of joint ventures, regional distribution, the search for agglomeration effects, and links with local government industrial policies).

In contrast to Japan and South Korea, China initially based its modernisation strategy on welcoming western FDI (from the United States, Europe and other Asian countries), in the hope of acquiring technology it did not have. In Japan and South Korea, company upgrading took place through a process of "reverse engineering", a process based on first mastering, then enriching and developing standard technologies, sometimes by achieving significant technological leaps (Freeman 1987). This process was also supported by adopting strategic industrial policies, that were targeted and cooperative (State-Enterprises), aimed at growth technologies (electronics). In China, domestic firms were only able to benefit from the spin-offs derived from the presence of western firms, in a second phase, once these firms had been established in the country and had created networks with suppliers. Only then could Chinese firms gain new skills and enter domestic markets which had been dominated by foreign companies. Low entry barriers in many areas, as well as the industrial policies conducted by central, provincial and municipal governments helped with the process of benefiting from spin-offs, company acquisition and the upgrading of local firms. Lastly and most recently, innovation policies and a significant rise in R&D (Fabre and Grumbach 2011) have sought to accelerate the catch-up of Chinese firms through access to technology, to achieve an increase in their performance in both domestic and international markets.

In the automotive industry, for example, Chinese partner firms have often played a passive role, acting as mere (neutral) platforms, providing grounds, plant, and labour to foreign operators. The foreign partners acted in the market (developing sub-contracting and distribution networks), while the Chinese partners took care of the bureaucracy (relations with authorities). Strongly competitive environments (low entry barriers) and strong market growth facilitated the entry of numerous competitors – public, semi-public and private – into the sector, helping raise supply and reduce costs (Richet and Ruet 2008).

Inward FDI has played an important role in the adjustment of firms and of trade. It generates more than half of Chinese exports and imports, accounting for 30 % of industrial output and creates 22 % of profits in the industrial sector, while only employing 10 % of labour, given its high level of productivity. Though it is hard to evaluate spin-off effects on other sectors, which are indeed real, industries receiving FDI do have higher levels of productivity. Generally speaking inward FDI has contributed positively to the strong growth of GDP. The central government has been able to combine a strong policy of regulating FDI, with a certain level of decentralisation regarding hosting, attraction, and the adoption of local industrial policies at the regional and municipal level, as shown by the car industry (Thun 2006).

It may therefore be asked whether FDI has allowed China to bridge the gap with the developed market economies.[1] It is hard to reach a clear and unequivocal view on this, due to the differences between sectors in terms of their foreign presence, the nature of markets, technologies and the degree of competition.

The impact of industrial cooperation is appreciated in a qualified way by the Chinese authorities. They view it as an essential contribution to the modernisation of their economy, while underlining its limited impact on the shift to high value-added production, the appropriation of know-how, and specialisation in numerous sectors (Yasheng 2003).

Sino-foreign cooperation through the creation of joint-ventures has not induced a rapid transfer of technology, despite agreements concluded between operators.[2]

---

[1] China's share in value added (less than 8 %) and its share of profits (1.8 %) in the production of iPhones are often used to illustrate its weaknesses in the value chain of high technology products.

[2] The joint-venture format has evolved, especially in less strategic sectors. Thus, in the automobile industry, firms producing component parts may be 100 % owned by foreign investors, though for final assemblers the limit is 49 %.

3 The Internationalisation of Chinese Firms: Growth, Motivations and Strategies

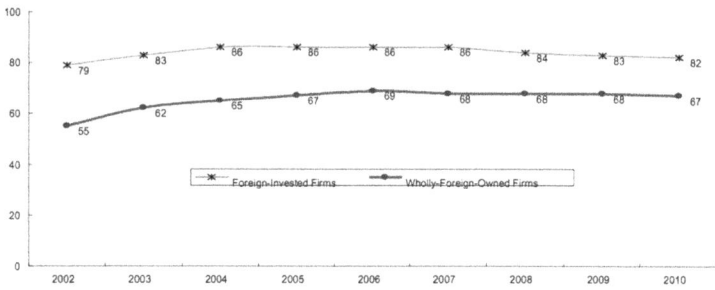

Fig. 3.1 Contribution des firmes à capitaux étrangers aux exportation à haute valeur ajoutée de la Chine (%) (Source: Xing 2012)

Chinese firms file less patents than their counterparts and innovate less. A large share of Chinese exports, be they upstream or downstream in the production process, are of low value-added products (Hanemaan and Rosen 2012), even though companies with foreign capital account for nearly three quarters of high value-added exports (OECD 2012) (Fig. 3.1).

There are several causes of this limited transfer:

- The protection of intellectual property (one of the main points of disagreement between China and its western partners, along with the undervaluation of the RMB). It is notoriously deficient and pushes western firms to limit transfers.
- The nature of agreements and the behaviour of Chinese partners. In many cases, Chinese partners have acted passively during the launch phase of cooperation. This reduces internal and external spin-offs (the transfer of knowledge, the appropriation of know-how).
- China's entry into the WTO has allowed foreign firms to protect their know-how better, especially by creating subsidiaries which are 100 % foreign owned.

Nearly half of all Chinese exports are of low value-added. Exports also contain a high level of imports: more than 25 % for automotive engines and more than 45 % in information technology (OECD 2012). The decision by the government to raise R&D spending substantially (which accounted for 1.83 % of GDP in 2011), is aimed at accelerating the acquisition of technologies that China still lacks.[3]

These facts explain why the Chinese government has a selective policy concerning FDI inflows, which focuses on the impact they could have in terms of providing technology to host companies. The Catalogue of Foreign Investments which was recently published by the Council of State Affairs sets out sectors targeted by the authorities (Bulletin économique de la Chine 2012). Such targeting reveals the level of technical competence reached by Chinese firms in several sectors (chemicals, pharmaceuticals, metallurgy, green technologies, textiles, high-voltage electricity distribution, etc.). It shows the threshold effects concerning technological improvements achieved and the volumes of production envisaged in

---

[3] The same level of spending as France. R&D spending is equivalent to 2.7 % of GDP in the US, 3.3 % in Japan, 2.3 % in Germany and 3.3 % in South Korea.

targeted sectors. Today, FDI constitutes a certain form of subsidiarity in the eyes of the government: how is technology integrated into capacities of Chinese firms?

These choices draw on the priority of the 12th 5-year plan, which sets out seven emerging strategies: alternative energies, new materials, biotechnologies, new generations in the field of new technologies, environmental industries, and alternative automobiles (electric cars). Today, these sectors account for only 4 % of output, but are planned to rise to 15 % by 2020 (BBVA 2012).

3.2 Chinese OFDI: Its Growth, Origin, Sectoral and Geographic Distribution

The Chinese economic model which has developed over the last three decades is different to those of Japan and South Korea, at least as far as its first phase is concerned in terms of access to technologies, the accumulation of competencies, the role of the State and the implementation of catch-up policies.

China has specialised in the production of low value-added goods, and has applied a mercantilist policy. As a result, it has been able to accumulate in a few decades financial and monetary surpluses which it can use to achieve other objectives. These surpluses include sovereign wealth funds, the purchase of foreign securities, and FDI. The latter still only accounts for a small share of these assets. In 2010, China's foreign assets stood at $4,126 billion: FDI was only $310.8 billion, and portfolio investments $257.1 billion, respectively 7 % and 6 %. Despite the strong growth of OFDI in the developed economies, levels still remain low. In contrast, the rise of China's OFDI has led to worries about its control of strategic assets, which are often considered as national, industrial jewels in some countries, such as the purchase of Volvo by the Chinese car firm Geely (Balcet et al. 2012), and worries about China's growing influence in the major developed (Subramanian 2011). The acceleration of the pace of Chinese OFDI is due to a number of factors including the strong growth of the Chinese economy which requires increasing raw materials and fossil fuels (oil and gas).

Over the last 20 years, inward FDI for the developed market economies (DMEs) has continued to rise, accounting for 69.9 % of the global IFDI stock ($12,501 billion), compared to 27.9 % for the developing economies. The Asian economies account for 16.3 % of this total, and China alone for 2.7 %. For OFDI, the DME's share fell from 93 % to 82.3 %, whereas the developing countries' share rose strongly from 6.9 % to 15.3 %, with Asia's share of the world stock rising from 3.2 % to 11.5 %, and China's from 1.1 % to 4.5 %.

The growth of Chinese outward FDI has been marked by several phases (BBVA 2011; Hanemaan and Rosen 2012). Each phase has been linked to political choices and central government incentives ranging from strict control, to gradual relaxation and then encouragement with adoption. At the start of the 2000s, proactive policies known as "going global" were adopted as part of the 10th development plan. In the second half of the last decade, these policies contributed to accelerating the internationalisation of Chinese companies across all continents (Box 3.1).

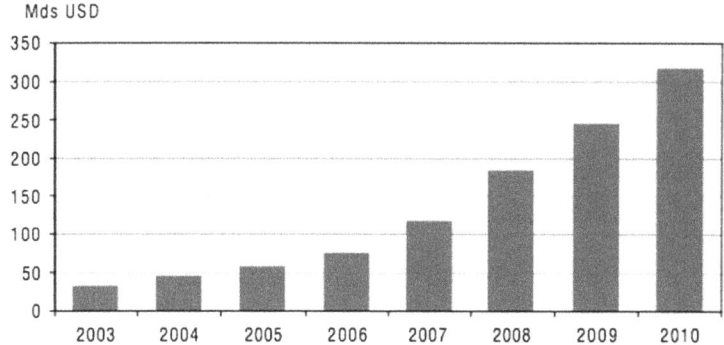

Fig. 3.2 The evolution of Chinese FDI abroad (Source: Bulletin Economique Chine 2011, Mofcom)

Figure 3.2 summarises the sectoral and geographic distribution of Chinese outward FDI, and Table 3.1 shows the distribution of value added. These figures raise a few points. The first concerns the two types of investments, notably *round tripping investments* from Hong Kong made by Chinese firms. These concern capital which is not repatriated to China, but which stays in Hong Kong to avoid foreign currency controls by central government. Such Hong Kong investments are largely understated in official Chinese statistics, only 4.9 % (*China Daily*, 31/9/2012). Subsequently, the search for tax havens in the Caribbean (the British Virgin Islands and the Cayman Islands) has led to the creation of platforms for investments in third countries, notably in Latin America, which is a favoured destination of Chinese outward FDI, especially in the raw materials sector, as well as in agriculture.[4]

The sectoral distribution of Chinese OFDI involves a large variety of sectors, with four leading sectors accounting for 75 % of all investments.

Part of China's outward FDI is directly linked to the expansion of commercial activities related to exports (transport, insurance and financial services). The search for raw materials, especially hydrocarbons, is also important. China's top multinational firms in terms of capitalisation and turnover are operating in these sectors. They are present in Asian markets, the Middle East and Canada. The search for strategic assets is being carried out to meet the supposed limits, as far as China is concerned, of the transfer of technology and appropriation of know-how provided by foreign multinationals based in China.[5] This seems to have slowed down since

---

[4] Pierre Salama (2012) points to the contradictory position of the Brazilian economy, whose strong export growth (especially towards China) and GDP growth are being accompanied by a precocious deindustrialisation processes.

[5] Measuring know-how precisely is generally difficult as apart from data on patents filed there is little quantitative information available, except at a micro economic level (workshops and companies).

Table 3.1 The stock of Chinese outward FDI in ($ millions)

Industry	2010	In %
Leasing & business service	97,246	30.65
Finance	55,253	17.41
Mining	44,661	14.07
Wholesale and retail trade	42,006	13.24
Transport, storage & post	23,188	7.30
Manufacturing	17,802	5.61
Information transmission, computer services	8,406	2.64
Real estate	7,266	2.29
Construction	6,173	1.94
Scientific research, technical services	3,967	1.25
Production and supply of electricity, gas & water	3,411	1.07
Residential & other services	3,230	1.01
Agriculture, forestry, husbandry, fishing	2,612	0.82
Water conservancy, environment & public utility	1,133	0.35
Management	450	0.14
Accommodation & catering service	346	0.10
Culture, sport & recreation	36	0.01
Public management & social organization	24	0.007
Total	317,211	100

Source: Adapted from BBVA (2011).

China's accession to the WTO, because of the greater possibilities of protecting intellectual property (Fig. 3.3).

Lastly, as far as the legal form of companies is concerned, they are mostly State-owned enterprises (nearly 70 %), or publicly listed companies in which the State has a share, influencing the internationalisation strategy of these firms. Box 3.2 shows the importance of mining investments compared to other sectors.

> **Box 3.1. Chinese Round Tripping Investments**
> There is a statistical bias when analyzing the flow of Chinese outward foreign investments and assessing the reality and importance of round tripping investments (Sutherland and Matthews 2009). An important part of Chinese outward FDI are located in tax heavens. Chinese investors use these locations (Hong Kong, Cayman Islands, British Virgin Islands) in order to take advantage either of local taxation policies, to escape capital control on the home market. Reintroducing capital in China favours the change of original companies into foreign invested firms with tax advantages.
>
> The location abroad can also enjoy several financial benefits: valuation of assets, access to external financial markets, greater facilities for raising capital in other financial centers.

(continued)

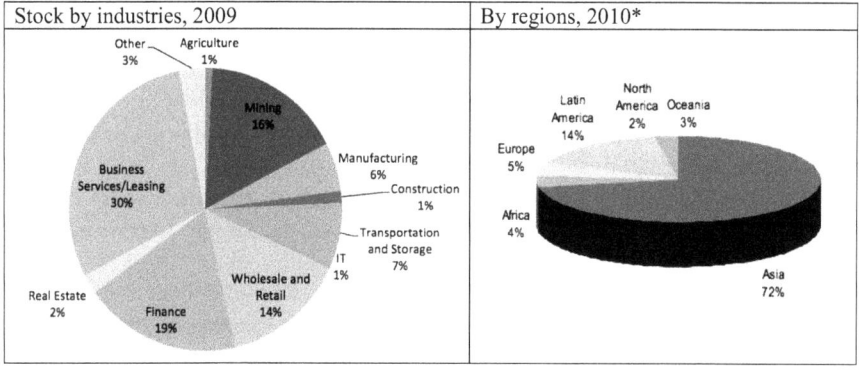

Fig. 3.3 Chinese outward FDI by industry and region (Source: Mofcom, BBVA (2011)). *Within Asia's total of 72 %, 66.9 % is in Hong Kong, while within Latin America, the British Virgin Islands and the Caymans account for 11.7 %

Box 3.1 (continued)

Sixty three percent of total Chinese FDI in 2010 went to Hong Kong (87 % of Chinese FDI in Asia). The second largest regional stock is Latin America and the Caribbean (14 %) with both tax havens mentioned hosting for 92 % share of the Chinese FDI in this region (Davies 2012).

Box 3.2. China's 10 Largest Multinational Companies (Stock of Capital Invested Abroad)
1. *China Petrochemical Corporation (Sinopec)*. Fully owned by the State. Its main activities include: oil, natural gas and petrochemicals. It is the largest Chinese producer and distributor of refined products.
2. *China National Petroleum Corporation (CNCP)*: a state owned enterprise with a wide range of upstream and downstream activities related to oil and natural gas.
3. *China National Offshore Oil Corporation (CNOOC)*: an integrated state owned enterprise in the energy sector.
4. *China Resources Holdings Co.*: a state owned conglomerate with a wide range of activities including real estate, food products, brewing, petrochemicals, retail trade, textiles, cement and electricity.
5. *China Mobile Communications Corporation*: a state owned enterprise operating in telecommunications: mobile telephony, Internet and multimedia services.

(continued)

Box 3.2 (continued)
6. *China Ocean Shipping Group Company (COSCO)*: China's largest shipping company with exclusive ownership of 25 subsidiaries.
7. *CITIC Group*: a state-owned enterprise with 44 subsidiaries. Its main activities are in finance and investment.
8. *China National Cereals, Oils and Foodstuffs Corporation (COFCO)*: trade in grains, vegetable oils and food products. Strong diversification since 1992.
9. *China Merchants Group*: a strongly diversified conglomerate belonging to the State, but based in Hong Kong. It mainly operates in three fields: transport and related infrastructure (ports, motorways, transport of energy and logistics), financial investments and asset management, as well as the development and management of property.
10. *Sinochem* Corporation: a State-owned enterprise operating in the oil sector, fertilisers and chemical products.

These 10 companies are State-owned enterprises under authority of the SASAC (State-owned Assets Supervision and Administration Commission) of the State Council.
Source: Mofcom, OECD (2008).

3.3 The Motives of Chinese Companies' Internationalisation

The internationalisation of Chinese firms as part of a slow process, linked to the phases of economic reform and openness, two choices by central government and to incentives that have been introduced regularly. There is a strong correlation between institutional reforms, political liberalisation and the development of outward FDI (Buckley et al. 2011; Ren et al. 2012) as shown in Fig. 3.4.

Four major motives have pushed Chinese firms to internationalise (Zhan 1995; OECD 2008; Gugler and Boie 2008; Wang 2012):

– *Access to markets*

Access to markets, especially when nearby, follows trade flows and the penetration of markets by Chinese exports. Entering a market is made easier thanks to accumulated know-how. It is a way of circumventing tariff barriers, creating local or regional distribution networks, and getting close to regional markets which are expanding strongly. Another motivation is linked to strengthening competition and the rise in domestic overcapacity, which reduces firms' profit margins. Through local investments, Chinese firms acquire new know-how (which is produced outside the domestic market) and can experiment their internationalisation strategies by limiting risks and costs in case of failure. The accumulation of competencies acquired in the market in areas of medium technology (consumer goods) or high-technology (ICT) has acted as a springboard for the internationalisation of certain firms, some of which have become world leaders in their field, such as Haier,

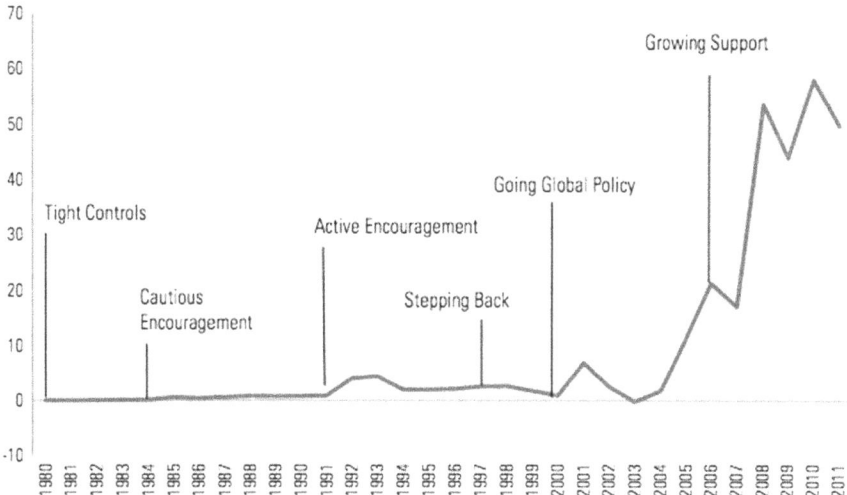

Fig. 3.4 The liberalisation of the capital export regime and outward FDI, 1980–2011 (Source: Hanemaan and Rosen 2012)

Huawei and Lenovo, which are amongst the best known. In contrast, other companies which had the same levels of competence domestically, sometimes with government help, partly failed in their internationalisation strategy via acquisition (TCL, and SAIC in Korea). Such failures have been due to the fact that acquisitions have been difficult to integrate into groups' strategies, or because the acquiring company pursued and an asset stripping strategy (acquiring firms with the aim of only controlling a part of them).

– *The search for efficiency*

This factor was less important at the start of the internationalisation process, given China's low production costs. The rise in domestic costs in recent years, however, has led to firms relocating to other Asian countries (Vietnam and North Korea), in labour-intensive industries (textiles). Today, in the province of Guangdong, the rapid and consequential rise in wages (up more than 20 % within 2–3 years) has contributed to offshoring to neighbouring economies with lower labour costs.

– *The Access to resources*

This is certainly a leading motive of internationalisation by Chinese firms. The Chinese economy has to ensure the availability of resources needed for double digit growth, taking into account both the limits and depletion of national resources (with the exception of coal) and its plant and equipment, which are largely run down and which consume high levels of raw materials. The technological choices set out within the framework of the 12th plan (2011–2015) stress the use of substitutable energies, but the energy transition risks taking a long time. There are several State-owned enterprises among all the top internationalised firms, which are actively supported by central government, and which operate in oil and natural gas extraction. The access to resources is not constrained by proximity. Chinese companies are working at a global level: in the Americas, Africa, the Pacific, and Central Asia. Nationalist conflicts in the China Sea, between China, Vietnam, the Philippines and Japan have been sharpened by the discovery of oil reserves under the seabed.

– *The search for strategic assets*

The search for strategic assets has become one of the leading preoccupations of Chinese firms, both to consolidate their strengths in foreign markets as well as to acquire technologies they have not been able to obtain through cooperation with foreign MNCs present in China, or due to the weaknesses of China's innovation system. The financial reserves which China has accumulated, along with the liberalisation of regulations on outward FDI (reductions in controls on capital exports) on the one hand, and the fall in foreign asset values due to the international financial crisis on the other hand, have greatly increased opportunities for acquiring firms abroad. Accordingly, the "shopping list" of Chinese investments has lengthened, especially in Europe and the United States, which in turn has led to protectionist policies concerning certain sensitive assets (telecommunications). The acquisition of technology and of foreign brands has been a means to accelerate the rise of Chinese companies and improve their foreign reputation. Chinese firms have been able to obtain assets entirely in this way (companies and their networks), or just segments, which often have a technology content and which can be repatriated and integrated into production in China (sometimes accompanied by the temptation of asset stripping). This is an advantageous means of entering markets, allowing Chinese firms to acquire reputation and accede to technologies they do not have. Through mergers and acquisitions, Chinese companies have thus been able to acquire assets they seek to integrate in their global strategy.

By compiling data on outward FDI undertaken over a number of years, Chinese economists have highlighted the motives of Chinese firms. Two motivations standout in particular: the search for resources, and the search for strategic assets (Wang 2012) (Table 3.2) (Box 3.3).

Box 3.3. The Acquisition of Volvo by the Geely Company

Geely is a last-generation Chinese automobile company, which has brought together private companies that developed without direct support from the State, and which often followed technological spin-offs. The acquisition of Volvo by this company, which ranks 10th among Chinese car producers, has been much commented:
– How was it possible for a non-state company to acquire a Western firm considered as one of the jewels of global car production?
– How did Geely develop the skills and resources to acquire this firm?
– How does Volvo fit in with Geely's domestic and global strategy?

(continued)

Table 3.2 The distribution of outward FDI by primary motivation

	Number		Value	
	Number	%	Value ($ billions)	%
Total				
Search from markets	87	30	28.2	28
Search for resources	121	41	51.0	51
Search for strategic assets	78	27	20.0	20
Search for efficiency	7	2	0.2	0
Manufactured products				
Search from markets	49	27	6.9	22
Search for resources	61	34	9.9	32
Search for strategic assets	63	35	14.2	46
Search for efficiency	7	4	0.2	1

Source: Wang (2012)

Box 3.3 (continued)

First, Geely was able to acquire Volvo at half the initial price because of the financial crisis. The acquisition of Volvo is part of Geely's development strategy in China. To move upmarket, Geely has pursued external growth by acquiring assets it did not own, knowing that it could not obtain the level of technology to be competitive upmarket in China (where car companies are owned by foreign firms like BMW, Nissan, Mercedes, Toyota, Lexus, Buick, Chevrolet, etc.).

A division of labour has been set up between the Swedish and Chinese headquarters. The Swedish management retains control over international strategy and research & development, while contributing to the development of upmarket products for the Chinese market. The Chinese side of the company has built two new factories and research centre in China, with financial support from the three provinces which host these investments (an indirect form of support from the State).

The technology remains abroad, but the acquisition has allowed Geely to enter into competition in the largest car market in the world, namely China. The company is therefore internationalising upmarket to compete with firms operating on the Chinese market. It is also investing in developing economy markets to establish low- and medium-market production units.

Source: Balcet et al. (2012).

3.4 Some Theoretical Interpretations of the Internationalisation Strategies by Chinese Firms

For many specialists, the internationalisation of Chinese firms can be explained by the domestic institutional context in which it is occurring. This process seems to confirm the "international investment path" paradigm of Dunning, who established a link between domestic growth and increasing FDI. The other explanatory factor follows from technological and managerial spin-offs introduced by the presence of numerous Western foreign direct investments in China over the last three decades (Box 3.4).

The internationalisation of companies can be understood within a threefold context: (i) the profound reform of the Chinese economy, (ii) the internationalisation strategy expected and encouraged by the state and applied to companies, and lastly (iii) the importance of institutional changes, the interactions they have provoked by providing actors with greater room for manoeuvre. Companies which internationalise benefit from direct support, profit from opportunities, and know how to use their autonomy by drawing on experience accumulated over the years, within a competitive environment created by economic reforms.

The growth of Chinese FDI is very recent. It only really took off in volume terms, both in the number of acquisitions as well as greenfield investments, when China joined the WTO in 2001. This phase of acceleration was preceded by the accumulation of competencies within the framework of successive reforms concerning Chinese regulations governing foreign investment. State policy has changed considerably in recent years. It has created a favourable environment, rather than fixing strict rules to guide firms wishing to internationalise.

A distinctive characteristic of Chinese MNCs lies in the way firms acquire skills, as the necessary prerequisite to undertaking internationalisation. To Dunning's OLI paradigm (Organisation, Localisation, Internalisation) should be added the LLL model (Linkage, Leverage, Learning) by Mathews (2002), to account for this process. The latter shows how cooperation with high value-added firms, on a contractual basis stretching out over time, has allowed Chinese firms to take advantage of leverage and accelerate their apprenticeship and skills' development.

In the context of globalisation, which is characterised by the globalisation and disintegration of the international chain of value, the apprenticeship and accumulation of competencies has become easier. Despite their lack of resources compared to Western multinational companies, Chinese firms have accomplished their internationalisation successfully.

Williamson and Yin (2010) complete the analysis of institutional factors favouring the internationalisation of these firms. The authors integrate two dimensions: positioning in the market and the mobilisation of resources to explain how firms generate their competitive advantage. Companies which internationalise mobilise three types of capacities:
– Cost innovations by using cost advantages of domestic firms (i.e., the capacity to produce while cutting production costs), yet still maintaining quality;

Table 3.3 The growth characteristics of Chinese MNCs

First category of firms: the presence of advantages, followed by internationalisation	
1. Technological domination	Huawei, Jincheng
2. Economies of scale/low costs	Haier, Hisense, BOE, Holley
3. Economies of dimension/diversified groups	CWGC, Haier
Second category of firms: internationalisation, followed by acquisition of advantage	
4. Search for technology	TCL, Lenovo, Shanghai Electronic, Wanxiang
5. Search for markets	TCL, Lenovo
6. Search for resources	CNPC, CNOOC, Shougang, Baosteel, CNMC

Source: Du et al. (2008)

– Combined capacities in offering markets redefined products to integrate technology, leading to low costs;
– Dynamic capacities in terms of adjustment in the face of uncertainty by drawing on the high levels of flexibility, a quick learning curve.

On the basis of several case studies, Chinese researchers (Du et al. 2008) have drawn a distinction between firms which require competencies before internationalising, and those companies which internationalise without any particular skills and whose competitive advantage is created in the process (Table 3.3).

> **Box 3.4. The International Investment Path**
> The model of FDI development in China follows that observed in most developing countries, and which can be summarised as having three phases, leading to an investment development path as proposed by Dunning (1988). China is currently taking this development path (Marton and McCartthy 2007).
>
> Hanemaan and Rosen (2012) recall the different phases of the cycle, showing in a stylised way the path taken by China, albeit with a slightly weaker amplitude.
>
> Phase 1: to start with, prior to economic reform, there was no foreign investment in China, and no domestic firm had the resources to invest abroad.
>
> Phase 2: when economic reforms were introduced and growth accelerated, foreign companies took advantage of the relaxation of exchange controls and profit opportunities, so that FDI entered into the country.
>
> Phases 3 and 4: once the economy reached a certain level of GDP per capita, domestic firms began to invest abroad and outward FDI began, while inward FDI remained strong. As OFDI exceeds inward flows, the net position shifts from being negative to positive.
>
> Phase 5: once the country reaches the per capita GDP levels of developed economies, the net FDI position stabilises and fluctuates around an equilibrium, which is dependent on the business cycle and the country's economic structure.

Conclusion

It is important to look at the context, and the specificity of the framework in which Chinese firms internationalise. Important too are companies' characteristics relative to theoretical models, which so far have examined the development of multinational firms based on the advanced market economies.

Concerning China, the first point, which stands out is the significance of cooperation, learning (and spin-offs) within industries, the role of the State and its policies encouraging companies. The accelerated growth of FDI in the various regions of the world should also be noted. Lastly the current financial crisis has also increased the possibilities of the diversification of Chinese reserves.

According to certain analysts (Phoenix Weekly 2012; BCG.Perspectives 2012), only a few Chinese companies are really present worldwide. The following critiques may be identified in particular:
- Apart from major companies like Haier, Huawei, and the large Chinese oil companies, most firms invest or do business locally and are far from carrying out all their activities internationally.
- The international influence and visibility of Chinese brands remains weak. Acquiring international reputation involves substantial investments in advertising and communication, but also particular care concerning product quality and customer services.
- Chinese firms are seeking to obtain their international objectives through the merger and acquisition of foreign companies, in order to obtain advanced technologies, sales networks and reputation rapidly. But this strategy is not succeeding very well. According to a report, 90 % of 300 merger and acquisition operations carried out abroad by Chinese firms, between 2008 and 2010, ended in failure and stock market losses of 40–50 %.

In recent years, strong growth of Chinese outward FDI has occurred, especially since China's membership of the WTO. But it remains limited, for the moment, in volume terms across different destinations, notably in the developed countries (the acquisition of technologies and brands), and in developing nations (the acquisition of raw materials). China's central government, and indirectly, both provincial and municipal governments have been supporting the move to internationalisation through incentives and subsidies. However, firms' own motivations are determinant: internationalisation reflects their own strategies and is part of their policy to access production factors. Internationalisation is also motivated by domestic competitive conditions.

Several factors emerge from the accumulated experience of Chinese firms:
- The specificity of Chinese firms in terms of catching up and their learning curves;
- Advantages in terms of innovation, cost controls and integration into international networks.

However, the linkages between domestic and international strategies remain problematic. Many firms internationalise to acquire what they do not have themselves, or have great difficulties in obtaining. Only some large Chinese companies today are capable of developing strategies similar to those implemented by large Western multinational companies.

References

Alon I, McIntyre J (eds) (2008) Globalization of Chinese enterprises. Palgrave MacMillan, New York
Alon I, Chang J, Fetscherin M, Lattemann C, McIntyre JR (eds) (2010) China rules. Globalization and political transformation catching-up and development. Palgrave MacMillan, New York
Alon I, Fetscherin M, Gugler P (eds) (2012) Chinese international investments. Palgrave MacMillan, New York
Balcet G, Wang W-H, Richet X (2012) Geely: a trajectory of catching up and asset-seeking multinational growth. Int J Automot Technol Manage 12(4):360–375
BBVA Research (2011) China's outward FDI expands. Economic Watch, China
BBVA Research (2012) Innovation: where does China stand ? Economic Watch, China
BCG.Perspectives (2012) The 2012 BCG 50 Chinese global challengers: end of easy growth. https://www.bcg.perspective.com
BCG Perspectives (2011) The 2011 BCG Global Challengers: companies on the move. Rising stars from rapidly developing economies are reshaping global industries. pp 1–19, https://www.bcg.com
Buckley PJ, Vass H, Cross AC, Clegg LJ (2011) The emergence of Chinese firms as multinationals: the influence of the home institutional environment. In: Pearse R (ed) China and the multinationals. International business and the entry of China into the global economy. Edward Elgar, Cheltenham
Bulletin économique Chine (2012) Actualisation du cataloque chinois sur les investissements étrangers avril, (45):20–21
Chen C (2011) Foreign direct investment in China. Location determinants, investor differences and economic impacts. Edward Elgar, Cheltenham
Davies K (2012) Outward FDI from China and its policy context. Vale Columbia Center, pp 1–16, Columbia University, New York
Dent P (2012) Effects of absorptive capacity on international acquisitions of Chinese firms. In: Alon I, Fetscherin M, Gugler P (eds) Chinese international investments. Palgrave MacMillan, New York
Du Y, Kang R, Yinbin K (2008) Understanding the growth models of Chinese multinational corporations. Int J Chin Cult Manage 1(4):451–478
Dunning JH (1988) The eclectic paradigm of international production: a restatement and some possible extensions. J Int Bus Stud 19–1:1–31
Economist Intelligence Unit (2010) A brave new world. The climate for Chinese M&A abroad. The Economist, London, 48 p
Econote (2012) Chine: investissements directs à l'étranger: beaucoup de bruit pour rien, 7, mai, Société générale, Département des études économiques
Fabre G, Grumbach S (2011) The world upside down. China's R&D & innovation strategy. Séminaire BRICS/EHESS-FMSH, Paris, Miméo, 20 p
Fortune (2012) Global 500. The world's largest corporations, 23 July
Freeman C (1987) Technology policy and economic performance; lessons from Japan. Frances Printer Publishers, London/New York
Goldstein A (2007) Multinational companies from emerging economies. Palgrave Macmillan, Basingstoke
Gugler P, Boie B (2008) The emergence of Chinese FDI: determinants and strategies of Chinese MNEs. Conference emerging multinationals: outward foreign direct investment from emerging and developing economies, Copenhagen Business School, Copenhagen, 23 p

Hanemaan T, Rosen D (2012) China invests in Europe, Rhodium Group, New York, 77 p
Huchet J-F, Richet X (eds) (2005) Gouvernance, coopération et stratégie des firmes chinoises. L'Harmattan, Paris
Kim I (2009) Inward and outward internationalization of Chinese firms. SERI Q 2(3):23–39
Marton K, McCarthy C (2007) Is China on the investment development path? J Asia Bus Stud 1(2):1–9
Mathews JA (2002) Dragon multinationals. A new model for global growth. Oxford University Press, Oxford
McKay H, Song L (eds) (2012) Rebalancing and sustaining growth in China. Australian National University, E-Press, Canberra
OECD (2008) OECD investment policy review: China 2008. OECD, Paris
OECD (2012) China in focus: lessons and challenges 2012. OECD, Paris
Pearse R (ed) (2011) China and the multinationals. International business and the entry of China into the global economy. Edward Elgar, Cheltenham
Phoenix Weekly (2012) Les entreprises chinoises transnationales sont-elles vraiment transnationales? 1er août 2012
Ren B, Liang H, Zheng Y (2012) An institutional perspective and the role of the state for Chinese OFDI. In: Alon I, Fetscherin M, Gugler P (eds) Chinese international investments. Palgrave MacMillan, New York
Richet X, Ruet J (2008) The Chinese and Indian automobile industry in perspective: technology appropriation, catching-up and development. Transit Stud Rev 15(3):447–465
Richet X, Wang H, Wang W (2001) Foreign direct investment in the Chinese automobile industry. China Perspect 4(38):40–47, November–December
Rosen D, Hanemann T (2009) China's changing outbond foreign direct investment profile: drivers and policy implications. Perterson institute for international economics, policy brief number PB09-14
Salama P (2012) Les économies émergentes latino-américaines. Entre cigales et fourmis. Armand Colin, Paris
Subramanian A (2011) Eclipse. Living in the shadow of China's economic dominance. Peterson Institute for International Economic, Washington, DC
Sutherland D, Matthews B (2009) 'Round tripping' or 'capital augmenting' OFDI? Chinese outward investment and the Caribbean tax havens. Paper prepared for Leverhulme Centre for Research on Globalisation and Economic Policy (GEP), University of Nottingham 14th and 15th January, 2009
Thun E (2006) Changing lanes in China: foreign direct investment, local government, and auto sector development. Cambridge University Press, Cambridge
UNCTAD (2012) World investment report 2012. UNCTAD, Geneva
Vercueil J (2011) Les pays émergents. Brésil, Russie, Inde, Chine. Mutations économiques et nouveaux defis. Bréal, Paris
Wang B (2012) Upgrading China's economy through outward foreign direct investment. In: McKay H, Song L (eds) Rebalancing and sustaining growth in China. Australian National University, E-Press, Acton
Williamson P, Yin E (2010) Racing with the Chinese dragons. In: Alon I, Chang J, Fetscherin M, Lattemann C, McIntyre JR (eds) China rules. Globalization and political transformation catching-up and development. Palgrave MacMillan, New York
Yasheng H (2003) Selling China: foreign direct investment during the reform era. Cambridge University Press, Cambridge

Part II

Redesigning of Public Policies to Meet Competitiveness and Attractiveness Challenges, While Dealing with Business Lobbying

From Dirigisme to Realism: Chinese Industrial Policy in the Era of Globalisation

Jean-François Huchet

The 2012 "Fortune 500" classification of the world's largest companies includes 73 Chinese firms (32 for France and 68 for Japan), whereas there were none only 15 years ago.[1] Meanwhile, Chinese firms are increasing their overseas operations with nearly $60 billion of foreign direct investment per year, on average since 2008, compared to less than $1 billion annually before 2000. Fifteen years ago, Chinese exports were mainly composed of primary products and goods with a low technological content. Today they are rapidly concentrating on products in the information industry. Research and development (R & D), which was totally lifeless in the early 1980s, has also experienced brisk development since the late 1990s: China is now the world's second largest publisher of scientific journals and ninth in the number of patents filed in the United States in 2009.[2]

These signs of the emergence of China's industrial power raise a number of questions in the fields of economics and industrial policy, as well as in growth theory (Huchet 2010). After the Japanese and Korean miracles, the temptation is indeed very strong to apply to China – the civilisation at the origin of the Confucian political and cultural basis of Asia – explanations related to the omnipotence of the State and the effectiveness of industrial policy (Johnson 1982). What is really the truth? Has China followed the virtuous industrial policy footsteps of its Asian neighbours? What have been the terms of the industrial policy since 1978 and what effect has it had on China's economic takeoff? What directions might industrial policy take in the coming years, given the context of the increasing openness of China's economy? This paper aims to provide some answers to these questions.

---

[1] http://money.cnn.com/magazines/fortune/global500/2012/countries/China.html?iid=smlrr, consulted 31 August 2012.

[2] Royal Society, Knowledge, Networks and Nations: Global scientific collaboration in the 21st century, Royal Society Policy document, March 2011, 114 pp.

J.-F. Huchet (✉)
INALCO-Langues'O, Sorbonne Paris Cité, 65 rue des grands Moulins, 75013 Paris, France
e-mail: jean-francois.huchet@inalco.fr

Section 4.1 recalls some aspects of the historical legacy of the period before 1978, as well as some features of the first steps to economic reform in the late 1970s and early 1980s. These had a major influence on the objectives, the strategy and the efficiency of Chinese industrial policy. The second section presents the main outlines of China's industrial policy until the late 1990s, focusing primarily on the policy of creating "national champions", and the rationalisation of industrial structures, as well as on the development of the technological capabilities of firms. Industrial policy during this period was often characterised by excessive ambitions, given the mode of socialist institutions and businesses, along with the chronic underdevelopment of human and financial resources that plagued China until the mid-1990s. Policies launched during this period were largely imbued with socialist planning. They led to mixed results depending on the sector, but were often disappointing in terms of objectives. Other elements of the reform policy during this period which were not, strictly speaking, industrial policy, did in fact help transform corporate behaviour and the functioning of institutions, to increase the financial and human resources available. Finally, Sect. 4.3 looks at the transition from dirigisme to realism in the second half of the 1990s. This development occurred within an economic context that was generally much more favourable than in the 1980s. The improved tax situation allowed the Chinese government to have the financial means to launch credible and ambitious industrial policies. Institutions, including ministries, commissions, and agencies were restructured, while the vestiges of planning were cleared away. The State industrial sector was also significantly restructured, through privatisations, mergers, layoffs and employment along with social protection reforms which shattered the "iron rice bowl" that the socialist leaders had not dared to attack in the 1980s.[3] Finally, the massive investments made in the 1990s in the educational system of large cities and in infrastructure also contributed to improving the design and conduct of industrial policy. The less proactive industrial policy of the 2000s also diversified, both in terms of means and targets, aiming to provide support to the private sector and small- and medium-sized enterprises (SMEs). These businesses had been totally ignored during the first period.

4.1 The Historical Legacy of Industrial Policy

Despite the profound break in the economic development strategy that occurred when Deng Xiaoping seized power in December 1978, Chinese policy-makers remained firmly focussed into the mid-1990s on a vision of industrial development policy that was inward and planned. It is useful to recall some historical facts and aspects of the early stages of economic reform, which had a major influence on the content and evolution of Chinese industrial policy during the 1980s and 1990s.

---

[3] The "iron rice bowl" refers to a system of lifetime employment, free housing and basic social protection which prevailed in State enterprises and municipalities.

4.1.1 The Weight of *History*

Generally speaking, China's industrial policy has been influenced by four major events in the history of modern and contemporary China:
- A sense of humiliation and theft of its rank as a great millennial power in the face of Europe, the United States, and Japan which all forced China to sign unequal treaties. This has led to a strong will to find a prominent place on the world stage.
- The observation made in the late 1970s by Chinese leaders of its growing economic and technological backwardness with respect to China's Asian neighbours. Economic success is analysed as the result of proactive action by the State, within a capitalist system.
- A deeply rooted belief in the omnipotence of the State and its capacity to intervene following the combined influence of the "celestial bureaucracy" of imperial China and the assimilation of the Soviet planning model.
- Management of the policy favouring population growth promoted by Mao Zedong in the late 1950s. Despite a slowdown in the birth rate in the early 1970s, this policy resulted in a doubling of the population between 1958 and 1980 (when China's population exceeded one billion individuals) and the influx of young people (near 15 million per year) on the labour market in the late 1970s. The spectre of widespread unemployment that could undermine social stability and thus the communist regime has strongly guided the choice of the Chinese leadership, both at central and local levels. The communist State adopted a *laissez-faire* approach and tolerance for the proliferation of public and private companies which are under-capitalised and poorly innovative, but able to absorb this huge "industrial reserve army".

These four major factors in the history of modern and contemporary China have strongly conditioned the ambitions, the nature, objectives and results of the industrial policy pursued by the State over the last 30 years.

4.1.2 The Maoist Legacy

China took a great step in 1978 in terms of re-designing its industrial development strategy. Few countries, even in the communist camp, had been so cut off from the rest of the world, having experienced political movements such as the "Great Leap Forward" (1958–1961) and the Cultural Revolution (1966–1976), which were devastating to its economic organisation.

The industrial development strategy in the Maoist era was based on an essentially functionalist view of the economic system. Unlike the Soviet model, which favoured large production units, China's strategy was also concerned with local autonomy in production. Each government department had its own companies, each province, even each municipality had to adopt as complete a production system as possible. The period during which so-called "Third Front" companies were set up in interior provinces (1964 and 1973) only reinforced this dispersion phenomenon and the duplication of investments. Political movements orchestrated by Mao's Great

Leap Forward and the Cultural Revolution deeply destabilised the Soviet-style system of central planning China introduced between 1953 and 1958. The implementation of such Soviet planning was stopped at the institutional level between 1958 and 1978: no 5-year plan reached its objectives during this period (Riskin 1987). In 1990, just months after the Berlin Wall had fallen, 52,000 products were still being managed by central planning in Moscow, at the USSR's Gosplan. In China, in 1978, only 700 products were managed centrally, by the State Planning Commission in Beijing (Naughton 1995).

The Maoist strategy led to a prioritisation of industry subject to the planning level of production. Production units existed that were directly supervised by central government (*Zhongyang shu*), while other units were dependent on provincial or municipal governments (*Difang shu*). Naturally, companies that were under direct management by central government benefited from its logistical support. These large state-owned enterprises (SOEs) were considered as China's "industrial backbone" (*Gugan qiye*), while the projects they developed were the so-called "key points" (*zhongdian*) of the 5-year and annual plans. They received priority support financially and materially (access to raw materials and procurement) from central government. For these companies, planning was also developed in the USSR. Their numbers grew throughout the 1960s, then levelled off during the 1970s and 1980s at around 10,000. But they never dominated the entire economy, as in the USSR.

Planning did not play such an important role for businesses managed at the provincial level. The allocation of inputs was not organised centrally. At most, planning was undertaken in aggregate terms, province by province, with industrial provincial offices subsequently taking responsibility for ensuring a more precise allocation for each company. Most often this allocation of resources was organised at the provincial or municipal level. However, planning was far from covering all the activities conducted by firms in this category. Companies in search of inputs, and marketing their outputs were taken to develop horizontal relationships with other companies. These horizontal relations were in barter, not monetary form (Granick 1990). The majority of these companies were taxed as "3/80" (San Ba): the provincial government allocated 80 % of the necessary inputs, 80 % of specified material, and 80 % of the resources needed to purchase equipment. Mao bequeathed an industrial organisation which superimposed two systems: a planned and centralised Soviet-style system for a few large companies that provided only 30 % of total industrial output (compared to 74 % in the USSR), and a myriad of economic systems compartmentalised at the local level and characterised by a "semi-planning and semi-anarchy" (Granick 1990).

4.1.3 Change and Continuity Until the Mid-1990s

Until the mid-1980s, the communist leaders tried repair the aberrations in the management of the economic system put in place under the influence of Mao between 1958 and 1976, instead of introducing a market economy. Policies aimed to depoliticise economic life, to demilitarise company management and management by ministries, and to restore central planning, which had been largely discontinued. The authorities were locked in a dialectic process they could not get out of: they had to pursue reform both to correct the contradictions of existing reforms which could destabilise them, but which also held out the promise of generating growth to maintain a minimum of political legitimacy among the population. With each wave of reforms, the deregulation of the economy (and thus the parallel freedom of individuals and firms in the economy) gained increasing scope. But it was not until the bloody episode of Tiananmen in 1989 and the attempts to return to economic socialism by the conservative wing of the CCP were overcome, that the 14th Congress of the CCP in October 1992 was able to set aside the political, intellectual, economic barriers for lack of a possible alternative, and that the market economy was clearly adopted in the policy reforms of the economic system.

There was therefore a clear turning-point in the late 1970s, which was primarily aimed at a return to socialist normality, and peripherally, elements of reforms to make the socialist system more flexible, such as the opening of Special Economic Zones (SEZ) in southern China, the dismantling of People's Communes, and the opportunity to develop collective enterprises in rural areas. These 'peripheral' reforms proved to be the essential dynamics of the revival of Chinese industry. Yet they took place in indirect ways and often in a manner not anticipated by the regime.

A chronological analysis of Chinese industrial policy makes it possible to distinguish two periods clearly enough. The first lasted nearly 20 years, from 1978 to mid-1990. This period was marked by strong interventionism and inordinate ambitions in terms of the financial and human resources which China had. Furthermore, objectives were carried out in the framework of an economy still largely operating within a planned system. The second period began in the mid-1990s and was marked by greater realism, as well as an improvement in the design and implementation of industrial policy in China.

4.2 The Era of Dirigisme

During the first period from 1978 to the mid-1990s, industrial policy focused on three main priorities: (i) the creation of large national industrial groups; (ii) the assimilation of imported technology from abroad, and; (iii) reform of the national system of research and development (R & D). The general principles underlying this policy, the strategy to achieve the objectives, the types of companies covered by the industrial policy, and the means implemented were still largely rooted in socialism and the functioning of a planned economy:
– During this period, the principles were still based on a functional, productivist and centralised vision of the economy.
– The strategy adopted by the Chinese government was very proactive. The State was the centre of all decisions and directly intervened in companies via the transmission belt of public ownership and planning.

- Firms receiving state aid were all large SOEs, the so-called "backbone" of the industrial system (*gugan qiye*). Small and medium enterprises, let alone those that would grow out of the state sector, were completely ignored by industrial policy.
- Industrial policy was largely controlled by the powerful the State Planning Commission and central ministries that oversaw various industrial sectors. They determined the priority sectors and firms, and the volume of investments within the framework of 5-year plans.
- The financial, administrative and human resources used to carry out policies were both weak and disassociated from planning.
- Finally, the objectives put forward by the Chinese government in the context of industrial policy were quite ambitious: technological catch-up in areas in which China had lagged for decades behind the technological frontier; the creation of large industrial groups capable of entering the small world of the "Fortune 500" classification; strong integration of industrial production throughout the country to reduce imports; and the autonomy and empowerment of scientific and technological production (Conroy 1992).

4.2.1 The Ambitions of China's Planners

The Policy of Creating Industrial Groups and the Rationalisation of China's Industrial Structure

Chinese leaders have been strongly influenced by the experiences of Japan (with its *Kereitsu*), France (nationalisation and national champions) and Korea (*Chaebols*), countries in which the State has played a more or less direct, but no less important, role in the formation of major national industrial groups capable of generating cutting-edge technologies, and projecting economic power beyond their borders. In the detailed analysis of the late industrialisation of Japan, South Korea, and Singapore, the presence of large industrial groups with a multinational vocation has been viewed by Chinese leaders as the main reason for the speed of development and of the industrial dynamism of their virtuous Asian neighbours. In Chinese rhetoric, such groups were then exhorted to become the "national army" (*guojia dui*) representing China abroad, while being industry leaders at the national level (*zhuli jun*). These enterprises appeared as the key to solving all problems and structural deficiencies of Chinese industry. Their role was to break down barriers both geographically (business combines in different regions), but also in terms of ministerial dependencies (business combines linked to different government entities).

Consolidation was to occur around a few large state enterprises and progressively lead to the creation of increasingly important financial and technological synergies. The context in which these national experiences took place (a market economy that was competitive at the national level, the decision-making autonomy of companies) was largely concealed by the designers of China's industrial policy.

Only the very proactive and interventionist dimension of government policy was put forward, which overestimated the ability of the State to create industrial groups able to withstand international competition.

The Chinese authorities have sought to rationalise the industrial structure of the country. The policy of regional self-sufficiency, along with Mao's dictum of "relying on one's own strength", which he promoted from late 1950s until his death, resulted in the duplication of investments in thousands of small production units. These were under-capitalised and incapable of generating economies of scale. The proliferation of small SOEs was most widespread in the cement, fertiliser, steel, and electricity generation industries. For example, it is estimated that there were nearly 500 companies producing steel in the late 1970s (Perkins 1991). The policy of decentralizing investment authorisations, taxation and bank finance launched by Deng Xiaoping in the early reforms further aggravated this fragmentation of industrial structures. The negative impact of such fragmentation of industrial structures became apparent: over-production in virtually all sectors of the industry (hence low capacity utilisation), very low, or even with no returns on investment, the waste of savings, and initial signs of negative consequences for the banking in terms of bad loans.

The Management of Technology Transfers

As for technological progress, the strategy of self-sufficiency (*zili gengsheng*) remained the rule. The decision to allow foreign direct investment (FDI) in four "special economic zones" (SEZs) in southern China, quickly spread to 14 large cities and 256 districts. But it did not call into question the principle of "import substitution", which remained at the heart of the Chinese State's technology policy. The FDI Act in 1979 was a turning point, compared to the previous period when some "turnkey" plants were imported without foreign capital. For the first time since 1949, the FDI Act allowed foreign capital to enter Chinese soil. Such foreign capital was only allowed into re-export activities and into some key sectors (the automotive, nuclear, telephone and integrated circuit industries) that Chinese companies were unable to master. FDI had to be in joint ventures, in which the foreign partner could not hold a majority stake.

Re-export activities, by foreign-owned companies producing in China, mainly in SEZs and coastal towns, were not in direct competition with the large state enterprises, as they did not have the right to sell into the domestic market. For investments in the so-called priority sectors (the list was changed periodically), the FDI Act was designed to ensure a maximum transfer of foreign technology to ensure import substitution. Joint ventures (JVs) were subject to a set of rules on the degree of foreign technological innovation transferred, and the rate of local integration into production. This had to rise over time to help create Chinese suppliers of components and spare parts. Furthermore, the Act required joint ventures to transfer (after several years) their knowledge to their Chinese partners in the JV (generally, large SOEs), so the latter could become more independent in terms of technology.

Reform of the National R & D System

The national R & D system before 1978 was largely modelled along Soviet lines until the Cultural Revolution, and practically disintegrated for nearly 10 years thereafter. The system suffered the weaknesses of the Soviet model: a partitioning of R & D performed in public laboratories (many of which were for military purposes) *vis-à-vis* industry, the waste of scarce human and financial resources, bureaucratic excesses in the planning of innovation, very low efficiency in its contribution to the production of cost-effective technologies.

As of 1985, the central planners sought to boost the R & D system through a series of reforms. These are aimed at selecting public research institutions according to their excellence and opening up the R & D system by bringing together the productive sphere of the research. With the exception of laboratories of excellence, research institutions have been gradually led out of dependency on state subsidies, which previously funded the entire R & D system.

Despite the existence of a strong commitment in central government, the establishment of industrial policy very quickly ran into the practical functioning of the Chinese economy. In the late 1990s, nearly two decades after the launch of these three priority programs, the results were fairly mixed, even disappointing in terms of objectives. However, some more general reforms related to deregulation of the economy did have a positive impact on the operation of Chinese enterprises.

4.2.2 Failures and Surprises in the Policy of Creating Industrial Groups and the Rationalisation of Industrial Structure

The Failure of Administrative Logic in the Creation of "National Champions"

At the end of 1989, Chinese industry had 1,630 industrial groups that had been set up following authorisation by central and local government.[4] The industrial groups formed during the 1980s existed only on paper. They had no internal structure likely to lead to technical and financial complementarities following from concentration. Analyses very quickly pointed to three operating characteristics of the socialist Chinese economy as the main sources of problems in the creation of industrial groups: (i) the system of public ownership, (ii) the administrative dependency of companies *vis-à-vis* local governments, and (iii) the fiscal and monetary systems. The majority of consolidations into groups were conducted in an authoritarian manner by municipal governments, through administrative edicts forcing local companies in the same industry to merge. These mergers were often obtained to hide losses in some firms by linking them to other businesses in better financial health. An inter-sectoral coordination effort was made in the early 1990s (again at the municipal level), with local boards of management of State assets being set up

---

[4] In *Zhongguo Qiye Guanli Nianjian*, (Directory of management of Chinese companies), Zhongguo Qiye Guanli Xiehui, Beijing, 1990, p. 305.

in haste in major Chinese cities which were meant to conduct the local industrial policy. Despite this, the groups did not reflect the needs or strategies of their component businesses, which had to comply with the orders of the local authorities. It was also difficult, if not impossible, to create groups which crossed the territorial jurisdiction of a municipality or province. The payment of taxes, the management of earnings, the authorisation of investment finance, the appointment of directors and company management, all depended on local government, which exercised the right of ownership delegated to it by the central government in Beijing. As the groups were sources of tax revenue, patronage, and political prestige, no local government wanted to forego the benefits which ownership of such public companies provided. However, the vast majority of these groups were unable to deploy the financial, technological and business synergies for which they had been created, so that they remained mostly a collection of independent production units (Jian 1990).

Concerning the rationalisation of industrial structures, the policies launched by the central government produced meagre results. Thousands of under-sized producers, making the same products, were spread across the country: there were 8,000 independent producers of cement, compared to an estimated 1,500 worldwide; 123 automobile producers; 1,500 steel plants. An analysis of concentration ratios based on the census of industrial enterprises (conducted in 1995) showed there had been no positive developments in this area. Among the 25 major industrial sectors (despite contrasting trends by industry), the market shares of the top eight companies increased only in very small proportions, from 11.7 % to 12.2 % between 1990 and 1996. The 1995 census of industrial companies also showed an extremely low production utilisation rate in the 43 sectors surveyed: only four sectors recorded a capacity utilisation rate of 60 %. In 1994, 500 Chinese groups accounted for only 16 % of GDP, much lower than in industrialised countries, where the top-500 companies generally represent at least 30 % of GDP.

Decentralisation: An Engine of Growth and a Brake on Concentration

The difficulties encountered by the central government in streamlining industrial structures were largely due to the significant level of decentralisation of decision-making within the administration concerning investment.

This decentralisation took place with the background of the Maoist legacy that, for ideological and military reasons, had sought the fragmentation of the production. The political and economic environment in which decentralisation took place in the 1980s had evolved. On the one hand, large state enterprises remained within the system of centralised socialist planning at the national level, albeit with some management autonomy relating to daily business. They continued to have priority support from the central government for their financial needs, as well as access to raw materials and human resources, while representing the main source of tax revenue of the central government. On the other hand, for small and medium-sized SOEs controlled by central government or local authorities, China's leadership felt it was unrealistic to integrate them into a centrally-managed apparatus. Subsequently, decentralisation has profoundly changed the incentive system of local management, given changes in the business environment, including the increasing monetisation of the economy, particularly through the development of bank financing, the growth of tax revenues of local governments and a liberal political environment conducive to growth and personal enrichment which was advocated by Deng Xiaoping (Shirk 1993). Local officials could henceforth participate actively in local economic development, accelerate their careers in the hierarchy of the Communist Party of China (CPC) on the basis of purely economic criteria, develop local patronage, and enrich themselves by marketing their decision-making authority and by participating indirectly in the creation of new businesses.

Changes in the incentive system for managers, their grip on local bank financing channels (mainly through the appointment of branch managers in state commercial banks) led to fast growth in start-ups and investments. Entrepreneurship not only affected the collective and private sectors. In rural areas, start-ups were carried out under the status of collective ownership (more flexible and vague to the point of being qualified as hybrid).[5] In cities, the state sector continued to grow rapidly (from 65,000 to nearly 126,000 industrial enterprises in 1996) and remained by far the largest employer in industry, in the mid-1990s.[6] This movement to create state-owned enterprises in the industrial sector took place at a time when bankruptcies were non-existent and when the constraints to repay bank loans for public firms were almost zero. It is easy to understand why the policy of creating groups and rationalising industry largely failed. Paradoxically, this sustained creation of companies along with its attendant chronic over-production would lead to the emergence of competition in some industries and produce unexpected results regarding the emergence of China's industrial groups.

Competition and the Emergence of New "National Champions"

In this context of the proliferation of companies and overproduction, competition gradually developed in the late 1980s in several sectors, such as light industry, building materials, the automotive industry, textiles and chemicals. The downturns in the economy between 1989 and 1991, and between 1994 and 1998 heightened competition between firms, within an environment of chronic overproduction. With the exception of a few areas that were still monopolistic or regulated (like the electricity and oil industries), companies had to fight to win customers and market share, from this time onwards.

One of the paradoxical and unexpected effects of decentralisation for Chinese industrial policy-makers was the advent of large industrial dynamic firms of a new type, controlled by the State, and which were able to use the competition to their advantage. As of the early 1990s, some companies which had not been among the best-known and most-favoured by the State during the 1980s, launched price wars,

---

[5] Local governments were owners of companies in towns and counties, so their management was very largely privatised (Nee 1992).

[6] *Zhongguo tongji nianjian* (China Statistical Abstract), 1997.

improvements in product quality and after-sales services. They also aggressively development of their distribution networks across the country. This strategy triggered a virtuous cycle as they increased their market share, and economies of scale, helping to raise profits, which were then assigned to new investment in new products or to improve quality. These firms have built up their reputations on strategies that do not differ from those of large firms in capitalist economies. It should be emphasised that these firms were not included in the list of "national champions" identified by those responsible for industrial policy in the 1980s, though they were not deliberately discriminated against by central or local government. These groups include firms such as: Changcheng (Great Wall) in IT; Mudan in Beijing, or Panda in the province of Jiangsu; TV Plant No. 1 for electrical appliances in Shanghai; Haier, Changhong, Konka in electrical appliances (Richet and Huchet 2005); Stone and Legend (now Lenovo) in IT (Kennedy 1997); Baosteel in steel (Steinfeld 1998) or ZTE and Huawei in telecommunications. But, these groups were also far from being supported financially and logistically in the same way as large state enterprises considered as a priority, and which dominated their sectors during the 1980s. The very strong personalities of the leaders of these firms and the results obtained also led to a *de facto* privatisation of the management of these companies. Several case studies (Richet and Huchet 2005) have shown that the leaders have gained their independence over almost all management decisions of the company (except for the sale or purchase of assets, for which regulators still retain a degree of control). Their independence also comes from their funding strategy. Having not benefited from the generosity of the State in the 1980s, the initial financing received from banks was used efficiently and the profits generated by business reinvested in relatively well-planned new investments, plus avoiding too great a dependency *vis-à-vis* the state banking sector.

The results, however, were devastating for the companies that failed to adapt to competition, including large groups which were the priorities of industrial policy during the 1980s. With funding primarily based on bank lending, businesses that were unable to increase their market share very quickly found themselves unable to meet their repayments and had to borrow even more to continue to survive. In 1994, when the major reforms of the public sector were launched, these SOEs constituted a cohort of loss-making companies which were carried by the public banking sector and which the government was obliged to restructure or close in the second half of the 1990s. This shift from a market dominated by supply in the 1980s, to a market dominated by the demand in the early 1990s, with the introduction of competitive strategies by some companies, has been a very powerful factor in pushing forward the concentration of industry since 1997.

4.2.3 The Accumulation of Technological Capabilities

The targets set by the Chinese government were to make up for the technological backwardness of Chinese firms relative to their foreign counterparts; to establish "national champions" capable of innovation and able to compete with foreign firms and to achieve maximum technological autonomy in all branches of industry in order to reduce foreign dependence (and China's import bill). In the late 1990s, nearly 20 years after the launch of this policy, these objectives were still far from being achieved, despite some successes in some areas. China's failures, however, were not all useless. They were extensively analysed by the Chinese authorities, and helped modify the government's policy in the late 1990s.

Concerning technology imports (excluding FDI), state enterprises have mostly focused on conventional technology transfers: licence purchases, purchases of production equipment with assistance from suppliers, purchases of turnkey factories and procurement of "turnkey-type" products. Without these imports of foreign technology, Chinese companies could not have overcome the many technological bottlenecks due to the isolation of the Maoist period.

These imports were made at the cost of a huge waste of money and have been a means of survival and sustainability of largely inefficient firms in the public sector. Even though the size of the domestic market was propitious for the imperatives of economies of scale and scope, that are crucial in industry, it was not possible to achieve these because of the regional (or municipal) compartmentalisation of the administrative apparatus managing of public enterprises (Chen 1990).

State-owned enterprises suffered badly from very rigidities of the socialist system: lack of decision-making autonomy in relation to the supervisory bureaucracies, foreign exchange rationing, inadequate incentive systems for managers and employees, serious deficiencies in the management and organisation (Simon 1991), the allocation of own resources of companies for the benefit of firms' social services (the "iron rice bowl" in housing, hospitals, schools, health and retirement benefits) to the detriment of innovation (Geng 1991), weak linkages with public R & D institutes and rigidities arising out of the administrative control of investment decisions.

Thus, the assimilative capacity of foreign technology quite quickly became an important feature in discriminating state firms, as competition increased in the early 1990s.

Success in the assimilation of foreign technology was a major element in the emergence of "new national champions". But it was also important in the development of small firms in the collective and private sectors, which worked as subcontractors for leading public enterprises or foreign companies operating in China. Several field studies have shown that these companies have been able to assimilate foreign technologies: not only the hardware but also the *softer* parts of technology such as the organisation of work, the supply of spare parts and equipment repair (Jefferson et al. 1994). This openness and control of the black box of technology, has given them some form of independence from foreign suppliers in a context of shortage of foreign exchange, but also the ability to implement peripheral improvements, and over time to become gradually able to catch up with Western firms (Dalhman et al. 1987). In some industries, it is precisely this type of technological capacity, acquired through the incremental improvement of foreign technology, that allowed Chinese companies to improve their competitiveness or to become world leaders.

It is interesting to note that large parts of the industrial policy of the central government during the 1980s and early 1990s ultimately contributed very little to the technological success of the "new national champions" as well as the more dynamic collective and private firms. These firms were not priority actors supported by the State during the 1980s. The technological dynamism of a large share of these leading firms, which emerged in the mid-1990s in the competitive sectors, did not owe much to aid from central government included in its industrial policy. It was not until the second half of the 1990s and especially the 2000s that these firms were supported, but as part of a different strategic approach from that advocated by the State in the 1980s.

Despite the failures and waste, certain aspects of Chinese government action had a positive effect on technological catch-up by the "new national champions". Drawing on the lessons of centuries of industrial mercantilism, the Chinese authorities have pursued a policy of protecting the domestic market and the selective opening to foreign capital did foster the technological catch-up of a certain class firms. This policy was conducted in parallel with the gradual deregulation of the planned economy.

4.2.4 The Double-Edged Management of Foreign Capital

The impact of the policy of opening the economy to foreign capital has generally been beneficial to Chinese industry. The selective management of foreign investment, with on the one hand, FDI for re-exports only, and on the other hand FDI to produce goods for sale on the domestic market, but supervised by JV contracts for leading technologies, had several positive consequences:

- FDI for re-export, which was dominant until the mid-1990s by the Hong Kong and Taiwanese capital (nearly 3/4 of the total), was mainly located in the provinces of Guangdong, Fujian and Shanghai. Such investment allowed China to earn foreign exchange to finance purchases of foreign technology for Chinese companies. This FDI also contributed to create a set of small sub-contractors from the private and collective sectors. Often specialised by business, these formed a dense network of industrial partners, which were also in competition. Such outsourcing led to geographic specialisation with strong industrial districts that are among the most competitive in the world.
- For FDI authorised to sell on to the domestic market, and which was selected on the basis of technology or type of product manufactured, its presence in China had two important technological consequences (apart from saving foreign exchange). The first, and not least, has been to allow the Chinese economy to benefit from products such as automobiles (the JV with Volkswagen), integrated circuits (the JVs with NEC and Motorola), digital telephone exchanges (the JV with Alcatel), nuclear power (Areva), that Chinese producers were unable to produce. Technology transfers within JVs have generally been quite satisfactory. These product areas have had significant ripple effects via productivity increases and improved infrastructure. The JV also helped train local subcontractors who,

in many cases, after a few years, achieved commercial and technological autonomy to become globally competitive. The second, more indirect, consequence was the catalysing role played in the technological modernisation of Chinese enterprises in some sectors. JVs have been the undisputed technological leaders in many industrial sectors, and have pushed Chinese companies to pick up to speed in appropriating technology (Jefferson et al. 1994). Management by central government has avoided causing immediate, head-on shocks (of the type recorded in the former socialist countries following the sharp drop in tariffs after 1991) with Chinese firms, though the latter have still had to try to approach technological standards of JVs.

In terms of strategic positioning in the value chain, more is known about the effects induced by this policy of openness. Chinese high-technology exports remain largely dominated by foreign-owned companies (nearly 80 % of total) causing some crowding out of national producers in segments with higher value added. But even when Chinese producers dominate the industrial scene, their lack of visibility in terms of brand recognition and overseas marketing confines them to activities with very low profit margins. This hampers their ability to finance technological upgrading. It is not surprising therefore to see that Chinese industrial firms subcontracting for European, American and Japanese multinationals express the desire to move up the value added chain, in order to capture a greater share of profits on sales to consumers in developed countries. To achieve this objective, the control of intermediate companies that operate in the field of distribution is crucial to Chinese firms.

Finally, as far as the negative effects of the FDI strategy are concerned, it is worth mentioning that the best students leaving China's education system are attracted by foreign firms, thus limiting the impact of training on the human resources available to local industries run by large state firms.

4.3 Towards Greater Realism... and Efficiency

The late 1990s and early 2000s was marked by a progressive turnaround in the content and strategy of Chinese industrial policy. In some areas, such as the concentration and rationalisation of industrial structures, reform of national R & D, or the accumulation of technological capabilities, encouraging results emerged quite rapidly within a few years, portending to the greater effectiveness of industrial policy in the coming decades.

4.3.1 A Favourable Economic and Institutional Environment

The recent changes in industrial policy and the more encouraging results that have been recorded since the late 1990s are largely due to the positive results of the general reforms of the economy.

The Exit of Socialism and the Improvement of the Functioning of the Economy

In terms of the functioning of the economic system, China has now largely exited socialism. Since 1994, planning mechanisms have been dismantled, as characterised by the deregulation of prices, supply and distribution. The reform introduced in the early 1980s, and which allowed businesses to sell any production exceeding planned quotas set by the State Planning Commission on the open market, gradually led to the complete disappearance of planning. Today, just over 90 % of the retail prices in the industry and more than 80 % of agricultural prices are set by the market.

The financing channels of business investment have also been completely reformed. State banks benefited from the broad recapitalisation in 1998, at a total cost estimated at nearly $500 billion.

Concerning property rights, the last decade has been marked by a strong diversification of ownership and a significant retreat of the State. For political reasons, the path was more tortuous than in other socialist countries. But since 1997, between 30,000 and 40,000 SMEs have been privatised out of a total of 126,000 state-owned enterprises in the industrial sector in 1996 (Huchet 2006). The domestic private sector generates nearly a third of industrial production, and if foreign companies are included, private ownership in 2010 represented nearly 70 % of the country's industrial production (World Bank 2012). Such a review of all major operating mechanisms of socialist economies can be extended, leading to the conclusion that the Chinese economy exited the system in the early 2000s.

The Exit from of Socialism Has Had a Significant Impact in Terms of Industrial Policy

– The budget constraint on businesses has increased significantly to the point that it is now more and more difficult for companies that are leveraged to obtain bank loans to finance new investments. In parallel, banks have progressively improved their risk assessment of clients. Partial privatisation (stock market listing, capital entry by foreign banks) and the opening of banking to foreign banks since China's accession to the WTO, have increased pressure on both the State and banks, to improve the quality of their loan portfolios. These trends have led to further rationalisation of industries (via bankruptcies and mergers), promoting much faster concentration than existed in the 1980s and 1990s.
– The emergence of new actors in the private sector has led to a diversification of firms assisted by industrial policy. The importance of the private sector in the economy is such that industrial policy no longer focuses exclusively on the public sector. The criteria for awarding aid are more transparent, and less dependent on the status of the property. These changes are more marked at the local levels of government, which seek primarily to promote the development of their local economies.
– Regardless of their ownership status, companies are now subject to much less interference in their decisions about investment, financing, asset management or

the management of their human resources. They are thus able to formulate strategies for developing their activities which are much more independent, and implement incentive policies best suited to their employees. State enterprises no longer have to fund social protection entirely, which means they have more resources for productive activities and innovation in particular. Generally, their capacity to respond to opportunities arising in the business environment has become much faster and wider in scope. In this context, the State has been encouraged to play a more indirect role in its aid to companies.

4.3.2 Taxation Has Given the Central Government New Room for Manoeuvre

One of the most positive aspects of the reforms implemented since 1994 lies in the significant increase in tax revenues of the State, both for central government but also in the richest coastal regions. The decentralisation of the 1980s and the structural decline in the profits of state enterprises, that used to be the only source of income for the State, both lead to a very serious erosion tax revenues for the Chinese State. It also led to an imbalance in favour of the provinces, at the expense of the central government.

The major tax reform of 1994 and the various measures taken in the late 1990s concerning local finances (with control over extra-budgetary funds) have contributed – with the help of growth – to significantly improving the situation. The tax base of the State has been expanded, increasing sources of taxation. A better sharing of revenues between the centre and the provinces has been put in place, and most importantly, the State has managed to develop a tax administration that was largely deficient in the 1980s.

In nearly a decade, the results of this reform have enabled the State to envisage more solid support in some areas of industrial policy. After an annual increase of about nearly 20 %, total tax revenues in 2010 amounted to nearly 22 % of GDP and the share of the central government accounted for just over 55 % of the total, leading to a rapid rebalancing in favour of Beijing. Despite weaknesses (corruption, tax evasion, linkages with the lowest levels of government, regional disparities), the OECD predicts that the situation will continue to improve with the implementation of new reforms and the gradual modernisation the tax administration.

This improvement in the tax situation has also had a major impact since the late 1990s on the financing of infrastructural projects (with expenditures increasing from an annual rate of 3 % of GDP in 1983 to just over 8 % from 1998) and education. Significant improvements in these two areas have in turn had a positive impact on productivity in industry, the industrialisation of inland areas and, to some extent, on the conduct of industrial policy with a better educated elite working in government departments and agencies.

Notable increases have occurred in R & D budgets since 1997: annual growth has been running at 19 % (since 1995), to reach nearly $130 billion in 2011, or 1.83 % of GDP, and the resulting proliferation of targeted programmes with better finance should continue with this improved tax situation.[7] These developments should be more important in coastal areas, in which the greatest technological capabilities are concentrated.[8]

4.3.3 Institutional Reform

In parallel to the exit from socialism and the improvement of the tax situation of the Chinese State, the last decade has been a period of intense reform of the institutions in charge of the economy. This has had a direct impact on industrial policy. Among the various reforms, we can select three, given their involvement in China's industrial policy:
– Almost all the industrial ministries from the socialist system have been removed since 1997 (with the number of ministries falling from of 40 to 29). State enterprises, especially larger ones, are no longer linked to a particular ministry but instead to the SASAC (State-Owned Asset Supervision Administration), which manages the assets of the State. In addition, the powerful former State Planning Commission has been transformed into a National Commission for Development and Reform (NDRC).
– The reform of the management of public assets led to the creation of the SASAC in June 2003. It is now the only entity within government to oversee and manage the portfolio of assets held by the State. This reform has led to a considerable clarifying of the skills needed in public asset management, not only within the central government, but also between Beijing and the large municipalities (Huchet and Fernandez Stembridge 2006). The SASAC directly manages nearly 130 of the largest public groups, with combined assets of almost $870 billion. Technically, the SASAC is also responsible for the assets of other state enterprises, but it has delegated responsibility for their management to local municipal commissions, which are under the authority of municipal governments. This reform has greatly reduced the sectoral compartmentalisation of the socialist system, which interfered in the conduct of industrial policy.
– In the field of government management of the R & D system, several important changes have occurred since the late 1990s. The Group Leader Affairs Council (CHECK General Affairs Office) of State for Education and Technology was established in 1998. It aims to facilitate the coordination of technology policy throughout the country. Moreover, the former State Commission of Science and Technology was merged with the Ministry of Science and Technology (MOST), which is the main ministerial body in charge of technology policy.

---

[7] The Ministry of Science and Technology of the P. R. of China.
[8] Beijing, Shanghai and the province of Guangdong account for 40 % of the country's R & D spending.

4.3.4 Towards a New Face of China's Industrial Policy

The industrial policy of the Chinese State has been marked by three major developments since the early 2000s, and which are expected to strengthen in the years to come. We are witnessing a widening of the fields of action of industrial policy. On top of the existing, traditional areas of technological progress and the strengthening of the competitiveness of firms, these include: the decline in the energy intensity of industry; the fight against environmental degradation; and the promotion of industry in the interior regions of the west. These objectives have been presented as new priorities by the Chinese government. Otherwise, the action of the State's industrial policy is less interventionist and less proactive than during the 1980s and 1990s. Finally, industrial policy affects all types of companies and not just public firms, while there is now greater transparency about the criteria for awarding financial aid from the State.

In terms of restructuring and consolidation, the central government remains very active via the SASAC concerning the 150 largest companies in the country, but its action is no longer as dirigiste and proactive as it was in the 1980s and 1990s. Major restructuring in the monopoly sectors (energy, transport, telecommunications) already took place in the late 1990s. These large companies now have a wider range of action. Only large divestments or acquisitions of assets are still tightly controlled by the SASAC.

For state enterprises at the local level, the reforms of the banking sector now limit the State's role in subsidising loss-making SOEs with bank loans, as was the case throughout the 1980s and in the early 1990s. Finally, the demographic situation which was unfavourable in 1978 has now changed considerably. The active population will start to decline in 2015 and while the investment multiplier generates less jobs, and migrant flows to cities of persons looking for work will continue to be significant until 2025, the situation is not as preoccupying as it was in the 1980s. The need to promote an industrial model which is labour intensive but low in profitability (with all the consequences this has in terms of bad debts in the banking sector) is gradually fading away. Even though China is still far from having the levels of the most advanced industrial economies, the concentration ratio is increasing slowly without the State having to intervene in the proactive and interventionist manner of the 1980s and 1990s. A certain form of dirigisme is likely to continue to express itself in the new fields of industrial policy on energy and the environment. After stating in the 11th (2006–2010) and the 12th Plan (2011–2015) that the decline in energy intensity and the fight against environmental degradation are priorities, the State is attempting to foster the closure of obsolete companies and technologies, and promote the concentration of production in larger firms in the name of energy intensity.[9]

Strengthening the technological capacity of firms is also being addressed more indirectly than in the past. The State is focusing on building large research units

---

[9] Report by the Prime Minister at the opening session of the National People's Congress, 7 March 2008.

working in basic research and leaving companies to be more independent. The latter now account for nearly two-thirds of R & D. Companies have accumulated technological skills that enable them today (unlike the 1980s) to open the "black box" of imported foreign technologies, to select better imports to be more independent of foreign technology. With the exception of monopolistic sectors, in which the Chinese government retains a capacity to intervene directly via public property, and in the setting of norms and standards, its action in other sectors is increasingly focused on improving the environment in which firms carry out their innovation efforts.

Conclusion

Chinese industrial policy has been marked over the past three decades by significant change, both in content and in its results. Until 1997, it was actually in areas in which the State wanted to be the most active and more proactive that it was the least effective in its actions, as evidenced by the rather disappointing results in terms of the rationalisation of industrial structure and the creation of "national champions". The omnipotence of the Chinese State must therefore be qualified. Its ability to create strong firms commercially and technologically speaking was less than what other States were able to do in post-war Japan, or (South) Korea in the early 1960s.

Since the late 1990s, the Chinese State's industrial policy has evolved, and has indeed supported these developments. The State is gradually moving towards a more indirect form of intervention with the introduction today of more incentive policies to improve the environment in which companies operate. The restructuring of the public sector, banking sector reforms, lower trade barriers following the accession to the WTO in 2001, and the rapid development of the private sector have, within the space of a decade, drastically changed the environment of the industrial policy the Chinese authorities are implementing. Not only does the State no longer have all the levers to act proactively as it did during the 1980s and 1990s, but the Chinese government also appears to have largely learned the lessons of excessive dirigisme and proactive intervention.

References

Banque Mondiale (2012) China 2030. Banque mondiale, Washington, DC
Chen K (1990) The failure of recentralisation in China: interplays among enterprises, local governments and the center, Research paper. World Bank, Washington, DC
Conroy R (1992) Technological change in China. OECD, Paris, 276 p
Dalhman C, Ross-Larson B, Westphal LE (1987) Managing technological development: lessons from the newly industrializing countries. World Dev 15(6):759–777
Geng X (1991) Managerial autonomy, fringe benefits and ownership structure. A comparative study of Chinese state and collective enterprises, Research paper. World Bank, Washington, DC
Granick D (1990) Chinese state enterprises. University of Chicago Press, Chicago
Huchet J-F (2006) Privatisation et restructuration des PME d' État en Chine. Crit Int (32), juillet 2006

Huchet J-F (2010) Le rôle de l'État dans le décollage industriel de la Chine depuis 1978, Université de Rennes 2, Habilitation à Diriger des Recherches, Document de synthèse, 86 pp, 3 décembre 2010

Huchet J-F, Fernandez Stembridge L (2006) What's next for China state-owned enterprises. Far East Econ Rev 169(5):32–37

Jian Y (1990) Guanyu shenhua qiye gaige wenti de tantao (Réflexions sur l'approfondissement des réformes des entreprises). Gaige (5):45–46

Jefferson GH, Rawski TG, Zheng Y (1994) Institutional change and industrial innovation in transitional economies, Research paper series. World Bank, Washington, DC

Johnson C (1982) MITI and the Japanese miracle: the growth of Industrial policy, 1925–1975. Standford University Press, Standford

Kennedy S (1997) The stone group: state client or market pathbreaker? China Q (152):746–777

Naughton B (1995) Growing out of the plan Chinese economic reform 1978–1993. Cambridge University Press, Cambridge

Nee V (1992) Organisational dynamics of market transition: hybrid forms, property rights and mixed economy in China. Adm Sci Q (37):1–27

Perkins D (1991) China's economic policy and performance. In: Twitchett D, Fairbank JK (eds) The Cambridge history of China, Vol. 15, the people's republic, Part 2. Cambridge University Press, Cambridge, MA, pp 475–539

Richet X, Huchet J-F (2005) Gouvernance, coopération et stratégie des firmes chinoises. L'Harmattan, Paris, 212 p

Riskin C (1987) China's political economy. The quest for development since 1949. Oxford University Press, Oxford

Shirk SL (1993) The political logic of economic reform in China. University of California Press, Berkeley

Simon DF (1991) China's acquisition and assimilation of foreign technology: Beijing's search for excellence. In: Joint Economic Committee (ed) China's economic dilemmas: the problem of reforms, modernisation and interdependence, vol II. Congress of United States, Washington, DC

Steinfeld E (1998) Forging reform in China. The fate of state-owned industry. Cambridge University Press, Cambridge

Indian Firms in World Production: The State, Markets, and Innovation

Joël Ruet

The classical view of emerging India emphasises the importance of MNCs in the break with the country's previous development model, which was essentially based on a socialist industrial State. The reality is more qualified, and the continuity between the two eras is stronger than it seems.

The 5-year planning adopted by Jawaharlal Nehru, and subsequently by his daughter Indira Gandhi (who succeed Nehru in 1966 and who held power until 1975 and then again between 1977 and 1984) did indeed have a "socialist" reputation. But it was in no ways "Soviet". Indian planning mainly consisted of allocating resources to sectors deemed priorities: real planning of production only related to some strategic area. Only a few industries were "reserved" for the public sector. Otherwise, Indian planning was characterised above all by a system of authorisations, whose excessive regulations went under the nickname of the "Licence Raj", or "reign of licences" in reference to the "British Raj" of British colonial domination. In practice, India had therefore set up a strategy of co-development. This strategy brought together the State and the company sector, within a variable equilibrium process. India's political economy system gravitated very strongly around the very cohesive relationship between the State and industry, as of independence. This relationship has been profoundly modified since the liberalisation reforms of the fiscal year 1991–1992, though marked by continuity, and India's large multinational firms today are the direct descendants of the conglomerates resulting from the Licence Raj, or start-ups that have emulated the conglomerate model which has become a "national" form of Indian capitalism. This conglomerate business model has allowed India's MNCs to benefit from counter-cyclical advantages across sector. And since the 2000s, it has had an immediate impact on their global strategy, in contrast to Chinese MNCs.

This raises the question of what the relationship is between these firms, which are already multinational, with the economy and market India itself. The major

---

J. Ruet (✉)
CNRS, CEPN-Centre d'Economie de Paris Nord
e-mail: joelruet@gmail.com

industrial firms and the large service companies are far from being leading job creators in India. But they play a central role in the development, modernisation, the spread of technology, as well as in the polarisation and concentration of industrial districts that are at the heart of India's competitiveness.

India's competitiveness, however, is regulated in the final instance by the permanence of the State in the economy, via public policy partnerships. This is not a question of "State capitalism", but more a return to the principles of a market economy borne by a new economic and political elite, though India has not entirely reconnected with the values of liberalism inherited from the British Empire. Nor is it the return to a certain form of Fabien Socialism supported by Nehru in the 1930s. But the role of the State as an actor in industry has been re-legitimised by neighbouring China, and could well have a bright future.

Section 5.1 sets out the identity established by Indian companies. The next section looks at their internationalisation. Section 5.3 examines the link between Indian MNCs and India itself, and their position with respect to small firms and the continued presence of the State.

5.1 From Light Socialism to Protected Liberalism: The Continuation of Conglomerate Firms in India

In 1947, 70 % of the equity listed on the Bombay (Mumbai) stock exchange was controlled by Indians. However, the drive to industrialisation in India, which in the nineteenth century could have aspired to early development as Egypt did, was greatly prevented by British colonial power. As a result, at independence India was largely "living in its villages", to use an expression dear to Gandhi. As leader of the country, Jawaharlal Nehru however did not intend to submit to such an agrarian fatality. With support from the "Bombay Club", bringing together the major families of the business world, he launched a system of economic planning with the aim of modernising the countryside and developing industry. Yet it took time to escape from the "tyranny of the monsoon" which had forever ruled the Indian economy, and productivity only really began to take off in the 1980s. Growth further accelerated after the reforms of the 1990s, to stabilise at a level of about 6 %. This new growth orbit was equivalent to an annual increase in per capita GDP of 3.3 %. Private industry grew at 8.4 % per year (compared to 5 % in the years 1947–1980), with productive plant and capital equipment expanding by 9.9 %, and exports growing by 8.4 % per year in the 2000–2008 period, before falling back to a level of about 6 % afterwards, down to 5.3 % in fiscal year 2012–2013.

5.1.1 Conglomerate Firms: An Inheritance of the Licence Raj and the Structuring of Openness

India's import substitution strategy (which was typical of the 1950s and 1960s) complemented public industrial investment with tariff protection. This type of broad economic regulation led to the creation of a national form of capitalism based on conglomerates: each time their expansion was blocked by the limits fixed by private investors in a given sector, these firms invested in another, having duly obtained the corresponding "licence". The result was that from the 1960s until the end of the Licence Raj in 1991–1992, an industrial structure was built up comprising large public and private groups, which had taken on a conglomerate structure by piling up licences. This system led to the birth of a conglomerate, oligopolistic form of capitalism.

Despite these developments, re-alignments and the emergence of new groups, a large number of India's industrial giants today were nurtured under the Licence Raj. Reliance – the country's largest group in terms of profits – is among these. It built up its fortune based on the authorisation to import and produce (exclusively) certain synthetic fibres. Thereafter it extended its activities using the same principles to petrochemicals, energy, and oil exploration. More recently, during the liberalised regime but with State support, it has entered high-tech and renewable energy sectors. There is thus a certain continuity between "Indian socialism" which ran from the 1970s until the mid-1980s, and Indian capitalism today, in as far as the relationship between the State and big private industry remains at the heart of the system. The State has thus piloted the economy via its own public firms and its monopoly of so-called "reserved" sectors (though these are not very numerous), but especially through the orientation of private industrial and banking investments into "priority" sectors.[1] India's mixed economy thus never resembled Soviet nor Chinese socialisms, which were purely public. Between 1947 and 1971, the relative share of the public sector never exceeded 25 % of GDP: this included public administration, while the share of manufacturing output was 14.4 % (in 1980).[2] In contrast, the hold of the State over the private industrial sector was complete. During this period, the system was effective from a political point of view, as national cohesion was stronger than most people thought it would be. The system was also effective socially as poverty reduction began and inequalities between India's states diminished. It was also economically effective in terms of public infrastructures, as well as rising labour and capital productivity.

In this economy, which was developed and managed by "people with knowledge", economic openness was pursued through consensus, to allow the conglomerates to refocus their business on competitive activities. At the start of the 1980s, an emerging generation of economists who were close to the Congress Party, including the present Prime Minister Manmohan Singh, accepted the obvious, namely the need to give a greater role to private investment. Indira Gandhi and her son Rajiv adopted a series of "pro-business" measures, though more than ever in the name of import substitution. But henceforth this policy had precise technological objectives. At first, during the second half of the 1980s, this involved relaxing

---

[1] Planned investment in India accounted for three quarters of all investment from 1980 to 1985.

[2] This was despite absolute growth: in 1950, five companies generated R290 million of investment, whereas in 2005, 240 national industrial firms accounted for R2.525 billion (R = rupee).

import restrictions on machine tool technologies, in order to allow some major industrial groups to end their technological backwardness. This was undertaken on a case-by-case basis. The joint venture in the car industry between the Indian firm Maruti and Japan's Suzuki is today a leader in a market experiencing rapid growth. It is also emblematic of this new logic. The idea is for the State, along with the business community, to identify sectors in which the modernisation of obsolescent plant and equipment demands greater openness. Thus, more than 65 % of industry has progressively moved out of the system controlling prices, production and investment. Officially, the umbilical cord between the "babu" (civil servant) and the "sethji" (businessman) has been cut... But the role of politicians has not yet disappeared. In 1991, under the leadership of Prime Minister Narasimha Rao (of the Congress Party), the country committed itself officially to reforming its industrial policy. This was known as "liberalisation", via the opening of several areas of the private sector and foreign investment, the dismantling of licences in other sectors, cuts in customs and tariff restrictions, and a (limited) policy of privatisation. These policies were still gradual and thanks to CII took account of the interests of Indian business: this involved opening up to the private sector in areas in which Indian industry could engage itself, and to FDI in sectors in which it had sufficiently restructured itself and improved productivity.[3] Lastly, liberalisation has entailed opening up customs. The latter change has been conducted smoothly, as the Indian state continues to be careful about protecting industry from renewed competitiveness.

5.1.2 An Economic Policy Aimed at Industrial Restructuring

A new generation of top civil servants and industrialists came to the forefront in these years. Dialogue between them was progressively led by the Confederation of Indian industry (CII), a new employers' association, during the 1990s. It took over from the FICCI and replaced lobbying based on "blueprints" and economic programs with direct personal influence. These trends notably occurred within a strongly changing environment of the political equilibrium between the national parties. Even if the reform was largely initiated by members or sympathisers of the Congress Party, the party did not have a monopoly reform. Nor did its members support the process fully. The reform process benefited from changing political support, and debates on reform contributed in turn to stabilising alliances. In the years 1984–1987, it was indeed the visionary spirit of Rajiv Gandhi and others who

---

[3] In 1991, only eight industries were still "reserved" for the State, and 18 continued to operate within the licence regime. 34 industries benefited from a regime providing automatic authorisation for technological agreements and foreign investment up to 51 %. Three other sectors were taken out of the licence regime, and the pace of change then became regular. Today, only two sectors are reserved for the State (the nuclear sector and railways), only six sectors require compulsory licences, and 16 sectors are 100 % open to FDI. Between 1999 and 2003, 73 articles were taken out of the "reserved" list for small industries, and a further 85 were taken off the list in 2004.

initiated the first changes. In contrast, 1987–1989 were characterised by criticism of reform within the Congress Party, and calls for a "pause" by industrialists. Support for reform strengthened between 1991 and 1995. But in 1995, Prime Minister Narasimha Rao called anew for a pause, before the general elections of 1996. However, the CII and big industry were sufficiently won over by the cause for (gradual!) reform, and wished to continue. The following United Front governments, and subsequently the National Democratic Alliance government, led by the Hindu nationalist party (BJP), pursued reform, with employers managing to extend their influence, and support over the latter, in a timely manner. This provided more than a little help to the modernising wing of the BJP, which is less nationalist and less religious. This fraction was represented by Yashwant Sinha and Jaswant Singh, who were ministers from 1998 to 2004, and who switched their respective jobs of Finance Minister and Minister of Foreign Affairs in 2002. They were also soon to be supported by the Prime Minister, A.B. Vajpayee. The reforming wing of the party thus strengthened its influence on the evolution of the BJP, which pursued policies favourable to the industrial redeployment of the large groups. In the general elections of 2004, an alliance led by the Congress Party help the latter returned to power. But the direction of core industrial policies remained unchanged, despite essential turnarounds in redistribution and social policies in favour of the countryside and India's deprived population, though these were more or less effective. The role of foreign openness, and the ending of the licence regime domestically were confirmed.

The key trends in India's industries have thus been led by both continuity and change in the State-industry relationship. The dynamics of change have come to embrace the underlying contours of a relationship in which India's political and economic elites have a mutual interest, while also exhibiting a degree of sociological overlap.[4] The pace and equilibria of this relationship between the State and industry have of course been modulated by the social and redistributive tensions in Indian society. But generally, there is a consensus which has largely marginalised the voices of disagreement, even if these remain quite numerous.

New sectors have progressively been opened up to private investment, such as electrical or telecommunications production, or to foreign investment, as in the manufacturing sector. Foreign capital may hold significant shares of equity in Indian companies (the 51 % level was granted in certain sectors as of 1991). But several limits on the control by foreign capital are set to remain from long time. Contrary to conventional wisdom, which holds that services are the alpha and omega of development, these are based, among other things, on a diversified industrial infrastructure: information technology and biotechnology are not all of the Indian economy. Services accounted for 57 % of GDP in financial year 2011 (industry for 26 %, and agriculture, 17 %). But India is a patchwork country that has an original development model, in which not industry alone takes over from

---

[4] Even if measures on quotas of political representation have changed this slowly over the long-term.

agriculture, but growth is also largely drawn by services. Only a small share of these services are high-tech: information technology represents 7.5 % of GDP in financial year 2012. In contrast, as far as the international de-specialisation and globalisation of firms are concerned, India does not have the vocation of being only the "world's back-office", and Indian multinationals are present abroad, both in services and industry. The reason for this is simple: conglomerate firms operate in both sectors.

The "external" side of Indian firms draws on its "internal" side, but it is different.

5.2 From One Conglomerate to Another: The Dynamics of Technological Catch-up and Upgrading in the Value Chain

In their internationalisation, Indian companies have benefited from a "reverse brain-drain", returning from the United States, as well as from investments in joint ventures that they have been able to use for a broader dissemination of know-how and technology. But above all, they have been early visionaries in drawing on the advantages of conglomeration.

The globalisation of Indian companies is not simply limited to exports as in the classical view of international economics. Instead, it involves a global strategy by companies, partnerships and the planning of the outsourcing of activities: finance, development, production, marketing, etc. right through to the globalisation of their productive structure and/or the integration into global production networks (for example, the integrated production system of Asia, but also the world production system).

5.2.1 IT Services and Industry and the Ambitions of the "World's Back-Office"

One of the most visible changes, and perhaps the most structural in the world economy, is the emergence of India in high technologies, in IT and biotechnology. In several sectors or segments of new technologies and high technologies, India has transformed or is in the process of transforming its cost advantage into a capacity for the acquisition and development of technology. This process constitutes a profound technological intensification of its trade. It is largely piloted by Indian companies, and not only multinational firms, which are their clients. Indian companies in these sectors have real strategies for growth, technological catch up and their own R&D. Furthermore, these trends have strong local foundations, as shown by the positive externalities and ripple effects on industrial districts and local production systems. Ripple effects also impact on services, housing, the hotel industry, and of course, telecommunications. This has been shown, for example, by recent developments in the cities of Bangalore, Hyderabad and even Gurgaon, in the suburbs of Delhi.

The explosion of the new technology sector constitutes the leading symbol of the entry of Indian companies into the world economy. In the 1990s, "brains" that were expatriated to the United States returned home to found their own IT companies (Infosys and Satyam), bringing with them contracts from their former American employers. For their part, the conglomerates developed IT subsidiaries, such as Wipro or TCS by Tata.[5] As a result, since 1994, growth in the information technology sector has been between 40 % and 50 % per year. Today, it accounts for about 2 % of GDP, but for more than a quarter of exports. Though IT in India began by carrying out low skilled subcontracting work, the situation today is completely different, as firms today offer world quality services and consulting. Some start-ups have indeed adopted other global strategy, right from their creation. Half the world's companies certified as "SEI-CMM5" – the highest quality standard for software – are Indian (there are no French companies). And some companies from the subcontinent are virtually integrated with their American clients, whose information systems they structure. This provides these Indian firms with influence and decision-making authority throughout the overall organisations.

IT has largely developed as a result of the "reverse brain drain" of Indian IT professionals. They were initially trained in India's excellent higher education system, before expatriating and subsequently returning to India to set up IT companies, with contracts already established with their former employers, especially in the United States. Simultaneously, large IT groups have developed within India's existing conglomerates. They start operating with American venture capitalists (or Indian investors who made money in the United States), and with contracts with large American software, telecommunications and consulting companies. Today, companies in the bio-technology sector are seeking to emulate these models for developing modular assets, which may lead to economies of scope, as well as specific assets that contribute to reinforcing market power in partnership relations with their clients. The importance of setting up partnerships within the context of globalisation in designing productive intra-company and inter-company productive organisations, which is characteristic of the contemporary restructurings of global capitalism, has been completely understood by the Indian State. It is multiplying its forms of support, in particular for research. The same is true for global firms which have shifted from analysing India in terms of cost reductions to beginning to see it in terms of partnerships. This has not escaped a number of India's large industrial groups. Some of them have restructured today to develop ambitious business models in order to position themselves on the world R&D market and Indian companies controlled 58 % of the global outsourcing sector revenues (source: Nasscom.org).

---

[5] See Bomsel and Ruet (2001), Maria, Ruet, Zérah (2002), or Ruet (2007) for a view of the different business models currently at work, or before their stabilisation.

5.2.2 Industrial Business Models

The real ground swell of India's – industrial – emergence, which is unfolding today was prepared during the 1990s. As of 1995, though the context was still relatively protected, India's conglomerates accelerated the reorganisation of their activities, in particular by multiplying strategic alliances with foreign companies. Though it did not neglect to develop itself in IT, the Mahindra & Mahindra conglomerate has sought to transform its position from assembling tractors and jeeps into becoming a car producer. This is the heart of its development strategy. The company concluded a technological partnership with Ford and did not hesitate a few years later to launch its own model. In 2005, it entered into a new alliance with Renault, then Renault-Nissan, with more beneficial conditions. Just like Mahindra, Indian industrial groups have integrated the world economy with a twofold give-and-take strategy. On the one hand, they provide their partners with a point of entry into a complex emerging market. In exchange, they acquire mastery of new industrial processes. On the other hand, they allow their partners to develop low-cost production, in return for which the latter take part in research and development.

Furthermore, Indian groups like Tata are already designing new car models at a third of development costs in Europe. Overall, India is in the process of becoming a production and re-export platform of global importance. This activity is integrated into the industrial "global production network" strategies of multinationals like Hyundai, Toyota, ABB, and Nokia.

The importance of partnerships in a context of design and production globalisation has been perfectly understood by the Indian State. It is multiplying its forms of support, especially in research and higher education, financing technology parks as well as developing strong links with the Confederation of Indian Industry. Indian groups are globalising visibly. They are setting up subsidiaries in Shanghai, London and New York, and investing in emerging countries like Mexico, Brazil and in South Africa. They are relocating IT work to South-East Asia or China. Reliance has bought up a Dupont subsidiary in Nemours and Germany, etc. To be sure, having experienced 24 % annual growth over the last 30 years, this group does indeed have the resources of its ambitions.

The historical internationalisation of the car industry has largely structured the models of other industries. Following initial partnerships, technological endogenisation developed strongly within the car sector, running from design through to production. Having initially been producers of trucks, jeeps and tractors, Tata, Mahindra & Mahindra (along with Ashok Leyland) were in a position to adopt a technology acquisition strategy in order to partially design their own car models, at the end of the 1990s, and finally to enter into true international commercial partnerships at the beginning of the 2000s. Case studies have shown up the original dynamics of these strategies, which contrast with the classical analyses of conglomerates. In contrast to the usual prescription that companies should concentrate on their core businesses (which has been partly implemented successfully in as much as a certain "rationalisation" has indeed taken place), the real industrial dynamics of these Indian groups has been their capacity to achieve inter-branch, positive externalities. Organisational or industrial competences achieved in partnership in one area have been transferred to others, thus raising overall profitability of investments along with rapid catching-up.[6] In addition, the cash flow generated in the IT sector by a group like Tata (through its TCS subsidiary) has allowed it to invest in the modernisation of its steel sector, as well as the development of its car production. Today, the purchase of the Corus steel group by Tata Steel allows it to develop new materials that will yield a comparative advantage to Tata Motors. When the first experiments in joint ventures between Maruti and Suzuki turned out to be positive, the possibility of foreign control of joint venture equity in fact helped accelerate domestic technological appropriation (compared to the Chinese case, see Richet & Ruet, forthcoming). Lastly, the result, which is apparently only paradoxical, is that foreign control is far greater over high technology exports from India than for such exports from China (see Goldstein and Lemoine 2013).

Global partnerships are the last, most difficult frontier to cross. In 2010, Schneider Electric announced that M. Anand Mahindra, head of the Indian Mahindra & Mahindra (M&M) conglomerate would join its Supervisory Board, in a similar way to Ratan Tata who had been a Fiat Board member since 2006. This alliance did not survive, even though the advantages were clear for both actors: M&M as a favoured point of entry into India for the traditional activities of the French group (industrial electrical equipment for use in major projects as well as by the general public) and in terms of energy efficiency, which was a new frontier for the group whereas M&M was already active in windpower and CO_2-efficient utility vehicles. In contrast, M&M was to have invested in the modernisation of its automobile production lines, its machine tools and its factories: Schneider's know-how and networks were precious. Lastly, the two groups were working on electric cars: the French firm was working on recharging systems, while the Indian company had just taken over India's leading electric vehicle producer, Reva. M&M pursued its international acquisitions, especially in Italy in mechanical design (i.e. Metalcastelli) and industrial design with the purchase of Auto Designing Co. Lastly, M&M attempted to create a link with the key Italy firm in the sector, namely Giugiara. These large innovative SMEs are key strategic assets for emerging actors seeking radical innovation (Tata textiles and Benetton also have a joint venture).

But the Indian companies, which capitalise on local industrial organisations at an international level, are also active in their domestic markets. This is notably so for the car industry, with its geographic concentration in India leading to the quasi-integration of certain suppliers and assemblers, as well as in the re-concentration of component parts producers in this sector.

---

[6] See the lobbying and financial roles of conglomerate groups, by Palepu and Khanna (1997), as well modeling of these phenomena by Raychaudhury & Ruet (forthcoming).

5.2.3 The National and International Industrialisation Paths of Indian Multinationals

Aside their international partnerships, Indian multinationals are also active in their home economy, which they continue to fertilise with their know-how. This raises the question of what their comparative advantage is based on apart from simple cost advantages.

Technological catch-up strategies are accelerating while the acquisition of know-how and intellectual property has begun. The search for collaboration with multinationals from developed countries or the creation of re-export platforms are only two examples of such strategies. Compared to many developing countries, India – just as China – is also characterised by having a critical size for the development of its markets. This directly benefits Indian firms. The internal markets alone give them important financial margins for expansion. This ultimately permits "cost leveraging" strategies, or strategies for transforming cost advantage into technological comparative advantage. The transition growth strategies and models implemented by Indian companies are based on a balance between development in emerging markets, including foreign emerging markets, and strategic partnerships to acquire technology. The key to the success of these commercial and technical strategies lies in the capacity of mastering the whole design and execution process, or in being associated with strategic developments via the creation of specific assets. This bet has already been won concerning IT, and is in the process of being validated for some bio-technological, pharmaceutical and automobile segments. Attempts at repositioning in the global textile chain are also at work, which interestingly enough, are not exempt from concerns about vertical integration. As far as leading edge technologies in industry are concerned (for example, aeronautical propulsion systems), much still needs to be done, and the role of the State will be essential. From a comparative point of view, the private nature of big industry in India and the country's longer capitalist history means that India is already beyond post-socialist transformation, whereas China still has to settle questions concerning private property rights.

The business models for entering global capitalism adopted by emerging Indian companies are based on the following stylised sequence:

1. Because they are integrating themselves into a production system, which is already globalised – and not only into markets – emerging firms already have global strategies;
2. The common substrate is a twofold comparative advantage of rapid capitalisation in their markets, combined with powerful technological catch-up as Indian firms come into contact with global production systems. This catch-up is very dynamic, because it benefits today from the entry of international groups into local production (technology is spreading, either through partnerships, via industrial districts of suppliers, or even through the purchase of technology portfolios);

3. The mastery of this advantage has been vital to historically globalised companies, and results from the rapid re-composition risks, competition, as well as opportunities and possible alliances.

This is a model which seems to hold in general for the firms of several emerging economies. But Indian companies are following their own conglomerate trajectories, even if they also demonstrate "variations" specific to the sectors in which they are operating. The key question of their evolution relates to the dynamic links between the capital accumulation process and the technological catch-up mechanisms of emerging economies. Shifting from a cost-based strategy to moving up the value chain, for example, is largely linked to a strategy based on joint ventures and the acquisition of technological portfolios.

They are upgrading their technology through acquisitions: 80 % of investments in mergers & acquisitions by Indian companies in the United States are focused on IT, Indian takeovers in Europe also aim at IT, pharmaceuticals, electronics and computers, and high value-added chemicals.

5.3 MNCs and Their Place Between Small Companies and the Return of the State

While the developments of the models in big industry have been both part-and-parcel of the evolution of India's economic policy and the globalisation of industrial production, they have nevertheless raised to question. Do they necessarily imply the spread of changes and processes (both in qualitative and quantitative terms) to small and medium-sized industries? Also, do they lead to a redefinition of models of economic arbitrage centred on the State? These two questions will only really be answered with time, but this section seeks to underline the potential for transformation by current trends. It also qualifies a simple linear reading of the "liberalisation process": the Indian State knows how to intervene forcefully.

5.3.1 Industrial Districts and Dissemination

Large companies disseminate both know-how and technology.

Looking to begin with at the industrial districts of the car industry, McKinsey forecasts that by 2015 the component parts sector will have a turnover of USD 40 billion. Sixty percentage of this output will be dedicated to exports, equivalent to 3.5 % of the world market. Six thousand small or very small companies account for about 20 % of the market are not directly linked to car companies, nor to suppliers, at least at Rank 2. But they are present in the spare parts sector, supplying about 65 % of total demand. It is not possible to know what their evolution will be over the next 10 years, even if there is concentration.

The client-supplier relationship is central to the extension (or even just preservation) of productivity gains and potential innovation. Even if India is an "emerging" country which is "poor on average", it is not "futuristic" to envisage

the development of high levels of certification such as SA 8000, ISO 14000. Instead, it is a necessity. There are two particularly dynamic districts which are engaged in the certification process. They are:
- A "western axis" around Maharashtra in the region of Bombay/Mumbai, Pune, Nashik and Aurangabad. It is linked to Mahindra & Mahindra, DaimlerChrysler, Fiat, Skoda, Bajaj and Kinetic;
- A "southern axis" made up of a zone, bringing together Bangalore and Madras, and involving Ford, Hyundai, Mitsubishi (Lancer), Toyota, Ashok Leyland, TVS, and Volvo.

Suppliers of international components are already present in India, and have transformed India into an exporter of parts with volumes running far ahead of the domestic market alone. Ohara et al. (2011) mentions the presence of "Delphi (GM), Visteon (the sourcing arm of Ford), MICO(Bosch) and Cummins International", and direct sourcing by Ford, Volvo, Toyota, GM, etc. as well as of Chinese trucks. Ultimately, suppliers which are backed by car producers have adopted a strategy of quality production and moving up the value chain, via measures favouring "process upgrading" and "product upgrading".

Programmes for industrial cooperation to optimise the use of materials, the quality of products or cut rejection rates have been implemented collectively by actors as varied as the Confederation of Indian Industry (CII), the Ministry of Industry (the Small Scale Industry Department), the Indian government, the Small Industries Service Institute (SISI), the Indian Machine Tool Manufacturers Association (IMTMA), the Karnataka Small Scale Industries Association (KASSIA), the Small Industries Development Bank of India (SIDBI), the Automotive Component Manufacturers Association (ACMA), the Institute for Autoparts Technology (IAT), partners within the progress partnership, the PPACIA, supported by UNIDO, and link to FIAT, Ford India, the ACMA, Ashok Leyland, Sundaram Clayton Ltd, the International Business Leaders Forum, and INSEAD. From an academic point of view, recent studies by Gulyani (2001) and Okada (2004) have largely set out the positive externalities related to these dynamic processes. So what is taking place outside the car industry?

More generally speaking about 32,000 small and medium enterprises account for 95 % of the companies working in manufacturing, which produce 40 % of the sector's value-added. They employed 17.8 million people. These firms were for long protected by the systems of "reservation" within the Indian economy. The suppression of import quotas within the WTO framework made such protection obsolete. Numerous observers are worried about the competitiveness of this sector, which is often characterised by technological obsolescence linked to very poor access to credit for investment. Some observers have stressed a trend to reconversion of some of these firms in imports and the distribution of very cheap products. Given the context in which big industry is restructuring itself and has tended to lose jobs since the 1990s, such trends in the small and medium-sized industrial sector, which has traditionally created employment, are worrying.

5.3.2 The Proximity of the State

Indian diplomacy and Indian companies are working hand-in-hand in Africa. Tata, for example, has been present in South Africa since the 1960s, and contributed to the rapprochement between the two countries after the end of Apartheid. Elsewhere in Africa, business is also at the heart of India's relationship with the continent. The Tata Group is once again spearheading Indian investments throughout Africa, having pursued such a strategy since the 1960s. The company has allocated $1 billion in investment in telecoms and the car industry in Kenya, Zambia, and Algeria, etc. It is also involved in urban development (the modernisation of buses). Indian entrepreneurs are making investments with long-term implications in IT, health, and telecoms in which they have bought up numerous mobile telephone networks. Indian diplomacy has been mobilised in support of such developments, to foster confidence in this sensitive area. Since 2002, the Indian government has supported the development of IT and medical services across the continent (the Focus Africa Programme), which mobilises private companies. As with China, the first Indo-African summit took place in April 2008, while the IBSA (India, Brazil, South Africa) agreements have an economic dimension: customs cooperation, and sectoral cooperation with the sharing of expertise and experience (in energy, agriculture, jewellery, tourism, as well as banking and finance). Particular attention is given to cooperation between SMEs in transport, aeronautics, infrastructure, shipbuilding and maritime transport. India also cooperates in areas of science and technology (materials, biotechnologies, and electronics) within the framework of ASEAN.

These programmes have been designed and deployed with the help of Indian employer associations, while India's international involvement is motivated both to act as a regional counterweight to China, to draw on the development model of the ASEAN countries, and to complete the "Look East Policy" which aims at linking India to the process of Asian regionalisation. In particular, India has a commercial partnership with Indonesia, another former leader of the non-aligned world. Numerous Indian companies are present in this country, operating in IT, automobile components, banking, etc. The two countries are also cooperating in the defence sector.

Large Indian conglomerates have obtained contracts in Indonesia. This has strengthened India's diplomacy and in return has allowed private Indian investments running into billions of dollars in strategic resources, like coal.

But while the State is supporting arrangements by Indian companies in Africa, it is challenging them domestically.

In mid-November 2011, Rahul Bajaj, managing director of Bajaj Automobile, and former director of the Confederation of Indian Industry (CII) – stated his concerns about the fact that the State could bail out the country's second-largest airline company, Kingfisher Airlines. He stated bluntly that, "it's a market economy, and the dying must die". The Indian Prime Minister Manmohan Singh responded rapidly by reaffirming fiscal orthodoxy and stating that it was for the banks to restructure their loans to Kingfisher. The company's debts stood at €1.1

billion, leading to a debt asset ratio of 82 %. The airline company had indeed avoided bankruptcy, because the banks already own 23 % of its equity, subsequent to a previous restructuring, and because its owner, the billionaire Vijay Mallya, had put up the agribusiness subsidiary of his conglomerate, his villa and two helicopters as collateral. But Kingfisher got support above all from the State Bank of India (SBI), the country's leading bank, which converted €180 million of debt into preferential shares and which drew on a new credit line of €150 million. As the SBI is a public bank, this action amounted to quasi-nationalisation. It is not clear, therefore, that MM. Singh and Bajaj share the same view of fiscal orthodoxy, or that Mr. Mallya does not have his own interpretation of what orthodoxy is.

In reality, the Kingfisher affair is only a detail in the broader context of the increasing power of public finance in India. The federal government, in fact, had already generously accepted at the end of November to recapitalise Air India, the public airline company, to the tune of €1.5 billion (the company's debt being four times as great). A further €3 billion was added to expand the fleet, while the ever-benevolent SBI was asked to reschedule the airline's debt. But more was to come, when the SBI announced it was making the largest loan of its history to allow the (public) electricity company National Thermal Power Corporation (NTPC) to expand capacity from 35 gigawatts (GW) today, to 128 GW (equivalent to France's total electricity production) by 2032. India's private competitors will surely appreciate the fact that State-industry relations are still thriving.

Conclusion

India is fully engaged in the dynamics of economic emergence.

Indian companies also have strong commercial and technological advantages in petrochemicals, pharmaceuticals and IT, and developing strengths in car design and assembly, renewable energies and aeronautics, etc. India's captains of industry are also clearly aware of the country's long-term potential as a "workshop": the world's largest refinery constructed in one piece was built in India by Reliance Energy, and this does not even include additional refining capacity added in several other projects.

There are no pure or exclusive models. Instead, a wealth of initiatives is all part of this history, with some sequences which can be stylised. The drive to internationalisation by Indian industry comes on top of regional specialties or previous booms in other sectors. India's specialisations are both fluid and integrated into its national territory. The focus of analysis therefore has to be midway between the economics of the firm and macroeconomics. It must have a long-term vision of the paths taken by regional industries.

As a whole, the country is clearly engaged in a long-term modernisation process. But the dynamics of the most advanced activities are no longer limited to the private sector. They are being disseminated to small industries, which remain fundamental to the future of the country.

There are huge investment failures: the maintenance and modernisation of public infrastructures are strongly deficient. In transport, health and education, public services are lacking greatly. This is due to a large extent to archaic information and decision-making systems, despite the fact that India is a software powerhouse.[7] Furthermore, India has to be able to redistribute more fairly the fruits of its growth: poverty remains endemic (nearly 35 % of the population is living on less than one dollar per day), while the total tax take only represents a meagre 13 % of GDP. As it used to be said in the United States, "what is good for General Motors is good for America", so too in India the industry would want to say that "what is good for Tata, is good for India as a whole".

References

Bomsel O, Ruet J (2001) 'Digital India 2001', report to the French Government. Centre Français du Commerce Extérieur, CERNA-Ecole des Mines, Paris, 169 p
Goldstein A, Lemoine F (2013) L'économie des BRIC, Collection Repères. La Découverte, Paris, 126 p
Gulyani S (2001) Effects of poor transportation on lean production and industrial clustering: evidence from the Indian auto industry. World Dev 9(7):1155–1177
Maria A, Ruet J, Zérah M-H (2002) Biotechnologies in India, report to the French Government, 247 p
Ohara M, Vijayabaskar M, Lin H (eds) (2011) Industrial dynamics in China and India: firms, clusters, and different growth paths. IDE-JETRO Series. Palgrave Macmillan, London, 288p
Okada A (2004) Skills development and interfirm learning linkages under globalization: lessons from the Indian automobile industry. World Dev 32(7):1265–1288
Palepu K, Khanna T (1997) Why focused strategies may be wrong for emerging markets. Harv Bus Rev 75(4):41–51
Ruet J (2005) Privatising power cuts ? Ownership and organisational reform of state electricity boards in India. Academic Foundation, New Delhi, p 339
Ruet J (2007) Emergence des firmes multinationales "du Sud" et lecture du capitalisme. Annuaire Français des Relations Internationales 2007, Paris, 19 p

---

[7] There is no space to go into this problem here, but it has been well identified: see, for example Ruet (2005).

Joint Ventures, Technology Acquisition and Emerging Multinationals: The Case of the Chinese Automotive Industry

Giovanni Balcet

This Chapter focuses on the complex relationship between international joint ventures (JVs), technological catching up processes in industry, and emerging multinationals in China. It stresses the role of history, policies and institutions, within an evolutionary approach.

To discuss this issue, we focus on the automotive industry, a vertically integrated sector, on which strong political emphasis has been put since 1994, when it was defined as a "pillar industry" (as telecommunications, defence industry and public transportation). At the beginning of the XXI century the Chinese market boomed, becoming in 2009 the first in the world, exceeding the US market, and five times larger than the Indian market, that had a similar size 10 years before. Macroeconomic performances and industrial policies contribute to explain this performance (Balcet and Wang 2012).

However, this industry is still highly fragmented, while it looks very complex from the institutional point of view. It is highly regulated, compared with others sectors. Companies are both State-controlled (by central ministries, or more frequently by Provinces or Municipalities) and private (Richet and Ruet 2008).

The following relevant research issues will be discussed: which driving forces are behind this growth process? which relations exist between technology acquisition and international growth? which competitiveness factors explain the early multinational growth of Chinese carmakers? to which extent national regulations and industrial policies supported the growth and shaped the market structure of this industry?

G. Balcet (✉)
Dipartimento di Economia e Statistica, "Cognetti de Martiis", Università di Torino, Lungodora Siena, 100, 10124 Turin, Italy
e-mail: giovanni.balcet@unito.it

6.1 Trajectories of Transition: History Matters

In China, transition trajectories starting from a centrally planned economy evolved in the last decades to a "triple mix" configuration, mixing planning and market, private and public ownership, centralised and decentralized decision making (Balcet and Valli 2012). Institutions and policies deeply affected the growth trajectories (Huchet et al. 2007).

The take off of the automotive industry in China took place after 2001, when this country joined the WTO, strongly accelerating during that decade. However, the process of fast growth cannot be explained if the analysis – as it is often the case – starts from the deregulation and liberalisation processes, i.e. from 1978. On the contrary, the long decades of the centrally planned economy and the import-substitution stage of growth, notwithstanding the failures and bottlenecks, built the structural bases for the future rapid growth of this industry (Balcet and Ruet 2011).

The industrial bases, created during the Japanese occupation, and expanded after 1949 with the Soviet technical cooperation, affected the future path of growth. During the early industrialization era, the first automotive companies (FAW, First Automobile Works, Second Automotive Works, later renamed DongFeng, and Chang'An) have been created under the direct control of a State Ministry, through a vertical system of control. In the following decades, local governments exerced pressures for creating new facilities and jobs in their provinces, with the effect of duplicating and fragmenting the industrial structure. In 1978, 26 provinces on 31 had automotive factories (Huang 2008; Richet and Ruet 2008). The fragmentation, on the supply as well as on the demand side, continued and even accentuated after 1978, with the liberalization process, notwithstanding the attempts of rationalizing this industry made by the central government. Beside the new projects and the expansion of existing facilities promoted by provincial governments and municipalities, dynamic private newcomers launched industrial initiatives. In the 1990s and 2000s, also international JVs contributed to increase the initial fragmentation of the automotive supply. This trend produced conditions of over-capacity, and many small size factories, operating under an efficiency scale of production; but it also created the opportunity for processes of decentralised learning (Balcet and Ruet 2011).

This outcome of high fragmentation, notwithstanding the efforts of the central government to let few "national champions" emerge, may appear as a paradox, given that this industry is among the most regulated in China. To explain this trend, competition among provinces, as well as competition of provinces with the central government, should not be neglected. And the booming growth rate of domestic demand contributed per se to enlarge market opportunities for carmakers and component suppliers.

A process of two-ways internationalization took place since the 1990s, and especially in the new century: the major multinational carmakers and suppliers entered the domestic market, mainly via JVs, while Chinese companies, both State-owned and private, expanded abroad via exports, assembly plants and acquisitions

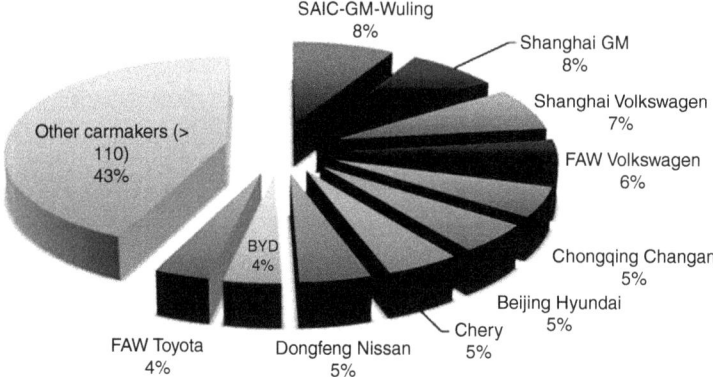

Fig. 6.1 China. Market shares in the passenger vehicle sector (2010) (Source: Balcet and Ruet 2011)

of foreign firms (Balcet and Wang 2012). The two flows are connected by the process of technological catching up, creative absorption of foreign technologies and know-how, and building of domestic innovation capabilities (Wang 2008).

Figure 6.1 shows the still highly fragmented industrial structure on the supply side in 2010, as well as the role of international JVs (see Sect. 6.2).

6.1.1 Corporate Governance and Ownership Patterns

The peculiar role of State-Owned Enterprises (SOEs), within a mixed and complex institutional frame, deeply affects this industry (Balcet and Ruet 2011).

State ownership, at central and local (province and municipality) level represents the dominant pattern of governance in China, along with JVs with foreign multinational investors. Private companies are a second but dynamic component (Wang 2009).

(a) Large SOEs such as FAW and Dongfeng are considered to be of direct relevance by the central government, while having also strong relationships with the hosting provincial governments. They became increasingly competitive throughout the 1990s and 2000s, with their indigenous models, while competing with foreign models made by their own JVs.

(b) Large companies, controlled by municipalities, such as BAIC and SAIC, based in Beijing and Shanghai respectively, played the role of major oligopolistic actors at the national level. SAIC was a pioneer of international JVs, since the 1980s.

(c) Other carmakers with a provincial ownership, such as Chery, Chang'An, GAIC and Brilliance, showed great dynamism both in promoting partnerships, and in accelerating international expansion through exports and FDIs (Balcet and Ruet 2011). They have been able to keep independent from the central government.

(d) Major private carmakers, such as Great Wall, Geely and BYD, developed different aggressive strategies for technological catching up, innovation and international growth. The same private actors maintained strict ties with provinces and the central administration, as it has been showed by the Geely-Volvo deal.

6.1.2 Regulations and Policies Matter

This industry is regulated by a complex and multi-level policy framework, where many institutions and policymakers interact (Wang 2009).

At the national level, the National Development and Reform Commission (NDRC) is a key technocratic institution. It is very influent in addressing strategic policy guidelines, and approving corporate strategies, through its Department of Auto Industry: its officials are considered to be excellent experts of this industry, not just bureaucrats. The approval of new investment projects, including new JVs, and the homologation of products have been among its key powers. Since 2008, some competences have been transferred from the NDRC to the Ministry of Industry and Information Technology (MIIT), including the registration of the product catalogues of JVs (so approaching to the Western standards); but the division of competences between these two institutions is not clearcut, and their relations are complex and sometimes contentious.

It is worthwhile to note a programmatic and influential document, issued in 2006 by NDRC. It stated the objective of four development stages for the automotive industry:
– The building of the industrial bases;
– The take off and the technological upgrading, via the JVs;
– The growth of national independent companies;
– The international growth (since the second half of the 2000s).

As we have noted, the announced proposal of a policy of industrial concentration and rationalization, making few "national champions" emerge, has not been effective till now, in front of the persistently fragmented structure of this industry. Other industrial policy requirements by the central government in the late 2000s concerned the promotion of new specific brands for JVs,[1] the expansion of the R&D centres of JVs and the development of electric vehicles.

Finally, also macroeconomic and industrial policies, including the post-crisis package (*Automotive Readjustment and Revitalization Plan*) launched in 2009, stimulated the growth process and contributed to the boom of this industry in the same year and in 2010.

Industrial pro-active policies at the level of provinces and municipalities influenced and stimulated FDI inflows, and the creation of new JVs. They represented factors of attractivity, through incentives and the efficient supply of infrastructures needed for the industrial production and modern logistics. The

---

[1] This requirement was "suggested" to foreign carmakers; but it became a condition for permission to expand the production capacities.

strategies of international JVs associating multinational carmakers with local State-owned partners (controlled by provinces or municipalities) have been sensible to the policies and priorities of regional and industrial development, for instance to the employment issues: it was the case, for example, of the IVECO (Fiat Industrial Group) JV in ChongQing, starting production in 2009.

It should be stressed, however, that the size and the fast growth rates of this market in the Chinese provinces represent per se major attractivity factors for foreign investors.

Since the early 2000s, and especially after the accession to WTO in 2001, Chinese flexible bureaucracy (at central and provincial levels) demonstrated its capacity to adapt to changes and to regulate this industry in an efficient way, favourable to growth.

6.2 Trajectories of Technological Upgrading

The catching up process in this industry, consisting of creative adaptation and recombination of foreign technologies, rather the simple transfer of technologies, took place through imitation, reverse engineering and international JVs (Balcet and Wang 2012). The process was made possible by the base of widespread technological know-how and engineering capabilities, created in the decades preceding the liberalization of the Chinese economy.

In this process, it should be noted the role of the major multinational component suppliers, following their clients – multinational car assemblers – in China, and diversifying in a second stage their clients. They are allowed to get full ownership of their factories in the country. It is the case, for example, of the French Valeo and the German Bosch.

International JVs plays a crucial role in this process, and were a key instrument of industrial policies. That's why we'll focus on them as a specific policy instrument.

6.2.1 Joint Ventures as Learning Instruments

Alliances, JVs and vertical relationships have represented crucial instruments to acquire assets from multinational partners, enhancing the capabilities and therefore the competitive advantages of Chinese firms.

Different theoretical approaches have been proposed in the literature in order to interpret international JVs (Balcet 2009).
- A first approach proposed the view that JVs may represent *second-best option* (Dunning 2005), in presence of restrictive rules. It is the case of this industry in China since the 1980s, where partnership in automotive assembly is imposed by national regulations.
- For a second approach JVs are related with *mature technologies*, to be transferred to developing countries. In this case, for the multinational, Western or

Japanese corporation, the main motivation is the access to growing markets, overcoming institutional barriers and the distance factor. Traditionally, transferred technologies could be mature or even obsolete, especially in the case of protected domestic markets, and MNCs could limit the technology transfer, or delay it, in order to preserve a gap. Also this second hypothesis has been relevant in the case of Chinese automotive industry, especially in its first stages of growth.

- JVs can be interpreted as a *"hostage"* in the case of complex and risky transactions. An institutionalized partnership can be an instrument aiming at stabilizing complex cooperative relationships, that would be difficult and risky to deal with purely contractual non-equity instruments.
- From a dynamic point of view, JVs can be viewed as a *"learning instrument"* in a broad sense, including the access to new technology and knowledge, learning of organizational and managerial skills, access to new markets, characterized by a strong distance factor. The last approach helps to understand the evolutionary nature of JVs (Balcet 2009).

In China, their role is still crucial as a guarantee for long-term partnership. China opened many sectors to majority ownership by foreigners, but the foreign ownership in car assembling remained restricted to JVs; while in the case of car component production (including engines) and of R&D Centres, full foreign ownership is allowed. Moreover, for a long time the government and NDRC directed the choice of partners and the locational choice of MNCs (Wang 2007).

Foreign carmakers are allowed to have a maximum of two JVs, while Chinese companies may develop several partnership. This is intended to create an asymmetry in favour of the Chinese partner. However, this policy also requires to the Chinese company the ability to manage a difficult integration of knowledge and technologies with different origins. In some cases, the integration of technologies by Chinese companies across multiple partners was difficult.

SAIC (Shanghai Automotive Industry Company) played a pioneering and firstmover role. A first step was represented by Shanghai VW, set up in Shanghai in 1984 between Volkswagen and SAIC, created at that time for this purpose. This early partnership soon became a major actor, shaping the market, upgrading the technological standards and influencing the consumer tastes, through success models like VW Santana and Passat.[2] The same JV allowed VW to benefit of a firstcomer advantage, deriving from a strong presence of its brads in the Chinese market before its fast growth stage. This advantage was later reinforced by a second JV with FAW, created in 1991 in Jilin Province. SAIC consolidated its role of oligopolistic actor through a second key JV, created in 1997 with GM.

---

[2] The success of these models, shaping the domestic market, may be compared to the success in the same years 1980s of the models produced by the Maruti-Suzuki JV in the Indian market.

Guangzhou Peugeot was another example of early JV (1985) involving GAIC and PSA, but less successful. In the following decade, the French PSA Group promoted another JV, Dongfeng Citroën (1992), in Hubei Province (Richet and Wang 2005).

BAIC, controlled by the Municipality of Beijing, developed a long-term successful process of technology acquisition and assimilation through several JVs: in a first stage with Chrysler (Beijing Jeep), and later with Hyundai and Daimler. This carmaker reached a strong market position in the commercial vehicle segment, through its brand Foton.

Brilliance, market leader in minibus production, tried to diversify into the premium car segment via a JV with BMW, importing engines from Germany; at the same time it cooperated with Toyota on the base of a long term non-equity industrial end technological agreement, in the minibus segment.

In June 2012, the Italian Fiat Group, mainly present in China in the truck sector with its company IVECO, started producing passenger cars in a new greenfield factory located in Changsha in a JV with GAC, that is also partner with Toyota, Nissan and Isuzu.

In China, catching-up is often an ability to adapt processes, in a creative recombination, rather than simply copying them or transplanting them (Wang 2009).

During the 2000s, the Chinese partners became in general less dependent on foreign technologies, as they developed their internal capabilities. However, some of the Chinese State-owned automakers are still depending for key technologies from their foreign partners, including multinational suppliers (Balcet and Wang 2012).

A new pattern of JVs is emerging, based on an exchange technology/technology, beside the traditional market/technology exchange.

Finally, we must note the growing number of R&D, engineering and Product Development Centres created in China by all the major multinational carmakers. These investments activated linkages with domestic firms and universities, giving rise to agglomeration effects and clustering. It is the case, for example, of the integrated technology district of Jiading, within the Shanghai municipality.

The case of Ford R&D and Product Development facility in Nanjing is specially interesting, because it was originally created in order to control the quality of the supply chain, within a global sourcing strategy. In a second stage, it was reconverted to the mission of product and process innovation for the Ford – Chang'An JV.

Figure 6.2 shows the complex networks of partnerships of SOEs, provincial controlled companies and private companies with multinational carmakers.

On the domestic market, Chinese brands are in competition with multinational brands, produced by JVs. Since 2009, the Chinese government strongly supported the creation of specific brands for JVs.

Honda was the first to launch a brand for its Guangqi Honda JV, followed by the three-parties JV SAIC-GM-Wuling, and by Dongfeng Nissan. Daimler AG and BYD announced the launch of new brand for the electric car to be produced by their JV in 2013.

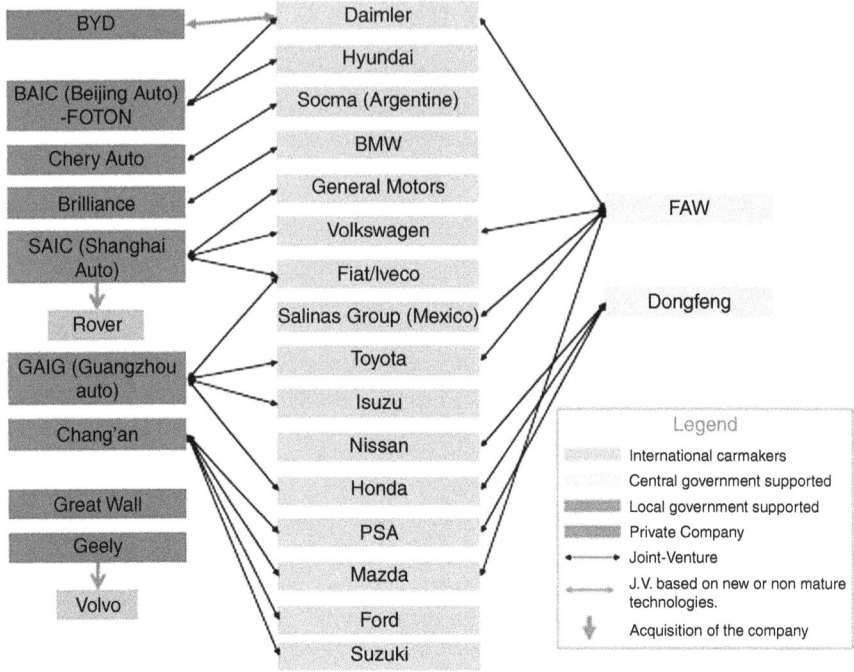

Fig. 6.2 Car industry in China: major actors, joint ventures and acquisitions (Source: Balcet and Ruet 2011)

6.2.2 Electric Vehicles, a Leapfrogging Opportunity?

Since the 1990s, the Chinese government gave importance to the development of electric vehicles, in order to reduce pollution and dependence on imported oil. In the second half of the 2000s, it made a significant policy move towards this new and promising industry segment, seen as a key opportunity for technological leapfrogging, with potential implications for the future global scenario of this industry. The stated objective was to become a leader in full electric vehicle segment (and to a lesser extent in the hybrid vehicle segment).

This strategic choice was based on the consideration of several potential advantages:
- The production experience in the field of batteries, where China is a top producer, with Japan and South Korea;
- The quasi monopoly in the rare earth metals production, crucial for producing new generation batteries;
- The huge market and production experience of electric bikes and scooters;
- The ability to build in short times and to manage complex infrastructures (e.g., smart grids), needed for developing this new segment.

All the major automotive groups launched or announced plans to develop electric or hybrid vehicles, as well as several minor producers and many component suppliers. A first comer in this field is BYD (Build Your Dream), a private company founded in 1995 as a battery company, specialised in cell-phones batteries, with no experience in the car industry. It decided to diversify in the electric vehicle new market, trying to exploit its competitive advantage and know-how in batteries. Its production is vertically integrated and diversified. After receiving an investment from Warren Buffet's company, in 2009 BYD made a JV agreement with Daimler Benz, for producing an electric car (Wang and Kimble 2010). However, after a rapid growth, due mainly to traditional engine cars, BYD slowed down its performances in 2012.

SAIC and Geely promoted alliances for developing electric vehicles with foreign suppliers, American and Danish respectively, that control key components. Also China's State-owned oligopolists in the energy industry showed strong interest in participating to the new business.

The government invested in infrastructure and introduced significant financial incentives in 2010. A program involving big cities, key ministries, NDRC and major carmakers, has been launched to subsidize the sale of plug-in electric and hybrid vehicles

However, coordination between central and regional policymakers has been insufficient. High prices of electric vehicles, weakness in basic R&D, technology problems with new generation batteries, the difficult definition of technical standards, and the lack of charging stations have been major obstacles to the take off of this segment.

6.3 Trajectories of Multinational Growth

The expansion of developing country multinationals in not a new phenomenon: since the late 1970s a relevant literature focused on "Third World multinationals" and South-South FDIs, mainly within Asian and South-American macro-regions (Lall 1983). However, during the 2000s a new trend appeared of South–north FDIs, while emerging country multinationals became very dynamic actors on the global scene (Goldstein 2007).

This stimulated the search for new theoretical explanations (Andreff and Balcet 2013). Some scholars extended existing theories, such as John Dunning's OLI approach, largely based on the experience of Western multinationals, to the new empirical developments (Buckley 2010). A common assumption of these theories is that a MNC has ex-ante competitive advantages over domestic firms, to overcome the initial disadvantages they face in the host country.

A second flow of theories, on the contrary, argue that emerging country multinationals may go abroad just to acquire the resources they lack at home: it is the case of asset-seeking strategies (Matthews 2006; Luo and Tung 2007). Emerging market companies can be expected to lack monopolistic or oligopolistic advantages in the strict sense, including patents or strong global brands. However they can possess other competitive advantages, ranging from their ability to obtain inputs on favourable terms to the access to cheap unskilled and skilled labour and raw materials, the ability for fast assimilation and creative recombination of transferred technologies, abundant financial resources, marketing skills and managerial abilities. Last but not least, the active support by the governments of many emerging markets, including state ownership, give rise to firm-specific advantages for these companies. It is the case of the Chinese new automotive multinationals (Balcet and Ruet 2011).

Since the 1990s, the fast growth of the Chinese automotive industry has been largely driven by the domestic market, where international JVs played a crucial role, and export have been less crucial the in other sectors. Moreover, some of largest carmakers have no international production. However, since the early 2000s a rapid internationalization process took place, starting with growing exports to developing and transition countries (Richet et al. 2007). The creation of assembling affiliates represented a development of previous exports, while different strategic asset-seeking motivations inspired foreign operations aiming to acquire technologies and foreign brands (Amighini 2012).

A wave of multinational expansion by Chinese companies in this industry took place since the early 2000s. The global financial and economic crisis accelerated the opportunities for foreign acquisitions.

It must be noted that many Chinese emerging multinationals are State-owned, i.e. by the central State administration, by Provinces or by Municipalities. This ownership pattern is related to the protectionist reactions against Chinese FDIs in some recipient countries.

A strong link exists with the catching up and partnership strategies, described in Sect. 6.2, because these strategies created the basic conditions for the multinational expansion abroad in the following years.

6.3.1 Emerging Multinationals: Asset Seeking Acquisitions as Specific Strategies

Two patterns characterize the multinational growth of Chinese carmakers.
- *Market-oriented strategies.* Previous export flows evolved into foreign assembly plants and SKD production, that substituted or were complementary to exports.

   Examples of this strategy are provided by SAIC, Chang'an and NAC (Nanjing Automobile, acquired by SAIC in 2007), that made FDIs in developing countries, Asia, Africa and Latin America. FAW and Great Wall launched production units in Russia, Ukraine and Bulgaria. Brilliance, with a strong competitive position in Africa in the segment of commercial and industrial vehicles, followed a gradualist approach in Egypt, moving from export to foreign production; while BAIC formed a JV to expand sales of minibuses in South Africa. Chery in the late 2000s developed an aggressive strategy of export and local assembly in Russia and in "difficult" countries, involved in internal and international conflicts, including Iran, Iraq and Syria.

- *The asset-seeking strategy*. In this case, the main driver for the multinational growth is represented by the acquisition of foreign assets, technologies and brands.

    A good example of this pattern is SAIC, that after a trajectory of trials and errors emerged as an international group. SAIC targeted in 2003 the Korean producer of SUV Ssangyong, and in 2005 acquired Rover technology, including engines and production lines.

    A very interesting case is that of Geely. This private company followed two parallel trajectories, of technology catching up and of asset-seeking foreign acquisitions. The first steps of the last trajectory were the equity participation taken in London Taxi, in 2006, and the acquisition of a leading Australian transmission producer in 2009. The last step is represented by the acquisition of Volvo in 2010 from Ford Motors, after a long negotiation process. While preserving its autonomy in Europe, Volvo started a new expansion of its production capabilities in China, announcing a huge investment plan in factories, R&D Centres and corporate universities. This acquisition benefitted of financial support by the governments of three Provinces, where the planned investments should be located (Balcet et al. 2012).

Asset-Seeking for Car Styling: Chang'An Design Centre in Turin, Italy

An interesting example of R&D asset-seeking strategy is given by Chang'An, a province-controlled carmaker based in ChongQing. It developed a mixed strategy of technological catching up and international growth, based on domestic JVs (with Suzuki Motors, Ford Motors and PSA), for the acquisition of foreign technology, and on a strong international expansion. The last strategy was based on export and early assembling abroad, to access markets in developing countries, and on asset-seeking FDIs in developed countries, for non-manufacturing activities (Amighini 2012). It is specially interesting to note that Chang'An built up an international network for R&D, design and product development. Beside five R&D Centres located in China, four other Centres have been created and developed in Japan (Yokohama), UK (Nottingham), USA (Detroit) and Italy (Turin).

The "Chang'An Automobile European Design Centre", created in 2005 for car styling, is an example of asset-seeking greenfield FDI. It has been attracted by the cluster effect in Turin area, where all the car styling supply chain is represented, giving rise to synergies of vertical integration design-product-services. The integration of creative styling and technologies, within the Italian design tradition, explains the attractivity of this area for a Chinese carmaker.

The ambitious mission of this Centre is to bridge European car styling tradition with Chinese demand, consumer tastes and production conditions. More than half of the Chang'An production in China benefitted from projects developed at the Turin Centre, thanks to a vertical coordination with the production platforms in Chonquing, while an horizontal coordination took place with other R&D Centres, including Shanghai and Nottingham (for engines). Ways for learning, technology transfer and acquisition included the mobility of managers and skilled labour. The process of creative adoption of new technologies faced challenges and bottlenecks.

Linkages with the Turin's district do not seem specially developed, except for relations with small and medium-sized service and engineering companies, and for the fruitful relationship with the specialised skilled labour market. This case is a good example of a complex and challenging, but successful asset-seeking FDI in R&D and design.

6.3.2 Chinese New Automotive Multinationals: Which Competitive Advantages?

In conclusion, let's try to focus on the key competitiveness factors, both country-specific and firm-specific, that explain the growth performances and the multinational expansion of Chinese carmakers.

Country-specific factors created significant competitive advantages supporting the growth, catching up and multinational expansion of Chinese carmakers, including economies of scale, static and dynamic and economies of scope, generated by the huge size and fast growth of the domestic market. Domestic savings and the expanding national financial system supported with cheap money corporate growth and international expansion (WIR 2006, 2013).

Also the national system of innovation and the educational system created essential conditions for the acquisition of industrial technology and the development of organizational capabilities that allowed industrial groups to go abroad.

The pro-active role of the State promoted industrial dynamics, creating the competitive framework needed to engage into technology upgrading, innovation and international expansion. State support to internationalisation played a crucial role, since the "Going Out" policy.

The diplomatic support of the Chinese State was a key success factor both for exports and for international production. SASAC (State Asset Supervision and Administration Commission), which holds the State assets, played an important role, representing the national interest in the process of outward internationalization and FDI. The support by the government has been important in takeovers as well, at the financial level (credit, access to foreign currency, or later access to national technology centres and their human resources to fast integrate the knowhow of the acquired company). It was the case of the acquisition of Volvo by Geely in 2010.

The State support – as well as the State ownership – was at the origin of concern and protectionist reactions: it was the case of the move promoted in 2012 at the WTO by the US Obama administration against Chinese subsidies for car and autoparts makers.

Firm-specific factors include the capacity for fast assimilation and creative recombination of transferred technologies and knowledge, supported by the managerial and engineering abilities, leveraging resources through partnerships, and the acquisition of well-established brands via asset-seeking foreign acquisitions. Different strategies and trajectories characterize Chinese carmakers, including reverse engineering, imitation, product architecture innovation. In the upgrading process, JVs played a crucial role. In the late 2000s, the competitiveness of Chinese automotive companies benefitted from the new pattern of JVs, no longer based on the traditional exchange old technologies/new growing markets, but involving innovative technologies and launching their own brands.

Labour costs matter. Unlimited supply of low cost unskilled labor pushed corporate profits and growth, as well as exports. Low cost highly skilled labor, including engineers, chemists, managers and technologists, explains why the ability to absorb foreign-generated technology evolved into the capacity to introduce original improvements, incremental innovations and finally new products and processes. It is a major source of competitive advantages for Chinese companies going multinationals.

This factor represents on the one hand a locational advantage for foreign multinationals investing in these emerging countries, and on the other hand a competitive advantage for Chinese emerging multinational investing abroad, in particular in developed OECD countries. This is a paradox from the point of view of the current ortodox theory, based on a factor-endowment approach. This theoretical approach is therefore incapable to explain this new trend, and should be reversed (Andreff and Balcet 2013).

References

Amighini A (2012) Chinese FDI in the European automotive sector. In: Ciravegna L (ed) Sustaining industrial competitiveness after the crisis. Lessons from the automotive industry. Palgrave, pp 114–133

Andreff W, Balcet G (2013) Emerging multinational companies investing in developed countries: at odds with the HOS theorem? *The European Journal of Comparative Economics*, 10, n.1, April 2013, pp 3–26

Balcet G (2009) Economia dell'impresa multinazionale. Problemi e teorie, dal ciclo del prodotto alla globalizzazione. Giappichelli, Torino

Balcet G, Ruet J (2011) From joint ventures to national champions or global players? Alliances and technological catching-up in Chinese and Indian automotive industries. Eur Rev Ind Econ Policy (3)

Balcet G, Valli V (2012) Potenze economiche emergenti: Cina e India a confronto. il Mulino, Bologna

Balcet G, Wang H (2012) Editorial. Int J Automot Technol Manage 12(4), pp 313–317

Balcet G, Richet X, Wang H (2012) Geely: a trajectory of catching up and asset-seeking multinational growth. Int J Automot Technol Manage 12(4), pp 360–375

Buckley PJ (2010) Foreign direct investment, China and the world economy. Palgrave Macmillan, London

Dunning J (2005) Multinational enterprises and the global economy. Addison-Wesley, New York

Goldstein A (2007) Multinational companies from emerging economies. Palgrave, Houndmills/New York

Huang Y (2008) Capitalism with Chinese characteristics. Cambridge University Press, Cambridge

Huchet J-F, Richet X, Ruet J (eds) (2007) Globalisation of firms in China, India and Russia. Emergence of national groups and global strategies of firms. Academic Foundation, New Delhi

Lall S (1983) The new multinationals. The spread of third world enterprises. In: Lall S (ed) Multinationals from India. Wiley, Chichester

Luo Y, Tung RL (2007) International expansion of emerging market enterprises: a springboard perspective. J Int Bus Stud 38(4):481–498

Matthews J (2006) Dragon multinationals: new players in 21st century globalization. Asia Pac J Manage 23:5–27
Richet X, Ruet J (2008) The Chinese and Indian Automobile Industry in Perspective: Technology Appropriation, Catching-up and Development. Transit Stud Rev 15(3), pp 447–465
Richet X, Wang W (2005) Foreign direct investment in the Chinese automobile industry. A case study through a Sino-French joint-venture. In: Huchet JF, Richet X (eds) Gouvernance, Coopération et Stratégie des Firmes Chinoises. L'Harmattan, Paris
Wang H (2007) Foreign direct investment in China's automotive industry. In: Huchet J-F, Richet X, Ruet J (eds) Globalisation in China, India and Russia. Emergence of national groups and global strategies of firms. Academic Foundation, New Delhi, pp 243–258
Wang H (2008) Innovation in product architecture – a study of the Chinese automobile industry. Asia Pac J Manage 25(3):509–535
Wang H (2009) Made in China: joint-ventures and domestic newcomers. In: Freyssenet M (ed) The second automobile revolution. Palgrave MacMillan, Houndmills/New York, pp 383–403, Chapter 20
Wang H, Kimble C (2010) Betting on Chinese electric cars? Analysing BYD's capacity for innovation. Int J Automot Technol Manage 10(1):77–92
WIR (2006) World investment report. UNCTAD, Geneva
WIR (2013) World investment report. UNCTAD, Geneva

7 Multinational Corporations, Sub-national Governance and Human Resources: A Cross-national Comparison for Europe

Phil Almond, Anthony Ferner, Maria Gonzalez Menendez, Jonathan Lavelle, David Luque Balbona, and Sinead Monaghan

7.1 Introduction

In the context of the transnationalisation of productive systems and changing dynamics of competition to host foreign direct investment (FDI), it is commonly argued, both in economic geography and in discussions of the political economy of FDI, that relatively local, sub-national governance actors play an increasing role in attempting to connect regions to global production. This applies both to negotiating with current and potential investors, and to establishing wider business systems which will attract FDI and try to 'embed' it within the relevant geographical space.

This chapter therefore analyses the relevance of sub-national business systems and public policy in attempting to attract and retain FDI, on a cross-national comparative basis. It is based on co-ordinated in-depth case study research on the relations between sub-national governance institutions – including regional and local government, but also regionally significant business system institutions such as development agencies, skills institutions, employer organisations and trade unions – and multinational corporations (MNCs) located within selected regions of Ireland, Spain, and the UK. Each of the countries under investigation has, in the past, successfully competed for FDI at least partly on the basis of low labour costs and/or labour market flexibility within a Western European context. These positions, though, have been undermined by the expansion of the European economic space, as well as by more active competition for inward FDI by core EU countries and regions. From broadly comparable positions in the international

P. Almond (✉) • A. Ferner
Department of Human Resource Management, Leicester Business School, De Montfort University, The Gateway, Leicester, LE1 9BH
e-mail: palmond@dmu.ac.uk

M. Gonzalez Menendez • D. Luque Balbona
Department of Sociology, University of Oviedo, Spain

J. Lavelle • S. Monaghan
Kemmy Business School, Limerick, Ireland

competition for investment, regions in the three countries are under pressure to 'upgrade' and provide specific resources to international firms. However, they do so with different business systems, as well as political systems, particularly as concerns the role for actors below the national state level.

The chapter proceeds as follows. The first main section briefly reviews arguments around sub-national governance in the contemporary competition for FDI. After a methodological note on the project on which our analysis is based, we discuss in detail three main elements of the sub-national governance/multinational corporation (MNC) nexus, on a comparative basis: first, the articulation between different levels of public intervention, including both relations between different geographical levels of governance, and the articulation between state and non-state governance actors; second, we compare the roles of inward investment agencies; third, the extent and nature of relations between governance and MNC actors is examined and compared. The concluding discussion synthesises the comparative findings and suggests directions for future research.

7.2 Sub-national Governance and FDI

Arguments around the importance of the institutional construction of resources – including physical infrastructure, but also labour market resources and the availability of access to supplier and knowledge – for internationally mobile firms is a key feature of the literature on contemporary economic globalisation and MNCs (Jackson and Deeg 2008; Keune et al. 2004). Within this, work across different levels of analysis suggests that sub-national governance is (or should be) of increasing importance.

At a macro-level, political economists (e.g. Jessop 2000; Cerny 2000) have posited that, following the demise of Keynesian/Fordist regulation of national capitalisms, state emphasis has shifted from the protection of nationally-owned productive capital to securing positions in international contests for mobile investment. As economic policy has shifted towards the supply-side within broadly neo-liberal regimes, a 'rescaling' of governance (Brenner 2004) has occurred: coordination has shifted both upwards (to supra-national) and downwards (to sub-national) actors. 'Tailoring' institutionally-derived resources to the exigencies of specific firms is seen as being easier to coordinate at relatively local levels. As this occurs, powerful MNCs, as quasi-customers of governance systems in rival geographies, shift from being, in the terms of Crouch (2005) 'institution takers', responding to the 'constraints' arising from the imperative regulation of host governments, to having increased power to affect the nature of host systems.

Relatedly, at the meso-level, 'new regionalist' research in economic geography has used resource-based arguments about the contemporary importance of tacit knowledge to the sustained competitive advantage of firms (Barney 1991), and argued that the diffusion and management of such tacit knowledge is strongly supported by spatial proximity, being difficult to exchange over long distances (e.g. Maskell and Malmberg 1999). Thus, for many economic geographers, as Gertler notes in a significant review of this literature;

> tacit knowledge is seen as a prime determinant of the geography of innovative activity, since its central role in the process of learning-through-interacting tends to reinforce the local over the global...(This) helps explain the perpetuation and deepening of economic concentration in a world of expanding markets, weakening borders, and ever cheaper and more pervasive communication technologies. (Gertler 2003: 78)

To the extent that this is true, many MNC units are seen as being considerably more embedded in sub-national business systems than more extreme visions of 'footloose' MNCs would entertain. In fact, many analysts have claimed that the degree of MNC 'embeddedness' in local economies has increased in the last two decades, with a move away from routine 'branch plants' to units exercising more strategic functions with the firm, and with closer links to regional firms and institutions (Clark and Beaney 1993; Cooke et al. 2005; Morgan 1997). Within this vision, the resources present in locations are important both to investment decisions and the extent to which FDI offers possibilities for local development. From a policy perspective, how sub-national relationships shape such resources, and thus 'embed' MNCs, is taken to affect the nature of the commitment such firms will make to their host regions and countries, with effects on the nature and volume of employment as well as on productivity. At this point, the literature on economic geography unites with that of policy-oriented business academics in stating that, for such countries, competition for investment is likely to be in higher value-added activities (Delbridge et al. 2006), with the aim of becoming a "location competing on unique value and innovation" (Porter and Ketels 2003: 5). In order to achieve this, it is widely argued that sub-national institutions are central to the creation of networks and innovation and in fostering "skills ecosystems" (Finegold 1999), or the capacity to 'absorb' tacit knowledge (Cohen and Levintal 1990) which can respond flexibly to changes in demand (Delbridge et al. 2006; DfES et al. 2003). There is some debate within this broad consensus about whether individual dealings with specific MNCs (i.e. 'aftercare' initiatives) are more or less a public priority that broader attempts to develop appropriate labour market skills (Young and Hood 1995; Amin et al. 1994; Phelps et al. 2003).

Finally, at a more micro-level, the spatial and organisational fragmentation of production – a core feature of contemporary globalisation, enabled by improvements in information and communication technologies and declining transport costs, but driven by the financialisation of productive firms – has provoked a stream of research around global value chains (Gereffi et al. 2005) and global production networks (GPNs) (e.g. Coe et al. 2008; MacKinnon 2012). The latter has as its unit of analysis "the globally organised nexus of interconnected functions and operations by firms and non-firm institutions through which goods and services are produced and distributed" (Coe et al. 2004: 471). Similar ideas have for some time inspired research on whether MNC subsidiaries are becoming more 'embedded' in terms of local linkages (Hudson 1994), with an increased "depth and quality of the relationships between inward investors and local firms and organisations"

(Phelps et al. 2003: 28), and an increased potential – and requirement – for branch plants to compete for higher level functions in the MNC. As local units of MNCs increasingly compete for global/supra-national mandates, rather than merely replicating parent country operations, and as the number of relatively sheltered units within large domestically-owned firms has rapidly declined, regional development becomes increasingly dependent on the existence of localised economies of scale and scope, and on configurations of institutions capable of 'holding down' parts of GPNs. As the strategic needs of the key decision makers in GPNs often change rapidly, regional actors need not only to develop resources – such as high levels of skill – but also to ensure that the institutions responsible have sufficient flexibility to deal with new or recalibrated needs. While national institutions obviously remain important in setting frameworks within which this can occur, it is again implied that the relevant 'institutional entrepreneurship' (Crouch 2005) is often located at more local levels.

Each of these strands of literature, at least when discussed summarily, is obviously somewhat heuristic, and qualifications are necessary. Clearly labour cost, market access and natural resources remain important reasons for MNC location in many cases, and even where tacit knowledge is key to competitive advantage, the capacity of MNCs to transmit such knowledge across geographically dispersed locations should not be underestimated (Burrell and Coe 2001). Equally, as we discuss in more detail elsewhere (Almond 2011), moves towards greater sub-national coordination of business systems are likely to be affected both by institutions for sub-national political autonomy which often are established (or not established) for primarily political rather than economic reasons, as well as by 'institutional density' in national and regional economies (particularly, the balance between market, associational and state governance as discussed in the comparative capitalisms literature, e.g. Amable 2003; Whitley 1999).

Our empirical analysis therefore analyses the extent and nature of sub-national governance interventions, and governance-MNC relations, across peripheral or semi-peripheral regions in three countries which are broadly comparable in terms of position in contests for FDI, but which have important differences both in business system orientation and in the nature of sub-national political governance. The aim of this comparison is to establish the extent to which one can claim that sub-national governance/MNC relations follow some of the narratives presented above, and whether the ways in which this does or does not occur is related to features of regional and national forms of political and economic coordination.

7.3 Methodology

The research is based on an internationally comparative cross-sectional research design across two regions in each of Ireland, Spain and the UK. Two regions were investigated in each country in order to permit intra-national comparisons. The first stage of data collection required the identification of the sub-national boundaries, and thus, the participants. Each country research team generated a profile of the sub-national business system within each location, generating a database of key state and civil institutional actors who had a functional presence within the sub-national location *and* an evident affiliation to current or prospective FDI within the sub-national location.

In the case of Spain, which has a clear structure of regional political government, two of the 17 'autonomous communities' were chosen (Asturias, an old industrial region on the North Coast, on which the current analysis is mainly based, as well as the Madrid region). For the UK, we selected two top-level regions within England, on which the then-Labour government had instituted regional development agencies (RDAs), responsible for a range of meso-level governance activities, including the attraction and retention of FDI. For Ireland, where statistical regions have little reflection on the ground, we chose two specific regions where there was a history of meso-level economic development institutions – the Shannon and Gaeltacht regions.

Pilot interviews were held with key institutional actors within the location, predominantly inward investment/economic development agencies who are considered the "main interlocutor" to MNEs in a location to validate the database and ensure all relevant institutions were included. Following the interviews, actors were asked to identify other institutional actors within the sub-national location who engage with FDI. The result of this process ensured that all active sub-national institutional actors were identified. Unanticipated institutional change during the course of the English research led us to interview a number of individuals with new or changed roles towards the end of the project.

Prior to the data collection stage of this research, a standardised semi-structured interview format was collectively designed by all research teams, pertaining to the interaction of institutional actors with FDI within the sub-national location. Two broad interview formats were devised to account for the different perspectives of the sub-national institutional actors and MNC directors/managers. Specific dimensions of the interview schedule included role within the region, direct and proximate interactions with sub-national institutional actors, HR and labour markets and perceived strategically important MNCs within the location. The interview format also provided sufficient flexibility and scope to explore unique country- or sub-national-specific issues which may arise during the course of the interview. Interviews were recorded for accuracy and transparency. No individual, organisation or institution was identified, and anonymity was guaranteed. A standardised coding structure for qualitative interviews was also verified by all research teams prior to data collection, and used to code all interviews.

As this research is cross-national and inter-regional, the data analysis required a more robust and coordinated approach. In terms of analysis, a set of themes were deduced from prior literature to provide an initial framework to guide analysis. However, all research teams were encouraged to identify unique themes within their findings. Firstly, qualitative data from each sub-national location was collated, coded and analysed. Following this, each country compared the data from both sub-national locations to identify national level similarities and variance. Finally, data from all the sub-national locations were considered in their totality.

7.4 Articulation Between Levels of Public Intervention

This section will, first, identify the broad nature of institutions involved in the 'state-MNC nexus' (Phelps and Fuller 2001) in the three countries. It will then examine the more or less encompassing roles of inward investment agencies both in direct investment marketing and in shaping wider sub-national business systems. Finally, it will explore empirical evidence on the nature of relations between governance actors and MNCs present in the relevant regions.

7.4.1 Governance and Articulation Between Levels

It was expected that the ability of regions to create differentiated localised capacities, such that sub-national business systems have some degree of autonomy from the national business system, might be related to levels of regional political autonomy. For this reason, the wider project on which this chapter is based examined two countries with extensive sub-national political autonomy (Spain and Canada) and two where this is much more limited (Ireland and England).

Spain has among the highest degrees of regional political decentralisation in Europe, being divided into 17 Autonomous Communities with directly elected governments. Alongside extensive competencies in health, education, planning, transport, social assistance and culture, they have exclusive competence for regional economic development. As such, they are responsible for FDI attraction/retention strategies. The main limits to such extensive autonomy are budgetary (regional governments substantially depend on transfers from the national level), and through national law limiting grants/funds to private firms to accord with EU competition regulations.

References by fieldwork interviewees to "the government" frequently meant the regional rather than national government. Regional governments of the left (as in the Asturias case) have tended to be more active economic coordinators than those of the right. Until the 2012 Labour Reform, regions also had some ability to impose conditions on collective redundancies, meaning these were somewhat harder to obtain where governments were of the left. Asturias also has a regional tripartite social pact, formalising the role of the regional development agency, but also, *inter alia*, knowledge economy/society strategy, and employment and training policy.

England is unusual among large liberal market economies in having a highly centralised system of political governance of the economy, with no significant tier of government between the national and local authority levels. From 1998 to 2010, this was partially mitigated by the existence of ten (non-elected) Regional Development Agencies (RDAs) covering all of England (see below). More recently, the Conservative/Liberal Democrat government abolished RDAs, and with them any substantial degree of state governance of the economy between local authority and national levels. Newly established Local Enterprise Partnerships (LEPs) – sub-regional alliances between neighbouring local authorities and employers – provide some very limited degree of coordination at sub-regional levels. Local authorities are sometimes significant economic development and inward investment actors, especially in the larger Northern cities. Finally, the ministry of Business Innovation and Skills (BIS) and its national investment agency (UKTI) have always been significant players, and have grown in relative importance under the current government.

Ireland also has strongly centralised political administration, with fully 94 % of public expenditure decisions made at a national level (O'Broin and Walters 2007), and a fragmented sub-national infrastructure. Regional development agencies exist in the two regions we investigated (see below), but these are subordinate to a national agency.

7.5 Roles of Inward Investment Agencies

Inward investment agencies have a number of common features and roles across all the regions we have examined. They compete in investment marketing, guiding new investors through the local host environment and institutional system, including labour supply, skills, technological and research capacity, as well as the management or brokerage of whatever incentives are permissible within the national/EU system. They therefore draw on institutional resources of host locations – such as educational institutions, local and regional government, private service providers and sector specific bodies – to secure investment. They also, although not always to the same extent, deal with issues raised by existing MNCs within their geographical ambit – what was traditionally referred to as 'aftercare' – and attempt to broker relationships between foreign MNCs and wider business system actors (including supplier networks, skills agencies, etc.). In this way, RDA investor development officials sometimes become significant 'soft governance' actors in aiding the coordination of skills provision on an ad-hoc basis, and by acting as gatekeepers over available public-funded finance.

They differ from each other in three ways which are relevant in terms of a discussion about FDI and sub-national business systems: in *geographical level*; in *autonomy and governance*; and in the extent to which their role is *narrow or more encompassing*.

In terms of *geographical level*, as we have seen, the Spanish system is basically regional, as economic development is a regional level responsibility. Certainly in the Asturias case on which the current analysis is mainly based, the only significant agency, IDEPA, is a creation of the regional government.

In Ireland, by contrast, the most relevant agency is IDA (Industrial Development Authority) Ireland, a national statutory body. This body, established as long ago as 1949, has an extensive remit and is a relatively powerful governance actor. Although it has some regional presence, and is complemented in places by regional agencies of secondary importance, the attraction and retention of FDI in Ireland, a much more key part of Irish economic policy in general than elsewhere, operates via a hierarchy, with a predominantly national level orientation. This tends to override regional focus, as where FDI locates within Ireland is not a primary consideration for IDA Ireland (although see below).

Finally, in England the situation has been more complex and unstable (see Almond et al. 2012). From 1998 to 2010, the responsibility for inward investment was divided, with somewhat opaque boundaries, between RDAs and the UK national body UKTI. There was some role also for local-authority funded sub-regional agencies, particularly in large cities. Aftercare was largely in the hands of RDAs, except in the cases of the largest, "nationally strategic" investors which had, and retain, relations with national civil servants. Upon the abolition of RDAs, the responsibility for attraction passed to a private-sector contractor working for the national UKTI. This body is mainly targeted around new investment, leading to several interviewees questioning where aftercare responsibilities now lay.

Do geographical levels matter? We would argue that they do, first in terms of access to local, often tacit knowledge, about the capabilities, resources and needs of regions. Second, there is the issue of the regionalisation of the targets that agencies are managed by. In the English case, there is no regional-level structure, or regional focus of UKTI-sponsored inward investment work, which is nationally targeted. IDA Ireland is better networked into pools of local business system knowledge, and does pay at least lip-service to attracting investment outside the principal destinations of Dublin and Cork.

Turning to our second variable, the *autonomy and governance of inward investment bodies*, again there is substantial variation. In Spain, while regional bodies such as IDEPA have substantial day-to-day autonomy, they are under the control of regional governments. In a Spanish context, this means that they are relatively political institutions, with their leadership subject to change following the political fortunes of the regional government. This permits differences of emphasis between regions; for example we have evidence that regions governed by parties regionally closest to a free market model – Madrid being a prime example here – place less emphasis on aftercare than is the case in Socialist dominated Asturias, within an assumption that new investment is maximised through minimising exit barriers. It is also worth noting that in the Asturian case, IDEPA is nominally a tripartite agency, although neither representatives of collective labour or indeed collective regional employers report significant influence over its actions. Rather, IDEPA uses the presence of such institutions 'in the room' to attempt to communicate the pre-requisites for international competitiveness.

In Ireland, IDA, as a national government agency, has a fair degree of autonomy, and is extensively networked with ministers as well as the corporate class. The system is specifically designed to prevent local autonomy for other economic development agencies in the field of inward investment. Regional policies are largely created and imposed at either national or European level and therefore, these agencies have limited decision-making power and tend to operate in line with national level policy. Nevertheless, within the regions we examined, Shannon Development maintains full autonomy to engage with FDI within the Shannon Free Zone (essentially a business park with beneficial tax status, established in

1959), while Údarás na Gaeltachta have considerable autonomy for smaller FDI projects within the Gaeltacht region.

Finally, in England, issues of autonomy for such agencies are of a more existential nature, given a lack of political consensus on the desirability of regional governance. RDAs, while having a regional remit, were nationally-controlled institutions reporting to central government and with their boards appointed by Westminster. The current national arrangements, meanwhile, are a contractual arrangement, liable to change if results are not judged satisfactorily, or potentially in the event of a change of government. Given the necessity of meeting targets, there is little capacity for the private-sector provider to engage in 'institutional entrepreneurship' in going beyond its direct brief.

Our final, and crucial, variable, is the extent to which inward investment bodies become relatively 'encompassing', that is, wider business system actors. In the Spanish cases, and in the English regions prior to 2010, sectoral clustering and productivity initiatives were in the remit of the relevant regional inward investment bodies. These can be seen as attempts to provide an impulse to stronger associational governance among firms, within business systems where inter-firm cooperation is, for slightly different reasons, traditionally difficult. The aim of this, particularly in the Asturias case, is to develop an indigenous base of firms capable of slotting into global production networks.

In the English case, given the lack of formal regional government, RDAs had substantial formal strategic responsibilities for coordinating local and regional institutions in a number of spheres (innovation, skills, environment, transport, social inclusion, etc.), having been created to coordinate responses to 'market failures'. As far as this analysis is concerned, they had a particularly significant role as a 'broker' between MNC subsidiary units and the wider public sphere, particularly in their role as an intermediary between private firms and England's poorly articulated network of skills institutions and actors. Significantly, in an economy in which dialogue between employers on skills needs has historically proved difficult to establish, they also served, through their investor development work, as interest aggregators in this area. Our fieldwork shows several instances in which RDAs identified specific skills issues among neighbouring large firms, and played a role in the coordination of the skills provision required. Thus, although formal sub-national autonomy of the business system in England was limited, the presence of RDAs did provide MNC subsidiary units – particularly those which were regionally important employers – with a regional interlocutor with some decision-making powers over the distribution of public funding. It is difficult, however, to see how this function will be replicated in the emerging system.

In Ireland, although at a national level, IDA Ireland also has an important de facto role in business system development roles. It very strongly engages in relationship building with MNC subsidiaries, and there is evidence that IDA Ireland may coordinate and shape the business system as it affects specific firms insofar as they draw on services of other agencies to attract and retain FDI, most clearly evidenced through the 'itinerary tour'. Additionally, IDA Ireland often coordinates interaction with particular service providers in response to infrastructural issues such as broadband and airport services, and coordinates with other national bodies with responsibility over micro-economic policy. Given the relatively small size of Ireland, and IDA's extensive networking capabilities, coordination with more localised providers of institutional resources does not appear to be particularly problematic.

7.6 Governance Actor/MNC Relations

This section summarises findings on governance actor/MNC relations more generally. It discusses, first, the extent to which foreign MNCs engage in lobbying, and/or largely bypass regional institutional systems. Second, it looks at the extent to which such firms can be seen as being regionally embedded and/or have local interactions. Finally, we will look at the issue of 'strategic interlocutors' in the public sphere for subsidiary managers at times where decisions are being made globally that are decisive at local level.

Evidence on collective lobbying by MNCs is fairly limited, although this should be qualified by stating that our analysis concentrates mainly at the level of the regional operations of firms, and it is in some cases likely that lobbying 'behind closed doors' takes place mainly by executives working in small national headquarters operations, often located in capital cities, rather than at production unit level. While informal networking and information-sharing between local managers of different MNCs does occur to varying extents, this seems mainly to be about finding effective ways to reach the exigencies of global management systems within the local environment (particularly in the Spanish case), or on informal collaboration around encouraging repeat investment (particularly in Ireland): there is, on the whole, little appetite among MNC managers and directors to become very actively involved in official institutions of industrial relations or skills, beyond their immediate needs. In other words, the productive systems of MNCs were often created at one remove from formal qualifications, and employment systems often at one remove from national and regional industrial relations actors, with a heavy reliance on firm-based systems.

Sometimes regional actors are complicit in this. The clearest examples here are from Asturias, perhaps because it has a relatively densely institutionalised framework (and relatively strong trade unions). Particularly among new entrants, there are clear examples where regional or subsidiary-level compromise allowed for the creation of various forms of non-union HRM or of micro-level social partnership arrangements, both of which would be extremely difficult to establish in large Spanish-owned firms. While the exact processes by which non-union systems in large subsidiaries emerged are somewhat unclear, it seems very likely that regional trade union federations 'buying into' narratives of industrial renewal through FDI was important here.

More broadly, as we have seen, the importance of regional levels of coordination is highly variable, rather than flowing directly from functional changes in the economy as some of the geographical literature mentioned above sometimes implies. Sub-national levels are most clearly important in Spain, where, given the substantial autonomy of regional governments, regions have been able to seek FDI through intra-national variations in elements of the effective business systems facing potential investors. There is obviously a risk that, within a country comprised of what some of our interviewees regarded as 17 'mini-states', such competition becomes 'zero-sum'. Indeed, heavy reliance on grants in the 1980s and 1990s, and the subsequent closure of some plants which were publicly funded, has contributed to an unusually negative image of MNCs among much of the Spanish public. On a broader basis, interviewees involved in the defence of existing large plants, particularly trade unions, were well aware of the problems of potential 'regime shopping' within Spain.

At the same time, foreign MNCs in general did appear to be more integrated within sub-national business systems in Spain than was the case in the UK or Ireland. In general, strategic initiatives at the subsidiary level seemed to receive fairly effective support from governance actors, either through regional inward investment agencies, or more directly through relations with regional Ministries. In Asturias in particular, subsidiary-level actors had been successful in attracting global or European-level mandates, including significant research and development activity. The existence of clear and relatively powerful regional-level interlocutors was generally acknowledged as important here. While the qualifications and skills of the Spanish workforce within MNCs were not generally seen as problematic, managers dependent on relatively localised supply chains did have concerns with entrepreneurial and managerial capacity within the 'industrial tissue' of smaller enterprises which often had previously fairly captive markets in nationalised enterprises. This was also a concern of investment agencies, particularly in the more industrial economy of Asturias. This did lead the managers of some subsidiary units to engage in quality initiatives with indigenous firms, through open days, membership of quality clubs, etc., going beyond immediate market needs, on a fairly ad-hoc basis.

Similar initiatives, although not exclusively on a regional basis, could also be seen in England and Ireland. In England, for example, there is some, although on the whole limited, evidence of very large MNCs attempting to set national skills agendas to fit qualification needs in areas such as aerospace, although these rarely extend beyond trying to conjugate institutionalised skills systems with the direct needs of the individual firm.

In general, though, the picture in England is of much less interaction than occurs in the other two nations here. This begs the question of whether this should be seen, even from a managerial/economic development perspective, as a 'problem', or whether the strong liberalism of the UK economy means that there are in fact fewer problems to solve. In this regard, it is notable that UK directors of a number of large foreign-owned MNEs have highlighted potential problems arising from centralised actors' lack of knowledge of regional economic issues, and, from 2010, of the lack of a recognised regional interlocutor for discussing strategic issues.

Local innovation, and MNC managers making active efforts to engage with very local actors in the skills and education sectors – e.g. local colleges and universities – clearly does occur, but there are clear issues of resources, and of difficulties for private actors in understanding the dynamic complexity of the UK skills system without the expert brokers that RDA inward investment officials represented. Thus, perhaps ironically, the English system may have become too 'liberal' even for the large firms for whom this liberalism was partly designed.

Any sort of internationalisation of domestic systems through MNC actors is much more evident in Ireland. One specific, and generally underestimated, factor here is the concentration of managerial 'talent' in the foreign-owned sector. Interviewees repeatedly argued that, over time, Ireland had developed a cadre of managers who had become schooled in an MNC environment; they had developed skills and political acumen, not only on technical issues of management but also in developing and influencing corporate decision-makers, attracting new mandates and generally embedding MNCs more deeply in Ireland. This very high degree of informal networking also somewhat overrides the 'skills ecosystem' role of some institutional actors, with solutions sought more by direct networking rather than, as is more the case in England, navigating the complexities of the formal skills system.

Another common type of governance-MNC relationship is the 're-investment coalition'; this, involving political actors and trade unions as well as development agencies, is particularly common in subsidiaries operating in GPNs in which regular and predictable contests for repeat investment are a structural feature (contests for the production of new models in the auto industry are perhaps the archetypical example of this). In discussing this, and the issue of re-investment from large foreign-owned MNCs already implanted in the region, it is important to point out that, on the whole, subsidiary managers are much more interested in having a representative of the 'state' (at whatever level is most relevant) with whom to discuss their own immediate concerns – whether these be globally-driven threats of removal of investment, or more day to day issues of ensuring human resource supply – than to actively shape the overall nature of business and employment systems. For strategic issues, significant investors tend to deal with regional civil servants in Spain, while the IDA performs a similar role in Ireland. The state of flux of UK development institutions means that MNC managers were not able to identify a single interlocutor in the period following RDA intervention – something that was seen as a significant issue by some – although the very largest MNCs did have official access to national civil servants for issues of significant strategic importance.

Conclusion

This analysis sought to examine the relevance of sub-national business systems and public policy in attempting to attract and retain FDI, on a cross-national comparative basis, in the context of arguments about the regionalisation of public policy aimed at attracting and retaining investment.

Our chief conclusion here is that the establishment of some form of nexus between governance actors and inward investors at sub-national levels is highly contingent. The evidence from Spain is largely supportive of ideas about the regionalisation of investor support and wider business system provision, with the important rider that this has not happened for the reasons elucidated by much of the literature in economic geography, but rather because of the particular – and contested – political compromise about the regional level of government. In England, the New Labour government (1997–2010) did attempt to increase the importance of regional coordination, at least partly for more technocratic reasons allied to an interpretation of literatures on regional competitiveness under globalisation, but this level of governance itself failed to become sufficiently embedded to avoid being removed by a government of the right, with fairly limited opposition. In Ireland, meanwhile, coordination of FDI remains highly concentrated at national level, albeit within an industrial policy dominated by the aim of attracting and retaining foreign investment.

Among the relevant governance actors, we placed specific emphasis on inward investment and economic development agencies. These obviously exist at a variety of geographical levels, sometimes in a relatively coordinated way and sometimes on a much more ad-hoc basis. We also examined the extent to which these are narrow or relatively encompassing institutions. While there are clearly risks that strong institutions can create forms of dominance of foreign firms over regional (and sometimes national) governance, it is nonetheless clear that, given the extent of competition between locations for investment, the existence of clear interlocutors for the regionally-based managers of foreign MNCs is significant in trying to ensure repeat investment. Where this is not the case, as in the emerging system in England, there are clear misgivings both among corporate and economic development actors.

Finally, while sub-national governance systems, and the infrastructure they control – including, notably, labour market supply – are of importance in contests over the attraction and stability of investment, it seems that, at least for the (mainly large manufacturing) firms studied as part of this project, the degree of active embeddedness of foreign MNCs in regional systems remains much more limited than often predicted in much of the new regionalist and some of the GPN literature. There is an obvious contradiction between embeddedness in localised economies, and global firms seeking to maximise the benefits and bargaining power of (potential) mobility. Such active engagement as does occur is often the result of the efforts of local managers in firms where local manager identity is at least as much with the local or national operations as with the global firm, particularly in attempting to mobilise local institutional actors in order to better compete in contexts for new or repeat investment. This, though, is dependent on local institutions having enough valency, as well as flexibility, with which to execute such forms of coalition.

References

Almond P (2011) The sub-national embeddedness of international HRM. Hum Relations 64(4):531–551

Almond P, Ferner A, Tregaskis O (2012) The changing context of regional governance of FDI in England. Eur Urban Reg Stud. doi:10.1177/0969776412459861

Amable B (2003) The diversity of modern capitalism. Oxford University Press, Oxford

Barney J (1991) Firm resources and sustained competitive advantage. J Manage 17(1):99–120

Brenner N (2004) Urban governance and the production of new state spaces in Western Europe, 1960–2000. Rev Int Polit Econ 11(3):447–488

Burrell T, Coe N (2001) Spaces and scales of innovation. Prog Hum Geogr 25(4):569–589

Cerny P (2000) Political globalization and the competition state. In: Stubbs R, Underhill G (eds) Political economy and the changing global order. Oxford University Press, Oxford, pp 300–309

Clark M, Beaney P (1993) Between autonomy and dependence: corporate strategy, plant status and local agglomeration in the Scottish electronics industry. Environ Plann A 25(2):213–232

Coe N, Hess M, Yeung H (2004) 'Globalizing' regional development: a global production networks perspective. Trans Inst Br Geogr 29(4):468–484

Coe N, Dicken P, Hess M (2008) Global production networks: realizing the potential. J Econ Geogr 8(3):271–296

Cohen W, Levinthal D (1990) Absorptive capacity: a new perspective on learning and innovation. Adm Sci Q 35:128–152

Cooke P, Clifton N, Oleaga M (2005) Social capital, firm embeddedness and regional development. Reg Stud 39(8):1065–1077

Crouch C (2005) Capitalist diversity and change. Oxford University Press, Oxford

Delbridge R, the AIM scholars (2006) The organisation of productivity: rethinking skills and work organisation. Advanced Institute of Management Research, London

DfES (2003) 21st century skills: realising our potential: individuals, employers, nation. HMSO, London

Finegold D (1999) Creating self-sustaining, high-skill ecosystems. Oxf Rev Econ Policy 15(1):60–81

Gereffi G, Humphrey J, Sturgeon T (2005) The governance of global value chains. Rev Int Polit Econ 12(1):78–104

Gertler M (2003) Tacit knowledge and the economic geography of context, or the undefinable tacitness of being (there). J Econ Geogr 3:75–99

Hudson R (1994) New production concepts, new production geographies? Reflections on changes in the automobile industry. Trans Inst Br Geogr 19(3):331–345

Jackson G, Deeg R (2008) Comparing capitalisms: understanding institutional diversity and its implications for international business'. J Int Bus Stud 39(4):540–561

Jessop B (2000) The crisis of the national spatio-temporal fix and the tendential ecological dominance of globalizing capitalism. Int J Urban Reg Res 24(2):323–360

Keune M, Kiss J, Tóth A (2004) Innovation, actors and institutions: change and continuity in local development policy in two Hungarian regions. Int J Urban Reg Res 28(3):586–600

MacKinnon D (2012) Beyond strategic coupling: reassessing the firm-region nexus in global production networks. J Econ Geogr 12(1):227–245

Maskell P, Malmberg A (1999) Localised learning and industrial competitiveness. Camb J Econ 23(1):167–186

Morgan K (1997) The learning region: institutions, innovation and regional renewal. Reg Stud 31:491–503

O'Broin D, Waters E (2007) Governing below the centre: local governance in Ireland. New Island Books, Dublin

Phelps N, Fuller C (2001) Taking care of business: aftercare and the state multinational enterprise nexus in Wales. Environ Plann C Government Policy 19(6):817–832

Phelps N, MacKinnon D, Stone I, Braidford P (2003) Embedding the multinationals? Institutions and the development of overseas manufacturing affiliates in Wales and North East England. Reg Stud 37(1):27–40

Porter M, Ketels C (2003) UK competitiveness: moving to the next stage, vol 3, DTI economics paper. ESRC, London

Whitley R (1999) Divergent capitalisms: the social structuring and change of business systems. Oxford University Press, Oxford

Young S, Hood N (1995) Designing developmental after-care programmes for foreign direct investors. UNCTAD. At http://archive.unctad.org/en/docs/iteiitv3no2a4_en.pdf. Accessed 29 Nov 2012

Part III

Multinational Companies Across Home and Host Countries: Transfer, Hybridization, Adaptation of Business Model and Labour Relations?

Internationalisation Process, HRM Strategy and Transfer in Chinese MNCs' Subsidiaries in the UK

Miao Zhang, Christine Edwards, and Jiaying Ma

8.1 Introduction

In recent years, the internationalisation process of Chinese MNCs has attracted the attention of those researching international business and management. Research has mainly explored the motivation, entrance models and characteristics of the internationalisation process of Chinese MNCs as late comers to international markets (e.g. Cui and Jiang 2009; Rugman and Li 2007; Rui and Yip 2008; Luo and Tung 2007; Child and Rodrigues 2005; Buckly et al. 2006; Mathews 2002; Yeung 1994). For example, some authors have suggested that in contrast with MNCs from advanced economies who use their own knowledge and skills when they locate overseas (knowledge takers), Chinese companies as late comers are more likely to be knowledge seekers (Rugman and Li 2007; Bonaglia et al. 2007). However, others have argued that Chinese companies also have some distinctive national characteristics that may give them advantages when they operate aboard (e.g. Rui and Yip 2008), the most important being the support and influence of the Chinese State (Luo and Tung 2007; Zhang and Bulcke 1994). However, research has mostly been conducted at national or parent company level. Little is known about the behaviour of overseas subsidiaries of Chinese MNCs in relation to whether and how "knowledge seeking" takes place, what HRM strategies they use in order to promote transfer, and how different factors influence their knowledge seeking process if they do so. In this paper, we attempt to explore these questions through case studies of three UK subsidiaries of Chinese MNCs.

We start with a discussion of the literature on MNCs from developing/emerging markets and the questions it raises for exploring strategy adopted by Chinese MNCs operating in the UK. After describing the research method and cases, the findings

M. Zhang (✉) • C. Edwards
Kingston Business School, Kingston University, Great London, UK
e-mail: miao.zhang@kingston.ac.uk

J. Ma
International Department, China Central Television, Beijing, China

are presented. They describe the strategies used by three Chinese MNCs in the period between the 1990s to 2000s when they expanded their business in the UK. It shows how a variety of factors influence the scope and process of strategies for transfer. The research found that despite being at a similar stage of internationalisation as the Japanese in the 1980s, the strategies adopted by Chinese MNCs to speed up their internationalisation process are different. This suggests that national characteristics exert significant influence on the internationalization process and on the HRM transfer strategy and practice of MNCs.

8.2 The Chinese Internationalization Process and the UK Context

It is widely assumed that MNCs from developing/emerging markets use a different strategy from MNCs from developed countries when they join international markets (e.g. Luo and Tung 2007; Mathews 2002; Rui and Yip 2008). Some authors argue that the motivations behind the international operations of MNCs from developing/emerging markets, are related to capability development (e.g. Rui and Yip 2008). Therefore, HRM policies and practice may be designed to facilitate reverse knowledge transfer from mature to emerging markets and play a crucial role in the success of the firm in diverse cultural environments (Wilkinson et al. 2010). However, it is also argued that emerging country MNCs tend to be smaller with considerably fewer resources and international experience than their counterparts from developed markets. This limits their ability to absorb and transfer advanced management practices across their subsidiaries. Therefore, they may follow rapid and abnormal internationalization paths, for example, by leapfrogging through acquisition of host country companies (Wilkinson et al. 2010).

Two main arguments have emerged from the research on the motivation of Chinese MNCs operating overseas: one is that they are "knowledge seekers" (e.g. Rugman and Li 2007; Rui and Yip 2008) and operate in economically advanced countries in order to learn and develop their capacity to compete in international markets. Thus, there is some 'knowledge spill-over' taking place from overseas subsidiaries back to the home firms (Zhang and Edwards 2007; Luo and Tung 2007). However, others have argued that Chinese companies also have national characteristics and home-based resources, most notably state support, which may give them competitive advantage in international markets (e.g. Rui and Yip 2008; Luo and Rui 2009). However, the impact of the State on the internationalization process and management transfer is also subject to differing interpretations. On the one hand, the Chinese government has played a crucial role in promoting outward investment and in supporting Chinese MNCs (Rui and Yip 2008; Zhang and Edwards 2007; Luo and Rui 2009). State-owned companies have been given financial support to build up overseas business and learn from international experience in order to speed up their internationalization process. On the other hand, strong government control and intervention in the national business system and Chinese MNCs' overseas operations may impede their capacity to innovate and compete in international markets (Rui and Yip 2008). Thus, despite a growing literature on China's outward investment, a number of questions remain. In particular, little previous study has been undertaken at organizational level, or examined the role of HRM strategy as a vehicle for knowledge transfer in overseas subsidiaries' internationalization strategy. An exception is a study of Chinese MNCs operating in the UK in 1990s by Zhang and Edwards (2007). However, any subsequent developments and changes in their internationalization process in the 2000s have not been documented.

The UK is one of the most internationalized world economies, and owing to very open economic conditions and a well-regulated market environment has attracted vast amounts of foreign investment (Guest et al. 1996; Ferner and Varul 1999). It therefore provides an ideal location for foreign companies to learn the most advanced international practice. China has a long history operating in the UK and has rapidly expanded its investment in the past two decades to over $23 billion by the end of 2011 (UK Trade and Investment 2011). China was also listed as sixth in terms of all foreign direct investment in the UK and had the second largest number of foreign companies operating in London. In 2009/2010, there were 74 new investment projects from mainland China, and in excess of 400 Chinese companies operating in the UK in 2011 compared with around 30 companies in the 1990s (Zhang 2003). Therefore, Chinese companies in the UK provide an ideal case from which to explore Chinese MNCs' internationalization process and recent development, as well as the role of HRM strategy and transfer.

8.3 Methods

In order to examine international strategy and management practice in depth, three Chinese companies (Finance Co, Trade Co and Manuf Co) in the UK were selected for study. The case study companies are subsidiaries of large, "top" state-owned companies, which have been a major force in the Chinese outward investment and internationalization process (Zhang Toronto-full and Van Den Bulcke 1995; Young et al. 1996). They were established or expanded in the UK during the 1980s and 2000s, and vary in industrial sector, size and entry approaches.

Finance Co. has a very long history operating in the UK and was expanded to a company in the 1980s. Trade Co. was established in the UK in the middle of the 1990s, while Manuf Co. entered the UK in the mid 2000s. Trade Co started their business in the UK from scratch as a Greenfield site, while Manuf. Co was established through acquisition of a UK company in 2005.

There were two stages of data collection in Finance Co and Trade Co: the first in the 1990s and in the second follow-up interviews with key managers were conducted in 2011 and 2012. The study on Manuf Co was conducted in 2010. In all three companies semi-structured interviews were held with senior managers: Chief Executives, Managing Directors, human resources or general administration, and also with middle management; a total of 118 overall, including 72 in Finance Co, 31 in Trade Co and 15 in Manuf Co. Reports and information on company performance, workforce data, and other business documents were also collected. Personal interviews with the senior managers were focused primarily on the choice of management strategy and the MNCs' internationalisation process, and the influence of the external and internal environment on their management in the UK. For the middle managers and key staff, the interviews were focused on HRM practices and learning activities.

8.4 The Motivations of the Companies Operating in the UK

In the recent interviews with the three companies, it is found that the reasons of operating in the UK include: (1) to access to the UK and international markets; (2) to use UK advanced technology, labor skills and product brand to operate in both China and the UK markets (3) to learn and transfer UK's advanced technology and business management back to the home firms.

Finance Co. was a small branch of a Chinese bank that was expanded in 1980s in order to service the requirements of the growing Chinese business community in the UK and their investment activities overseas. To achieve this purpose, the home firm not only turned Finance Co into a registered company but also expanded it by setting up two new branches under its direction. It also established a totally new company (Finc 2) to access UK markets to find foreign investment for Chinese companies at home. However, it also had a major objective in terms of providing opportunities for learning and transferring market-orientated business and management practice back to the home firm. At that time, China had just started to move from a centrally-controlled economic system to market-orientated one, and Finance Co was asked to take responsibility for learning and transferring UK practice for the home firm. A third, although far less important objective at this time, was to make the profits to compensate for losses of the home firm in China. In response to the Chinese Government's policy of encouraging inward investment, western MNCs were setting up in China and making inroads into Chinese domestic markets (See Zhang 2003; Zhang and Edwards 2007 for the details). By the time of the follow-up interviews in 2012, the main task for this company was to service the now numerous Chinese organizations and business in the UK, and to compete with other Chinese and local finance companies. Learning and transfer is still important but no longer a priority.

Trade Co. was established in the mid 1990s. The purpose was to access the UK as an international financial centre and to learn how to conduct international trade. The first chief executive interviewed in 1998 stressed that to learn how to operate in the UK trade market was one of the main objectives for establishing the company:

> The UK provides us an excellent environment to learn the knowledge and experience as there are so many international companies operating here for us to learn

In order to achieve this purpose, three Chinese expatriates spent 5 years in London learning how to do business from working with UK colleagues (See Zhang and Edwards 2007). By 2012 however, company priorities had changed and the primary purpose was access to do business in the UK and international markets. Learning and knowledge transfer however, was still an important, if secondary, objective, as the current Chief executive interviewed in 2011 explained: *'Although the company has the relevant knowledge and established a position in the UK and international markets, learning and transferring still has a long way to go'*.

Manuf Co. was established in the UK in 2005 through the acquisition of a company in the North of England. This was the first Chinese acquisition in manufacturing industry in the UK. The purpose was firstly to use the brand of the acquired company to raise its home firm's reputation in both home and international markets, and secondly, to transfer the key technology and business knowledge of the company back to the home firm to improve the quality of its products. Currently, the company has just got through a difficult period of post-acquisition integration, and started its production and transfer process.

These cases show that the main purposes of the three companies are similar – to access the UK market and help the home firm to speed-up their internationalization process by using the UK as a learning and development base, although the priority of these purposes are different in three companies and in different periods.

8.5 HRM Strategy: Localization in the Companies

In order to achieve the above objectives, all three companies claimed that they had been adopting a HR localization strategy in their UK operations. The reasons given for doing so were threefold. (1) They were reliant on the UK employees' knowledge and skills in order to conduct their business; (2) the company could learn from the UK locals and transfer this knowledge back to the home firm. (3) The need to comply with UK regulations. However, the research found that the process and scope of localization varied in the three companies.

Finance Co. replaced a centrally-planned labor management system typically found in Chinese companies to one based on UK management practice in the 1980s. Further, over 80 % staff were recruited from the UK. One third of top managers and 75 % of middle managers were UK locals. However, by 2012, the proportion of UK top managers had fallen to one quarter. The managing director explained that there had been difficulties in communication and understanding between Chinese managers in the HQs at home and UK managers in the subsidiary and some had been replaced by Chinese managers in order to avoid conflict.

Trade Co started to use local staff in the middle of 1990s as the company expanded into the UK market. In the interview in 1998, they claimed that *'we have to use local employees to operate in the UK market as they know the market better than us'*. At that time, only the top manager was a Chinese expatriate, all the middle managers and staff were UK locals, and only three Chinese expatriates were in the company as trainees. However, in the follow-up study in 2011, only 30 % of staff was local and all others were Chinese expatriates. The managing director explained that: *'now we want to use more Chinese expatriates, one purpose is to give them opportunity to learn; on the other hand, they are cheaper than the locals and also easier to manage'*.

Manuf Co is different from these two companies, in that it uses a total localization strategy. Firstly, this is because UK local staff hold the key skills and technological know-how for the product, and they have had to use local staff to understand and transfer this knowledge. Over 95 % of staff are employed from the previous UK owned company. At the top, there are two Chinese expatriates and one local, but the rest of the staff are mostly from the UK with very few Chinese expatriates. Generally, it has retained both the local workforce and the local management system it inherited when it acquired the company.

Regarding the extent to which local management practice has been transferred into these UK subsidiaries. Over 85 % of the UK respondents in all three companies thought their company is like a UK company. In particular, they said that the main HR policies and practice are similar to the companies they had worked for in the UK. However, there are limits to the extent to which the companies have "gone native"; none of respondents interviewed think the company they work for is totally like a UK firm. In particular, when we came to look in more detail at the characteristics of the managerial orientation and HR function in these companies, it was found that there remain some strong influences from the Chinese national business system. For example, in all the cases, the parent company still controls overall business and labour planning and budgets. The most obvious influence from the parent companies is in the decision-making system. Bureaucratic procedures and the slow speed of decision making were mentioned by most respondents, which in their view impedes management effectiveness.

The data show that all three companies have employed an HR localization strategy using UK human resource management practice and local employees and practices to some extent in their management. However, all the companies have Chinese expatriates in the position of Chief Executive. UK managers usually were in charge of the operations, research and development, and sales functions, but all the heads of finance are Chinese expatriates. It was also found that the proportion of local staff has declined over the past 10 years in Finance Co and Trade Co. Furthermore, in the recent interviews, the Chinese expatriate managers in all three companies said that managing local staff and understanding the local environment remain their most challenging and difficult issues.

8.6 Cross-Organizational Learning and Reverse Diffusion

It was found that cross-organisational transfer activities have been taking place in all three companies. In the 1990s Finance Co and Trade Co, were providing on the job training and formal training programmes for the managers from home firms and other subsidiaries. In Finance Co, between 1980s and 1990s, although the company was small, it regularly took trainees from the home firm and also established a centre to provide management training programmes for the home firm. In the last 20 years, over a 1,000 of Chinese managers from the home firm and subsidiaries have been trained in this company (See Zhang 2003). In the follow-up study, these activities still remain in these two companies though not intensive as in the 1990s and knowledge transfer is mainly achieved through the expatriate's mobility.

However, in Manuf Co, we found much more intensive, formal and systematic learning and transfer activities taking place. Regular staff exchanges are the main learning and transfer mechanism. Each year the UK company sends 25 local staff to the home firm in China to train the Chinese staff and, the Chinese site sends 25 people to the UK site for training. Also, 5–6 Chinese engineers a year are sent to participate in the work of the UK Research and Development Centre. Thus the purpose of acquiring this company is not only to use its brand but most important is knowledge acquisition of its key skills and technology to improve its products.

8.7 National Influences and HRM Strategy and Transfer

The strategy and practice of Chinese MNCs in the UK is closely influenced by the Chinese government's internationalization policy. In the early 1980, China moved from a centrally-planned to a market-orientated economy and urged Chinese companies to use both inward and outward investment to 'borrow' market-orientated management experience. Finance Co's expansion in the UK was to service this purpose. By the middle of 1990s, the Chinese government was encouraging Chinese companies to 'go global' and access international markets. Trade Co was established in the UK to assist with this globalization process. By the year 2000, China had huge foreign reserves, and the Chinese government started to encourage Chinese MNCs to use acquisition to raise the country's overall competitive position and competency in global markets. Manuf Co's UK acquisition reflects this. Therefore, business strategy in these companies was and is still very strongly influenced by national characteristics and government policies.

The companies have had considerable financial support from the Chinese government and state-owned parent company. Finance Co and Trade Co have enjoyed freedom from short term financial targets and more autonomy than companies at home. It has allowed them to employ local staff and given time to engage in learning and transfer activities (see Zhang and Edwards 2007). Government finance also enabled Manuf Co to acquire a UK company. Without the government's support and home firm resources, these companies would have not had the chance to establish and survive in the UK. Even now, Finance Co and Trade Co's business in the UK is still directly supported by the Chinese government, and Manuf Co, is still dependent on home firm support to maintain the product line in the UK.

However, it could be argued that such dependence on government and home firm's resources has come at a cost. These companies have failed to develop and become self-sufficient and their competitive ability is constrained by their ownership. As state-owned companies, they need to follow government policy and the home firm's requirement rather than the business needs of the UK market. Their management is controlled by the home firm and government and they have limited autonomy to develop and manage their own business. The decline in HR localization in these companies reflects these influences. Two companies (Finance Co and

Trade Co) have operated in the UK over 20 years now, but their business development is still limited, and they are mainly reliant on the business from China rather than from the UK and international markets.

Furthermore, government support and home firm resources have protected managers from the usual pressure to meet financial targets and released them from the need to improve managerial capacity in order to compete in UK markets. Even though more recently the home companies have started to set financial targets for the UK subsidiaries, serving the home firm and markets has more priority. While financial support has it has given them time to learn it means that Chinese managers in these companies have to fulfill dual roles as both learners and managers while the UK managers have additional responsibilities as teachers and trainers. All this is made more difficult by a huge difference in the management systems and culture in the UK and China which remain to this day (Benson and Zhu 1999; Warner 2004; Zhang and Edwards 2007).

8.8 Discussion

The Chinese cases show that Chinese MNCs operating in the UK have learning and knowledge transfer as major priorities and use localization and cross-organizational activities for these purposes. Thus these cases support the argument that Chinese MNCs can be characterized as Knowledge Seekers. On the other hand, they operate overseas with significant home advantages in terms of generous government support and home firm resources. Without this financial support Chinese MNCs could not play a knowledge seeker role speeding-up their internationalization process through localization in developed countries such as the UK. However, the learning process is slow and the challenges of operating in different business environments and the need to learn acts as a drag on the ability of these companies to operate profitably in international markets.

The case of Chinese MNCs operating in the UK in the 1990s onwards how some similarities with and differences from Japanese companies operating in the USA in the 1980s, when they were at a parallel stage of internalization (Willard and Savara 1998; Yang et al. 2009). The motivation for investing in economically advanced countries for both Japanese and Chinese companies was to access the well-developed international markets. Both the Chinese and Japanese governments gave support for outward investment, but the Japanese government consistently rejected applications by foreign investors to set up wholly-owned subsidiaries or majority-owned joint ventures in Japan (Yammanura 1986). This protected Japanese firms from the distraction of fighting foreign competition at home and they were able to use resources gained from the domestic market for development (Yang et al. 2009). Thus when Japanese companies came to the USA, unlike the Chinese, they had well-developed technologies and management skills at home that they transferred into their US subsidiaries (e.g. Beechler and Yang 1994; Elger and Smith 1994). In contrast, Chinese government policy was to encourage both inward and outward investment in the beginning of Chinese firms' internationalization process. Chinese MNCs had to compete with foreign companies at home before they had developed their own capacity, and they were supported by the Government to learn the technology and management skills from operating in the developed countries.

As to management strategy, both Chinese and Japanese companies claimed to adopt localization in their HRM. However, the Japanese were a 'knowledge takers' when they accessed to the US market, and they clearly wanted to transfer their own knowledge and management systems (Beechler and Yang 1994; Yoshida 1987). Localization in the Japanese companies was only to the extent necessary to adapt to the local environment and USA regulation and we term it 'compliance localization' (see Zhang and Edwards 2008). In contrast, the Chinese as 'knowledge seekers' in the UK, used localization for learning and transfer purposes, a process we have termed 'absorption localization' (See Zhang and Edwards 2008). Although they adopted different strategies in HRM, both Chinese and Japanese companies experienced the similar challenges and difficulties when they operated in the developed western countries owing their Asian business and management characteristics and culture (Yang et al. 2009) However, we found the challenges and difficulties experienced by the Chinese MNCs in the UK to be much greater. As learners without key technological and international management skills, Chinese expatriate's business leadership and management is easily challenged by local staff with superior knowledge and skills.

Conclusion

The study demonstrates far greater complexity in the process and nature of internationalization in MNCs from developing countries operating in developed countries than previous analyses have suggested. It is argued that localisation could be a strategic choice for MNCs from developing countries to standardise their international management system and achieve competitive advantage in global markets, but the process varies and is hugely influenced by home and host national characteristics. However, we need to point out the limitations of this study. It was focused on state-owned companies from China, and while they have been dominant in Chinese outward investment in the past, recent research shows that private companies are becoming another powerful force (Yang et al. 2009). How these companies, which do not have financial support and resources from the Chinese government, access and survive in international markets, and what HRM strategy they use, will be an important topic for further research.

References

Beechler S, Yang JZ (1994) The transfer of Japanese-style management to American subsidiaries: contingencies, constraints, and competencies. J Int Bus Stud 25:467–491

Benson J, Zhu Y (1999) Market, firms and workers: the transformation of human resource management in Chinese manufacturing enterprises. Hum Res Manag J 9(4):58–74

Bonaglia F, Goldstein A, Mathews J (2007) Accelerated internationalisation by emerging multinationals: the case of white goods. J World Bus 42:369–383

Buckly PJ, Cross AR, Tan H, Liu X, Voss H (2006) An examination of recent trends in Chinese outbound direct investment. CIBUL working paper, Centre for International Business Studies, University of Leeds

Child J, Rodrigues SB (2005) The internationalization of Chinese firms: a case for theoretical extension? Manag Organ Rev 1(3):381–410

Cui L, Jiang F (2009) FDI entry mode choice of Chinese firms: a strategic behavior perspective. J World Bus 44(4):434–444

Elger T, Smith C (eds) (1994) Global Japanisation? The transformation of the labour process. Routledge, London

Guest D, College B, Hoque K (1996) National ownership and HR practices in UK greenfield sites. Hum Res Manag J 6(4):51–71

Ferner A, Varul M (1999) "Vanguard" subsidiaries and the diffusion of new practices: a case study of German multinationals. Br J Ind Relations 38(1):115–140

UK Trade and Investment (2011) UK committed to closer trade and investment ties with China, 11 Jan 2011

Luo Y, Rui H (2009) An ambidexterity perspective toward multinational enterprises from emerging economies. Acad Manag Perspect 23(4):49–70

Luo Y, Tung R (2007) International expansion of emerging market enterprises: aspiring board perspective. J Int Bus Stud 38:481–498

Mathews JA (2002) Competitive advantages of the latecomer firm: a resource-based account of industrial catch-up strategies. Asia Pac J Manag 19:467–488

Rugman AM, Li J (2007) Will China's multinationals succeed globally or regionally? Eur Manag J 25(5):333–343

Rui H, Yip GS (2008) Foreign acquisitions by Chinese firms: a strategic intent perspective. J World Bus 43:213–226

Warner M (2004) Human resource management in China revisited: introduction. Int J Hum Res Manag 15(4/5):617–634, June/August

Wilkinson A, Wood G, Demirbag M (2010) People management in emerging market multinationals. J Hum Res Manag

Willard GE, Savara AM (1998) Patterns of entry: pathways to new markets. Calif Manage Rev 30:57–76

Yammanura K (1986) Caveat emptor: the industrial policy of Japan. In: Krugman P (ed) Strategic trade policy and the new international economics. MIT Press, Cambridge, MA

Yang X, Jiang Y, Kang R, Ke Y (2009) A comparative analysis of the internationalization of Chinese and Japanese firms. Asia Pac J Manag 26(1):141–162(22)

Yeung HWC (1994) Transnational corporations from Asian developing countries: their characteristics and competitive edge. J Asian Bus 10(4):17–58

Yoshida M (1987) Macro–micro analysis of Japanese manufacturing investments in the United States. Manag Int Rev 27:19–31

Young S, Huang C, McDermott M (1996) Internationalisation and competitive catch-up process: case study evidence on Chinese multinational enterprises. Manag Int Rev 36(4):295–314

Zhang M (2003) Transferring human resource management across national boundaries: the case of Chinese multinational companies in the UK. Empl Relat 25(6):613–626, ISSN (online) 0142-5455

Zhang M, Edwards C (2007) Diffusing 'best practice' in Chinese multinationals: the motivation, facilitation and limitations. Int J Hum Res Manag 18(12):2147–2165, ISSN (print) 0958-5192

Zhang M, Edwards C (2008) Localisation strategy and internationalisation process in Chinese MNCs: a case study with six companies in the UK. In: The third International Association of Chinese Management Research (IACMR) conference, Guangzhou

Zhang H, Van Den Bulcke D (1994) International management strategies of Chinese multinational firms. Discussion paper No. 1994/E/17, Center for International Management and Development, University of Antwerp

Zhang Toronto-full H, Van Den Bulcke D (1995) Rapid changes in the investment development path of China. Discussion paper No. 1995/E/21, Center for International Management and Development, University of Antwerp

Between Europe and Asia: Labour Relations in German Companies in Russia and China

Martin Krzywdzinski

9.1 Introduction

The evolution of industrial relations in Russia and China is a fascinating research topic. Both countries experience a rapid economic modernization in which foreign companies play an important role. At the same time, both countries stick to an authoritarian model of state and society, in which trade union activities and the representation of employee interests are restricted. How do industrial relations in foreign companies in Russia and China evolve? Is a capitalism without employee voice emerging?

Foreign companies which invest in Russia and China face the following strategic choice: do they try to transfer their home country practices abroad? Do they adapt to the local conditions? Or do they try to develop new models of employee voice? German companies represent a particular case. Industrial relations in their home country are influenced by strong trade unions, the co-determination – a unique model which provides works councils with veto rights on a number of issues related to work and employment –, and cooperative relations between labor and capital. There is a controversial debate about the behavior of German companies abroad: do they see their home country industrial relations as an asset and do they try to transfer them abroad? Or do they see them as costs and do they try to escape them by relocating production abroad?

While there is a lot of research on German companies and their industrial relations in Europe, there is hardly any empirical evidence about German companies in Russia and China. At the same time, these two countries represent interesting cases to test hypotheses about the behavior of German companies. As authoritarian countries, they can be expected not to provide a fertile ground for

M. Krzywdzinski (✉)
Social Science Research Center Berlin, Wissenschaftszentrum Berlin für Sozialforschung (WZB), Berlin, Germany
e-mail: martin.krzywdzinski@wtb.in

strong employee representation and cooperative labor-management relations in companies. Against this background, this article examines two questions:
1. How do the institutional systems in Russia and China constrain the strategic choice of German companies regarding industrial relations?
2. Do German companies in Russia and China transfer their practices of industrial relations to Russia and China?

The following analysis is based on the review of existing empirical research on German companies in Russia and China, and on own research conducted together with Ulrich Jürgens in the research project "Personnel Management Systems in the BRIC Countries" from 2008 to 2011. The article is structured as following: Sect. 9.2 presents a review of the research literature on industrial relations of German companies abroad. Section 9.3 deals with the institutional frameworks of industrial relations in Russia and China. The main question here is how institutions in Russia and China constrain the strategic choices of companies regarding industrial relations. Section 9.4 present empirical evidence about industrial relations in German companies in Russia and China. The article ends with a section presenting final conclusions of the analysis.

9.2 Industrial Relations in German Companies and Their Transfer Abroad: A Literature Review

Industrial relations in Germany differ considerably between industries, regions and companies of different size. While large companies in the automobile, machine, chemical and steel industries are characterized by strong unions and co-determination, unions are hardly present in new software companies as well as in smaller companies. Particularly in Eastern Germany the level of unionization and the density of works councils have remained clearly under the West German average. The model of industrial relations, which is roughly sketched in the following, especially applies to large, industrial companies, although it is often simply considered the "German model". The core-elements of this so-called "dual" system are the collective bargaining on industry level as well as the co-determination at the company level.

The German unions are organized as industrial unions i.e., a union organization organizes one (or several) industry. Competition between unions is in principle excluded. Industrial unions developed in Germany after the Second World War after the experience that conflicts between the communist and social-democratic unions had weakened the union movement. Industrial unions conclude contracts with employers' associations for the entire industry. Thus labor conflicts are taken out of the plants and resolved at the industry level – an important basis for cooperative relations between employers and employee representatives at the company level.

The works council represents the whole work force i.e., it is elected by all employees (every 4 years). The works council is obligated by law to a "trustful cooperation" with the employer and is not allowed to initiate or execute strike activities. The works council has a number of co-determination rights regarding personnel and social concerns i.e., the employer needs the assent of the works council. This holds true for basic rules of the pay system, performance-based pay, working hours, overtime, vacation plans, technical devices for controlling employee performance, hiring and transfer of employees, principles of teamwork, internal educational measures and social plans in case of dismissals. Moreover, the works council possesses the right to information and consultation in further social, but also in economic questions (e.g. investments etc.). Through the prohibition of strikes, the works council is obligated to cooperate with the employer, although it can block certain decisions of the employer. It is an "intermediate" institution, which is able to mediate the different and sometimes opposing interests of the employer and the employees (Müller-Jentsch 2007: 59).

The institutions of industry-level collective bargaining and co-determination, which are constructed to limit conflicts and promote cooperation, cannot be transferred abroad by the German companies. Abroad, German companies are confronted with different rules and other actors. In this situation, management finds itself having to make a "strategic choice" (Kochan et al. 1984): it can attempt to transfer its home country practices, it can adapt to local conditions or it can attempt to develop new forms of representing employee interests. Regarding the unions at the overseas locations this can mean recognizing the existing unions, encouraging the creation of new unions or the avoidance of union representation.

The choice of the management is indeed limited by the local institutions and actors. One should differentiate here between "constraining" institutions, which tend to force the acceptance of a certain model of industrial relations, and "permissive" institutions, which allow much leeway in the forming of industrial relations (Tempel 2001: 69).

The attitude of German companies regarding the transfer of their models of industrial relations and codetermination abroad is strongly contested in research discussions. The lion's share of research occupies itself with Central Eastern Europe, which has become a major goal for investments and transfer decisions of companies. One of the results of this debate is that German companies show a high variety of approaches to labor relations abroad. Voss and Wilke (2003) argue that a large number of German companies operate somewhere between a 'formal cooperative' approach, which tolerates the creation of unions in CEE plants, but where cooperation with trade unions is limited to the statutory minimum, and a negative attitude towards trade unions. But which factors determine this variety? The three following competing hypotheses are discussed in the research:

H1: German companies try to transfer their industrial relations practices abroad because these practices promote social peace in the companies and are seen as a comparative advantage.

This hypothesis relies on the argument of "institutional comparative advantage" which was developed by the "varieties of capitalism" approach (Hall and Soskice 2001: 57). The "varieties of capitalism" approach argues that FDI decisions of companies are strongly influenced by the comparative institutional advantages ("institutional arbitrage") of different national institutional system. Core activities of the companies which rely on the home country institutions are not relocated, are relocated to countries with similar institutions or to countries where functional equivalents for the home country institutions can be established. There is evidence that in particular big flagship companies of the German economy (e.g., Volkswagen) see cooperative industrial relations as part of their company culture and as a competitive advantage and try to transfer them abroad (Jürgens and Krzywdzinski 2009, 2010; Krzywdzinski 2011; Tholen et al. 2006).

A second hypothesis has been developed based on an actor-centered approach. It stresses the role of works councils and trade unions at the companies' headquarters (Bluhm 2003; Krzywdzinski 2011). Bluhm (2007) points to differences between large capital groups and small and medium companies (SMEs). In German capital groups, powerful works councils enforce the transfer of "social partnership" industrial relations to foreign sites whereas German SMEs are characterised by weak works councils which have no influence on work models at foreign sites.

H2: German companies try to transfer their industrial relations practices abroad only if strong works councils and trade unions in the headquarters enforce the transfer.

A third, opposing hypothesis has been developed by Meardi et al. (2011). In a study on German, Austrian and American automotive suppliers, these authors argue that German companies are even less prone to accept trade unions and an employee representation in their Eastern European plants than the American companies. They explain this from an actor-centered perspective: co-determination has been enforced on companies by strong trade unions and social-democratic governments and has never gained legitimacy among employers. German companies use FDI to escape from the co-determination environment.

H3: German companies "perceive their home-country IR arrangements as costs, rather than advantage" (Meardi et al. 2011: 40) and do not want to transfer them abroad.

To sum up, the German institutions of co-determination and industrial relations cannot be transferred abroad. The foreign subsidiaries of German companies are thus faced with the strategic choice whether to copy German practices or try to emulate them through "functional equivalents", whether to adapt to local practices and rules, or whether to try to develop new practices. German companies show a high variety of answers to this question. In particular big flagship companies of the German economy, however, tend to look for a transfer of their industrial relations models abroad.

9.3 Industrial Relations in Russia and China

The strategic choices of the companies are strongly influenced and restrained by the institutional and regulatory frameworks in the host countries of the investments. How do the institutions in Russia and China influence industrial relations in subsidiaries of German companies? Both countries go through a transformation from a socialist to a capitalist society. In the following we will analyze which institutions and actors of industrial relations emerge in this process and how they influence foreign investors.

9.3.1 Russia

The main Russian trade union is the Federation of Independent Trade Unions of Russia (FNPR). The FNPR was founded in 1990 as successor organisation to the All-Russian Central Committee of Trade Unions (WZSPS). This incorporated the 77 million members of the WZSPS; by 2010, however, member numbers had declined to about 25 million, according to union figures. Thereby, the FNPR nevertheless organised more than 90 % of all union members in Russia.

To understand the relationship between the state and the FNPR, it makes sense to take a brief look at its genesis in the 1990s. The structural changes in the 1990s represented a threat to the union: the FNPR was delegitimized by the role of its predecessor as a 'transmission belt' for the Communist Party; it tried to gain new credibility by opposing the radical liberalisation policies of the Yeltsin presidency, but after Yeltsin's threat to dissolve the union and confiscate its property during the Russian constitutional crisis in 1993 the union realigned towards a compromise orientation (Ashwin and Clarke 2003). After 1993, the FNPR renounced all confrontational action, instead placing an emphasis on its own representation and lobbying work in the Russian Duma.

After Putin's election, the FNPR decided, in the absence of alternatives, for cooperation with the president, as well as with the institutions and organisations that he created. After the 2003 parliamentary elections, the elected members of the FNPR joined the fraction of United Russia, and in 2004 the FNPR signed a formal cooperation agreement with United Russia, which was renewed in 2008 (Clarke and Pringle 2009: 88). The union places an emphasis on consultations within the framework of 'social partnership', although on a material level they have achieved little in concessions from the government. However, in return for loyalty to Putin's policies, the FNPR has achieved public recognition and privileged access to the legislative process.

In addition to the FNPR, only two major trade union federations have managed to establish themselves in Russia. These joined forces in 2010 under the name of the Confederation of Labour of Russia (KTR). Their joined membership is around 500,000 members (FES 2008). The KTR unions differ in their self-conception of the FNPR. The self-conception of the FNPR can be well characterised on the basis of a 2001 survey of workplace union leaders carried out by the Institute for Comparative Labour Relations Research ISITO (cf. Ashwin and Clarke 2003: 218). One of the questions in the survey concerned the utilisation of membership fees. It was noteworthy that an average of 49 % of total contributions were spent on 'material assistance' for needy union members; a further 38 % for 'mass-cultural work' (vacations, celebrations, sporting and cultural events). Only 2.5 % of the budget was spent on information, training, and labour law services. Almost no funds were available for the strike fund. The FNPR unions thus effectively behave as a department for social support, and for recreational activities for workers. By contrast, many of the company organisations of KTR arose spontaneously during disputes over working conditions and wages. A frequent reason for a move to VKT or KTR is disappointment of workers with a lack of support on behalf of the FNPR.

In regard to industrial relations in the companies, the Russian labour laws seek to establish a system of 'social partnership', which has the aim of limiting industrial conflict. Firstly, Russian labour laws limit union capacity for conflict in the workplace through high barriers to union recognition in companies (50 % of the employees have to be organized before a union has to recognized), and complicated strike procedures. But secondly, the union leader and his representatives are protected from dismissal. Although unions have no rights of codetermination in the German sense of the word, they do have comprehensive consultation rights with respect to work organisation and social affairs. The employer is required to consult with trade unions on matters of restructuring, technological changes with consequences for workers, issues of vocational training and further training, the shortening of working hours for operational purposes, the dismissal of workers, overtime, preparation of shift schedules, working on bank holidays, holiday scheduling, wage systems, the definition of labour standards, the imposition of disciplinary sanctions, and the definition of regulations for health and safety. On the initiative of the union, the employer must form a permanent safety committee with equal representation of unions and management. In practice, however, poor law enforcement in Russia makes the exercising of these rights difficult.

Overall, industrial relations in Russia take the form of an authoritarian-corporatist model, whereby the state concedes public status to the FNPR unions, and they take on the task of maintaining social peace in companies, while there are limitations above all on the trade unions' capacity for conflict. In sum we can derive two results regarding the institutional constraints on strategic choice of companies:
- The institutional framework of industrial relations in Russia provides much leeway for union avoidance strategies of companies by defining high thresholds for the recognition of trade unions and by a restrictive strike law.
- The companies are faced with two competing models of trade union representation (FNPR and KTR) and with the possibility that conflicts between the trade unions are fought out within the company.

9.3.2 China

The context of labor relations in China is characterized by the specific role, which Chinese labor law applies to the union. The union has by law the task of mediating between the employees and the company. It must balance the interests of both parties, but is also bound by the duty not to engage in industrial action. Along with the classical task of the negotiation of wages and working conditions, the trade union in China has some particular tasks defined by law: it should mediate in labor disputes (and not simply defend the employee side), it should support the Communist Party in "ideological" work, and it should promote the education of employees and technological innovation in the companies. The union law obligates the union to not only represent the interests of the employees, but also to care about the economic well-being of the company. The latter task also includes the "education" of workers, as stated in Article 7 of the union law:

> Labor unions shall mobilize and organize staff and workers to actively participate in economic construction and to strive to complete production and work tasks. They shall educate staff and workers to continuously improve their thinking, ethics, technical expertise and scientific and cultural attainments so as to create idealistic, moral, cultured and disciplined staff and worker teams.

The only registered union is the All-China Federation of Trade Unions (ACFTU), which is formally an organ of the Communist Party and is subordinate to its guidelines. The ACFTU has around 220 million members in China. The main organizational units below the national level are the province-level unions and (one level below) the company unions.

The ACFTU, like the Communist Party, follows the principle of "democratic centralism"; i.e., the elected union bodies have unlimited authority vis-à-vis their subordinate levels. The union chairmen at the company level are in the majority of cases determined by superior union bodies and not elected (Pringle 2011: 163). The union chairman at the companies is in almost every case either the secretary of the Communist Party or a member of the company management (Kojima 2010: 37). This origin of trade union leaders strengthens the tendency that the unions in the companies concentrate more on social integration activities as well as supporting of educational and productivity campaigns.

The weakness of the trade union model becomes clear in the repeatedly appearing waves of labor conflicts which could not be influenced by the ACFTU. Characteristic for labor relations in China is the lack of regulations for solution of collective conflicts. Although strikes are not forbidden in China, unions may not participate in them. Chinese labor law defines labor conflicts as individual quarrels between workers and companies. In the first step, the union is obligated to mediate in these conflicts. If no solution is found, a three-level conflict solution process is foreseen, via mediation at the plant level, arbitration by the local labor administration and, finally, a court procedure – a very slow process (Cooney 2007).

The waves of labor conflicts lead again and again to efforts toward reform of the ACFTU and the attempt to strengthen the representation of employee interests such as in 1988 (before the suppression of protests at the Tiananmen Square) or the middle of the 1990s (Taylor et al. 2003: 111; White 1996). Conflicts broke out also in the years 2009 and 2010, with the particularity that this time also branches such as the automobile industry were involved (Hui 2011). The conflicts led to discussions in the province of Guangdong about possibilities of strengthening the representation of employee interests through more democracy within the union and through the legal permitting of strikes (China Labor Bulletin, 11.3.2011, http://www.elb.org.hk/en/node/101005).

Although the ACFTU unions, because of their traditional self-understanding and their lack of experience with conflicts, still concentrate on the tasks of social integration and productivity campaigns, they formally possess extensive rights to defend the interests of the employees. Chinese labor law prescribes consultation with the union in questions of work safety, working time and overtime, the pay system and benefits, the social security of employees, disciplinary measures and dismissals. In a commentary to the Chinese labor law, Lauffs (2008: 292) writes:

> Even though applicable laws do not explicitly grant labor unions the right to veto or obstruct a company's decision, when read in connection with the legislation governing equity joint ventures and wholly foreign-owned enterprises, the Labor Union Law effectively provides a union with a veto right over decisions by the board of directors to the extent that the content of those decisions relates to employee rewards and penalties, wage systems, wage benefits, labor protection and labor insurance. This is because if an enterprise proceeds with an action without the labor union's attendance and cooperation – whatever that may be defined as – there is a risk that such action by the enterprise could be invalidated.

Besides the representation of employee interests by the union, Chinese labor law prescribes in state companies to hold meetings of employee delegates (Workers' and Staff Congress) and defines them as an element of "democratic management". They meet once or twice a year, discuss the reports of the management and vote on collective contracts and important rules related to the employees' interests. Although the Workers' and Staff Congresses are obligatory for state-owned companies only, the government promotes their development also in foreign-invested companies. In the latter case, the role of the Workers' and Staff Congresses is, however, usually restricted to consultations about the company's policy and performance; there is hardly any participation of the Congresses in managerial decision making (Warner 2007).

In sum we can derive two results regarding institutional constraints on the strategic choice of companies:
– The institutional framework of industrial relations in China strongly constrains the strategic decisions of the companies. It enforces a micro-corporatist form of a "productivity coalition" between management and trade union.
– The representation of employee interests is the weak side of this "productivity coalition". The lack of concerns for employee interests on the side of the trade union can lead to legitimacy problems ad conflicts.

9.3.3 Conclusions

Let us suppose that German companies would aim for transferring their industrial relations practices to Russia and China. Which conditions do they find for this transfer? Officially, both countries aim for establishing "social partnership" (in the Russian case) and "harmonious industrial relations" (in the Chinese case) which sound relatively close to the cooperative industrial relations and social partnership in Germany. Both countries, however, differ strongly from the German model.

In Russia, the labor law gives companies considerable leeway to avoid union organization. In addition, the companies are confronted with two competing trade union camps which both differ from the German unions: the so-called "alternative" unions (the KTR) put a strong emphasis on the direct articulation of employee interests but pursue at the same time a conflict-oriented approach to which German companies are not used; the so-called "traditional" unions (FNPR), by contrast, follow a very cooperative model of industrial relations but are often not close enough to employee interests.

In China, the formal rules of industrial relations resemble the German model, but the trade union identities differ strongly. The ACFTU union leaders often see their main responsibility in productivity campaigns and the organizing of social and cultural events for the employees; the articulation of employee interests is still a weakness of the ACFTU.

9.4 Industrial Relations in German Companies in Russia and China

Russia and China are gaining more and more importance as target-countries of investments from Germany. The amount of direct investment of German industrial firms in Russia in 2009 reached 4.2 billion Euros (cf. Bundesbank 2011). The most important industrial branches for German investment were the automobile industry (33 % of the German FDI in Russian manufacturing) and chemical industry (23 %). Russia is, for German investors in both industries, indeed a relatively new location, which quantitatively still is not very important: the investment in Russia in 2009 amounted to only 1.4 % of the amount of foreign investments of the German automobile industry. In the case of the German chemical industry, the amount of investments in Russia amounted to 2.1 % of total foreign investments.

The importance of China for German companies is greater. The amount of direct investment of German manufacturing firms in China in 2009 amounted to 11.6 billion Euros. The automobile industry was by far the most important industrial branch (39 % of the German FDI in Chinese manufacturing), followed by machine building and the construction of power plants (both 17 % respectively). Direct investment in China in 2009 amounted to 4.5 % of the foreign investment of the German automobile industry. In machine building it even reached to 7.0 %.

Despite the great importance of German companies as investors in Russia and China, up to now there are hardly any studies which deal with the peculiarities of labor relations in these companies. In the following the existing findings will be briefly brought together and own research results presented.

9.4.1 Russia

There is hardly any research regarding labor relations in multi-national companies in Russia and still less regarding labor relations in German companies in Russia. The comparative literature on management cultures offers some indication as to the question of the transfer of German models of labor relations to Russia. Groeger (2006) established in her study of expatriates in nine German companies from different branches (construction, chemicals, trade, services, information technology and food) that none of the company headquarters made an effort to transfer the German company culture to Russia. The headquarters only defined the budget constraints for the Russian subsidiaries as well as in some cases the general guidelines for the pay and premium systems. The question of transferring the company culture was left to the dispatched German managers and was dependent upon their personal attitudes. If we see the relation to the union and the works council as a part of the German company culture, we can conclude from Groeger's (2006) findings that there has been no systematic attempt to transfer the practice of co-determination to Russia – even if the author has not dealt with this theme herself.

A further indication regarding the transfer of labor relations practices is offered by comparative studies about the leadership styles in German-Russian companies. In a cross-industry study of German-Russian joint ventures, Holtbrügge (1996) has shown that some typical conflicts arise in the cooperation of German and Russian managers. The older Russian managers follow an authoritarian, hierarchical and control-oriented leadership style. The majority of older employees in Russia have become accustomed to the fact that the company is centrally led and that the company manager possesses unlimited authority to issue instructions. German managers perceive the Russian employees as lacking in self-initiative and independence. At the same time, young Russian employees often show a strong entrepreneurial spirit and claim that the German managers do not recognize the Russian employees as equal partners and over-estimate their own abilities to solve problems.

Piske (2002) has, on the basis of similar findings in German-Russian companies, developed a model of cultural conflicts. The foundation of the model are "ideal types" of "German" and "Russian" leadership styles taken from research literature (cf. Zavyalova et al. 2011). Piske (2002: 224) characterizes the Russian leadership style as short-term oriented, authoritarian, and control-oriented, while the German leadership style is characterized by a long-term orientation of decisions and encouragement of employee self-initiative. In those German-Russian companies studied by Piske (2002) the German part of the company management dominated. The German managers perceived a wide distance between their leadership style and the "Russian" culture and reacted with increased efforts to define general norms and rules. These efforts towards standardization were seen by the Russian managers as a threat to their identity and as a devaluation of their position and released activities of "cultural differentiation" i.e., the Russian managers attempted to maintain their own style of leadership vis-à-vis the generally defined norms and regulations. The interaction of standardization efforts by the German managers and the efforts towards differentiation by the Russian managers can lead as well to a positive spiral towards rapprochement as to a negative spiral towards conflict. According to Piske (2002), a rapprochement of both perspectives depends on the transparency of the processes and the involvement of the Russian employees in the definition of norms and regulations, the credibility of the German management and the investments in qualification and personnel development.

Even though the studies regarding of management styles do not deal with labor relations (and often present a relatively oversimplified picture of national cultures), they provide an indication of the hurdles in the application of co-determination practices in Russia. It can be expected that authoritarian and control-oriented leadership styles of Russian managers will come into conflict with attempts at implementing a co-determination system.

The following case of a German car manufacturer (building on own research) is a unique example of a company which tries to transfer the German system of industrial relations to Russia; it also shows the difficulties the company experiences. As one of the German car manufacturers, the company belongs to the biggest and most important German companies. It opened its plant in Russia in 2007. In 2011, the plant reached its full capacity utilization with around 5,000 employees.

The Russian plant is located in a middle-size city with around 300,000 inhabitants; the entire oblast (the administrative unit corresponding to a province) has approximately one million inhabitants. Although there is a considerable shortage of labor, the wage level in the oblast was and remains low, in particular compared to the level of wages in Moscow some 200 km distant. Given this situation, high demand for wage increases developed quickly at the plant. There was a short strike already in the summer of 2009, and a slowing-down of the work pace by workers fighting for higher wages and extra breaks during the intense summer heat. A union formed, which then joined the recently established Inter-Regional Union of Automobile Workers (MPRA). The MPRA was founded as an alternative to the traditional trade union in the automobile industry (ASM) which is member of the post-communist FNPR. The creation of an MPRA organisation led quite quickly to the founding of an ASM organisation with the support of the regional governor and the regional ASM structures. ASM remained comparatively weak, however, and had only 50 members in 2011. In contrast, the MPRA union continues with its organising activities. A wage increase was implemented in 2010 following strikes and demonstrations. A strike threat in the spring of 2011 achieved a further wage increase. The MPRA had about 400–500 members in 2011.

The German works council of the company responded with a mediation initiative to the threat of an escalation of competition between the unions, and to the conflicts between unions and management. Representatives from both Russian unions, works council representatives and trade union representatives from Germany, and management representatives from the Russian plant, met in two seminars and negotiated an agreement that was a complete first for industrial relations in Russia: a German-style works councils is planned to be established with representation for both unions. Both unions have also received recognition from the company, and have been granted an office and information boards; the chairmen will be exempt from work for 2 days a week – even though both are still far below the obligatory threshold for union recognition (50 % of the employees). Following the German template, joint committees of unions and management have been established to address issues of occupational safety, work organisation, and personnel issues.

This case represents a transfer of the German model, which is nevertheless yet to be proven in practice. The establishment of the works council is a risk for both unions; in this case, they must also succeed in the council elections. Given their degree of organisation, this is not assured. At the same time, wage disputes are ongoing, as well as disputes regarding the management style of supervisors and managers, which has the effect of repeatedly putting into question the achieved level of cooperation. Not least, there are repeated and ongoing tensions between the two cultures of interest representation: the 'cooperative conflict management' encouraged by the German works council and German management, and the MPRA's confrontational approach to organisation and mobilisation.

9.4.2 China

Also in regard to China, there are hardly any studies up to the present, which explicitly deal with German companies. The few existing studies concentrate on the automobile industry. Depner and Bathelt (2005) have, in a study concerning the development of clusters of German automobile industries in China, established that many German companies arrive in China relatively unprepared. "It appears that German firms often send executives to their Chinese operations who are primarily technical experts but lack the knowledge of how to manage a company successfully in an intercultural context. Sometimes these managers know surprisingly little about the expectations and patterns of behaviour of Chinese workers and managers" (Depner and Bathelt 2005: 73). According to Depner and Bathelt (2005) the strong position of the Communist Party in the companies, who must agree to all personnel-related decisions (transfers, dismissals), is one of the most important peculiarities of HR management in China that German companies have to deal with.

In a study on Shanghai Volkswagen Kiefer (1998) has argued that the company had indeed established training systems according to the pattern used in Germany, but in general, it had rather from the beginning oriented the production and labor organization on the model of lean production as at Toyota. Kiefer did not report on any attempts to transfer the German model of co-determination and industrial relations.

Lübcke et al. (2007) have researched practices of corporate social responsibility (CSR) of German companies in China. Their research comprises of a German car manufacturer, two German first tier suppliers as well as three Chinese sub-suppliers of the German firms. They conclude their results in the following manner: "For the most part our findings corresponded to our expectations, namely that CSR already had a firm place in the company policies of the major international companies, whereas further along the supply chain the importance of CSR shrinks. In the case of first tier suppliers, which cooperate in a joint venture with foreign companies, the acknowledgement of CSR certainly exists, while Chinese private second tier firms very often only have a weak relations to the CSR principles" (Lübcke et al. 2007: 86).

Lübcke et al. (2007) characterize as "exemplary" the work-conditions at the German final producer. The regular working hours of 40 h a week and the number of overtime hours are limited. Much emphasis is placed on work safety standards. The only deviation at the Chinese location from the work conditions in Germany is the high level of temporary workers (30 %). The work conditions in the German supplier firms in China differ from the German standard particularly in regard to the working hours, which lie close to the legal limits with 48–60 h a week (including overtime). The share of temporary workers is very high with the suppliers too.

The union chairmen at the companies studied by Lübcke et al. (2007) were exclusively composed of nominated (not elected) representatives. Their knowledge of the problems in the plant and their influence were characterized by German managers as relatively weak. Indeed, this by no means indicates a weak union. The German managers pointed out that they had to consult with elected union representatives at shop level – these representatives had more influence on the actual operations than the top union chairman. But the resulting fragmentation of the representation of interests was seen as a problem since a strong union chairman was lacking to coordinate the interests. Lübcke et al. (2007: 91) argue: "Even if one considers the partiality and interests involved in statements [of the German managers, M.K.], one hears here the wish for calculability of their union counterpart, which can be only attained by the unions which are actually active in those areas which are ascribed as their primary fields of activity anyway, namely representing employee interests in operative questions." From the viewpoint of the German companies, a central problem of the labor relations in China is how to establish an authentic representation of employee interests.

The following case of a German car manufacturer (building on own research) shows the slow evolution from the traditional industrial relations model in China towards a stronger concern for representing employee interests. The company is located in one of the main Chinese industrial centers and is a joint venture between the German manufacturer (50 %) and a Chinese car company (50 %). In 2010, it employed 22,000 persons. The trade union of the joint venture is part of the Chinese company's trade union. At the top of the union stands the union chairperson (simultaneously the secretary of the Communist Party at the company); the union chairperson also participates in board meetings of the company. Below the central union committee follow the committees at the plant and shop levels as well as the union groups at unit level. The union has a professionalized structure with a whole row of commissions at the company level and with special working groups at the company level and at area level which deal with topics such as safety, welfare, etc. The union committees at all levels are elected by the union members. In addition to the union structure, there is a Workers' Congress, which meets once or twice a year. It consists of 230 elected representatives, accepts the report of activities of the management and can vote on social affairs as well as work-related topics. There is a collective agreement, which is renegotiated every 3 years.

An important role for the communication between management and union is played by the so-called "dialog of equals" (*Ping Deng Xie Shang*), a regular consultation process, which is held two to four times a year. The "dialog of equals" rests on an agreement between management and union and consists of four phases: in the first phase, HR or the union submits a proposal; in the second phase, the proposal is discussed in a joint working group of the union and the management; in the third phase, the heads of management and union negotiate the draft formulated by the working group; finally, the results is signed and, in especially important cases, voted on by the Workers' Congress.

The "dialog of equals" is the highest level of consultation at the company. Alongside this, regular meetings take place at the plant and shop level between management and union. A further level of communication is the three joint committees of management and union: committees for disciplinary measures, occupational health, and for transfer from blue collar to white collar jobs. Moreover, there are regular consultations between management and the union at the shop level. In this way, there is a close involvement of the union in operative questions. According to the management of the company, the trade union does not simply accept the management's suggestions but develops its own demands and positions on all relevant topics. Step by step, the union is moving towards the function of representing employee interest, even if the traditional role of providing social assistance and organizing social activities remains strong. Since the company is obligated by law to transfer 2 % of the aggregate wages to the union organization, this then disposes over considerable financial means to spend on social integration activities.

Conclusions

How can we summarize the results of the analysis? The first question was which institutional constraints influence the transfer of home country practices of industrial relations from Germany to Russia and China. The institutional conditions in both countries are not particularly encouraging for such transfer. Officially, both countries aim for developing social partnership between labor and capital. But actually, both countries have established restrictions for employee interest representations. In Russia, the high thresholds for the recognition of trade union organizations provide leeway for union avoidance strategies of companies. In China, the trade union is subordinated to the Communist Party. The traditional trade union role is to promote productivity increases in the companies and to provide social services and organize social and cultural events for the employees.

For the companies, it is surely much easier to adapt to the local conditions and not to try to transfer the German practices of industrial relations. The existing research literature for the Russian case (e.g., Groeger 2006), limited as it is, does not provide any evidence for the transfer of German practices of industrial relations. In brownfield plants, the adaptation to local conditions most often means the cooperation with the traditional post-communist union; in greenfield plants it usually means not to have a trade union. The similarly scarce research literature about industrial relations in German companies in China (e.g., Lübcke et al. 2007) also indicates that German companies adapt to the local conditions. Industrial relations in their plants follow the traditional Chinese model, in which the union limits itself to organizing productivity campaigns, and providing social assistance to employees.

While adaptation to local conditions might be the most common behavior pattern, this does not automatically mean that the traditional forms of industrial relations in Russia and China are seen by the German companies as very attractive. The cases of the German automobile manufacturers in Russia and China show a strong interest in the development of an "authentic" employee interest representation. The management wants to know about employee interests and the existing trade union structures and industrial relations institutions in Russia and China are seen as quite ineffective in providing this information. In addition, the German trade union and the works council demand the establishment of an effective employee interest representation in the plants abroad. As a consequence, the companies invest a lot of efforts to transfer its model of cooperative industrial relations and works councils to its foreign locations – even though this transfer proceeds slowly and in small steps.

How do we interpret these cases? They provide some support for hypotheses 1 and 2: it is both the influence of strong works councils and the management's interest in cooperative solution of conflicts that influence the approach towards industrial relations. The cases discussed have stem, however, from big car assembly plants. They are not representative in the sense that we can expect similar behavior from most of the German companies and so they do not disprove hypothesis 3. But it would be also wrong to dismiss the cases presented as exemptions. German automobile manufacturers are flagship companies of the German economy and belong to the most successful and biggest German companies abroad by employment and number of locations. In some cases, they are by the foreign governments and trade unions as the role model for the reforms of labor regulation. And they are able to influence labor standards of their suppliers.

How will the industrial relations institutions in Russia and China evolve? Until now, there are only weak signs of reforms in both countries. At the same time, the evidence presented in this article shows changes at the company level which could in the long run lead undermine the authoritarian model of industrial relations.

References

Ashwin S, Clarke S (2003) Russian trade unions and industrial relations in transition. Palgrave Macmillan, New York

Bluhm K (2003) Flucht aus dem deutschen Modell? Arbeitsbeziehungen in polnischen und tschechischen Tochtergesellschaften. In: Beyer J (ed) Vom Zukunfts- zum Auslaufmodell. Westdeutscher Verlag, Opladen, pp 214–236

Bluhm K (2007) Experimentierfeld Ostmitteleuropa? Deutsche Unternehmen in Polen und der Tschechischen Republik. VS Verlag, Wiesbaden

Bundesbank (2011) Bestanderhebung über Direktinvestitionen. Deutsche Bundesbank, Frankfurt/Main

Clarke S, Pringle T (2009) Can party-led trade unions represent their members? Post-Commun Econ 21(1):85–101

Cooney S (2007) Making Chinese labor law work: the prospects for regulatory innovation in the People's Republic of China. Fordham Int Law J 30:1050–1097

Depner H, Bathelt H (2005) Exporting the German model: the establishment of a new automobile industry cluster in Shanghai. Econ Geogr 81(1):53–81

FES Friedrich Ebert Stiftung (2008) Gewerkschaften in Russland heute. FES, Bonn

Groeger F (2006) Einfluss von Expatriates auf die Organisationsstrukturen deutscher Tochterunternehmen in Russland. Hampp, München/Mering

Hall P, Soskice D (2001) An introduction to varieties of capitalism. In: Hall P, Soskice D (eds) Varieties of capitalism. The institutional foundations of comparative advantage. Oxford University Press, Oxford, pp 1–70

Holtbrügge D (1996) Unternehmenskulturelle Anpassungsprobleme in deutsch-russischen Joint Ventures. J East Eur Manag Stud 1(1):7–28

Hui SL (2011) Understanding labour activism: the Honda workers' strike. In: Scherrer C (ed) China's labor question. Hampp, München/Mering, pp 133–151

Jürgens U, Krzywdzinski M (2009) Work models in the Central Eastern European car industry: towards the high road? Ind Relat J 40(6):493–512

Jürgens U, Krzywdzinski M (2010) Die neue Ost-West-Arbeitsteilung. Arbeitsmodelle und industrielle Beziehungen in der europäischen Automobilindustrie. Campus, Frankfurt/New York

Kiefer T (1998) Volkswagen's Shanghai plant: between Chinese tradition and modernization strategy. In: Boyer R, Charon E, Jürgens U, Tolliday S (eds) Between imitation and innovation. Oxford University Press, Oxford, pp 342–360

Kochan T, Mckersie R, Cappelli P (1984) Strategic choice and industrial relations theory. Ind Relations J Econ Soc 23(1):16–39

Kojima K (2010) Direction of trade union reforms and corporatism in PRC: based on a survey of primary trade union chairmen (2004–6). In: Hishida M, Kojima K, Ishii T, Jian Q (eds) China's trade unions – how autonomous are they? Routledge, London/New York, pp 25–51

Krzywdzinski M (2011) Exporting the German work model to Central and Eastern Europe. In: Contrepois S, Delteil V, Dieuaide P, Jefferys S (eds) Globalizing employment relations. Multinational firms and Central and Eastern Europe transitions. Palgrave Macmillan, Basingstoke, pp 99–118

Lauffs A (2008) Employment law & practice in China. Sweet & Maxwell, Hongkong

Lübcke E, Ruth K, Yim I-S (2007) Corporate social responsibility 'Made in China', vol 60, ITB-Arbeitspapiere. ITB, Bremen

Meardi G, Strohmer S, Traxler F (2011) The social transfers of multinationals in central Europe: British, US, Austrian and German experiences reviewed. In: Contrepois S, Delteil V, Dieuaide P, Jefferys S (eds) Globalizing employment relations multinational firms and central and Eastern Europe transitions. Palgrave Macmillan, Basingstoke, pp 29–44

Müller-Jentsch W (2007) Strukturwandel der industriellen Beziehungen. Industrial Citizenship zwischen Markt und Regulierung. VS Verlag, Wiesbaden

Piske R (2002) Deutsche Akquisitionen in der Russischen Föderation: Führung im Spannungsfeld kultureller Differenzierung und organisationaler Integration. J East Eur Manag Stud 7(3):241–266

Pringle T (2011) Trade unions in China. The challenge of labour unrest. Routledge, London/New York

Taylor B, Kai C, Qi L (2003) Industrial relations in China. Edward Elgar, Cheltenham

Tempel A (2001) The cross-national transfer of human resource management practices in German and British multinational companies. Hampp, München/Mering

Tholen J, Cziria L, Hemmer E, Kozek W, Mansfeldová Z (2006) Direktinvestitionen deutscher Unternehmen in Mittel- und Osteuropa. Hampp, München/Mering

Voß E, Willke P (2003) Modelltransfer oder Anpassung an lokale Verhältnisse? Bertelsmann Stiftung/Hans-Böckler-Stiftung, Hamburg

Warner M (2007) Management-labour relations in the new Chinese economy. Hum Res Manag J 7(4):30–43

White G (1996) Chinese trade unions in the transition from socialism: towards corporatism or civil society? Br J Ind Relat 34(3):433–457

Zavyalova E, Kosheleva S, Ardichvili A (2011) Human resource management and development practices in indigenous Russian companies and foreign MNCs: a comparative analysis. Int J Hum Res Dev Manag 11(2–4):179–193

The Revival of State Interventionism and European Industrial Relations: Some Lessons from a Survey

10

Patrick Dieuaide

10.1 Introduction

Since the early 1990s, national industrial relations systems in Europe have experienced a number of upheavals linked essentially to pressure from international competition, the globalization of financial markets and the transition to a market economy by all former East European, Soviet bloc economies.

In fact, the classical model of industrial relations à la Dunlop (re-edited 1993), and constructed on the national foundations of large, integrated companies with strong unions and an active State in terms of legislation and regulation, has been openly called into question. Relations between these actors are increasingly dependent on changes in the international economic and financial environment and above all on firms' strategic choices (Katz et al. 1986). These relations are thus slackening continuously, while complementarities previously identified here and there at the institutional level have quickly given ground to a complex, changing and multi-level architecture.

It is possible to identify two areas of analysis in the recent literature seeking to explain the logic of the reconstruction at work.

- A first area of analysis examines the impact of "shareholder governance" on human resource management policies. A key result of this work is that there is no "one best way" in this field. Instead, local or "sub-national" management configurations exist, due notably to the heterogeneity of institutional frameworks, as well as the capital structure of companies.
- A second area of analysis strives to understand the place and role of industrial relations in the genesis and spread of technical and organizational

---

P. Dieuaide (✉)
Associate Professor, Research Center on Integration and Cooperation in the European Area, (ICEE), Université Sorbonne Nouvelle - Paris 3, Paris, France
e-mail: Patrick.Dieuaide@univ-paris3.fr

changes in companies. Some of the principle socio-professional characteristics of industrial relations which have thus been identified as being at the heart of these new productive models in companies include subjective involvement, geographical and professional mobility, as well as de-unionization and the loss collective bargaining's centrality.

The field survey conducted by the author and others on behalf of France's Ministry of Employment within eight French Multinational Companies (MNCs) present in the CEECs does not fundamentally diverge from this overall view.[1] However, closer examination of the material available does bring out two specific dimensions: the assertion of new objectives and forms of social dialogue between social partners; and the singular role of the State in organizing and setting up a new institutional architecture of industrial relations within companies. This contribution seeks to address these two particular aspects of the survey and review the way they are linked.

10.2 The General Framework and Issues of Analysis

1. It is not the purpose here to enter into the detail of the data and field analyses carried within companies (see in particular, Contrepois et al. 2011).

The work takes as given the widely recognized observation, which was verified during the interviews, that: the extension of the field of industrial relations to other actors (international trade union federations, local authorities, NGOs, experts from European committees, etc.), other types of action (international framework agreements, individualization and contractualization of the employer/employee relationship), as well as other levels of regulation (local, national, global) are largely linked to the transnationalisation of national productive systems (growth in emerging markets, as well as the development of horizontal and vertical FDI). At the same time, a "management by profitability" model is imposing itself, which adheres very closely to the principles of short-termism and the maximization of "shareholder value" (see Flow Chart 10.1).

---

[1] The field survey was conducted within the framework of a study commissioned by the DARES (of the French Ministry of Employment). Eight French multinational companies were involved, with each being present in at least two of the three CEECs studied (Hungary, Slovakia and Rumania). Three were operating in the energy sector, two in agri-business and three in the auto sector. The survey led to 115 interviews with employees, French and East-European unions (central delegates, members of the European Works Council), firms' general management and human resources management. It was carried out between 2006 and 2008, and the results of this work led to the publication of a report, available on Internet at: www.cevipof.msh-paris.fr, or at www.ICEE.univ-paris3.fr.

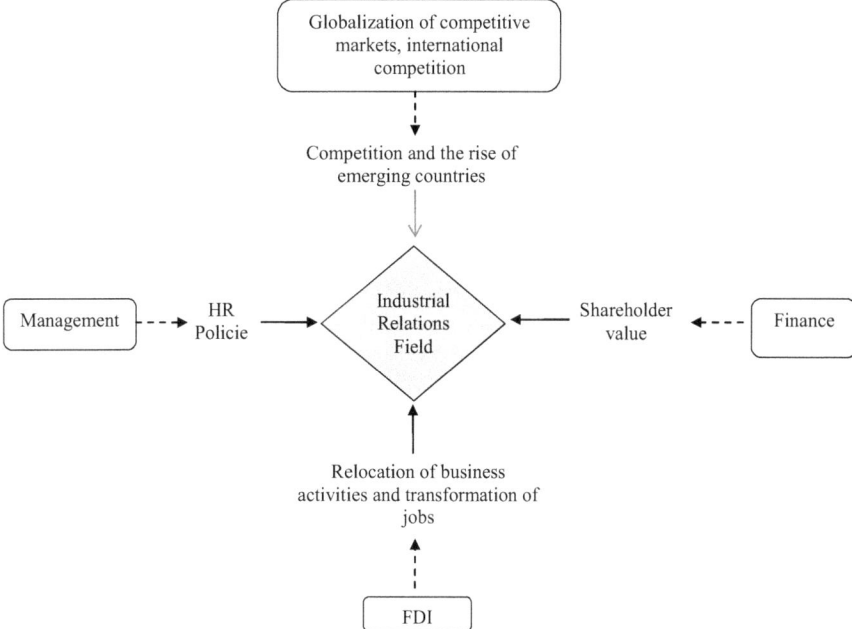

Flow Chart 10.1 Industrial relations within globalisation

These contextual elements are important in analyzing to what extent they restore industrial relations from a twofold perspective:

– First, the field of industrial relations is not as "homogeneous" as before. The distancing of economic power from the workplace, the fragmentation of decision making processes within companies through transnational value chains, the disconnection between markets and geographic areas fostered by the development of FDI, all act together to challenge the national space as being relevant to the game of social regulation.
– Second, pressure from many centres of economic and social influence (managers, shareholders, unions, local labour) on industrial relations systems challenge the very nature of compromises reached by social partners within companies. In particular, the place and role of collective bargaining in the social regulation game have been transformed.

Thus, we propose here to analyse the place and role of the State from this singular, "inside-out" position that industrial relations *vis-à-vis* frameworks instituted nationally and *vis-à-vis* the forms and modalities of social dialogue between different stakeholders. More fundamentally, as the survey tends to suggest, it is as if the State played a "gatekeeper" role with respect to socio-political compromises and the strategies of actors involved in the field of industrial relations. The point is to highlight the State's function not just in terms of adjusting institutional frameworks to the economic and financial requirements of globalisation. But it must also maintain a certain social cohesion between firms' strategies and local development.

Such a presentation is an extension of an approach to public action which is open, diversified and multilateral (Lallement and Mériaux 2001). It is interesting as it takes the State out of a scaled-down night-watchman or great watchmaker role in the field of industrial relations. If, in this conception of the State, it is party to the game of social regulation within companies themselves, then the State's involvement needs to be viewed in a differentiated manner, in terms of its mediation within global–local relations in which managerial and financial logic fit alongside social, industrial and territorial logic. Such a perspective leads to seeing the place and role of the State in industrial relations from the point of view of the *institutional complementarities* generated by the fallout of its actions.

2. In the light of the interview held with various MNCs, institutional complementarities deployed through the State directly affect strategic interactions between unions and employers (management and shareholders). More precisely, the survey reveals that the role of the State in industrial relations differs significantly between France and the East-European countries in which the MNCs in our sample operate.

A first explanation lies in the logic of financial globalisation (Michalet 2007), which is not affecting these two regions in the same way. In France, finance has imposed its views essentially through financial markets (in terms of shareholder value). In the East European economies, which have been in full post-communist transition, the State has found itself involved essentially in terms of foreign direct investment (FDI) (see Flow Chart 10.2 below).

A second element refers to the fundamental transformation of human resource (HR) policies by management, compared to 15 years ago. These policies have dropped the traditional functions of administering personnel. Instead they have shifted to managing skills and human capital. Employer/employee relations have been profoundly modified under the impulsion of new contractual regulations based on new objectives and new bargaining arrangements. This is a salient feature of the survey: under pressure from finance, a certain, strategic "HR management" has contributed to the emergence of new socio-political compromises. These compromises are specific to each geographical zone (see Part II). They are the foundation of a particular model of organising and managing social relations, which may be termed as a "Managerial Social Dialogue" (MSD). More specifically, MSD is taken here to refer to a general framework in which management not only holds power of initiative in contractual relations and bargaining, but also has the power to fix their contents and methods.[2]

---

[2] Without going into the details of the survey, Managerial Social Dialogue may be characterised using three dimensions:
- The strengthening of financial logic in HR policies, with the considerable development of financial incentives (individual bonuses, profit-sharing, employee savings schemes).
- A strong extension of contracting policy. The benefits are manifest in terms of the themes and goals of the social dialogue, whether these themes stray from or explicitly draw on ILO standards (prohibition of child labour, equal pay, the right to training, equal opportunities) or whether they are directly linked to management constraints of organisational flexibility (agreements on skills, flexible hours).

10 The Revival of State Interventionism and European Industrial Relations: Some...

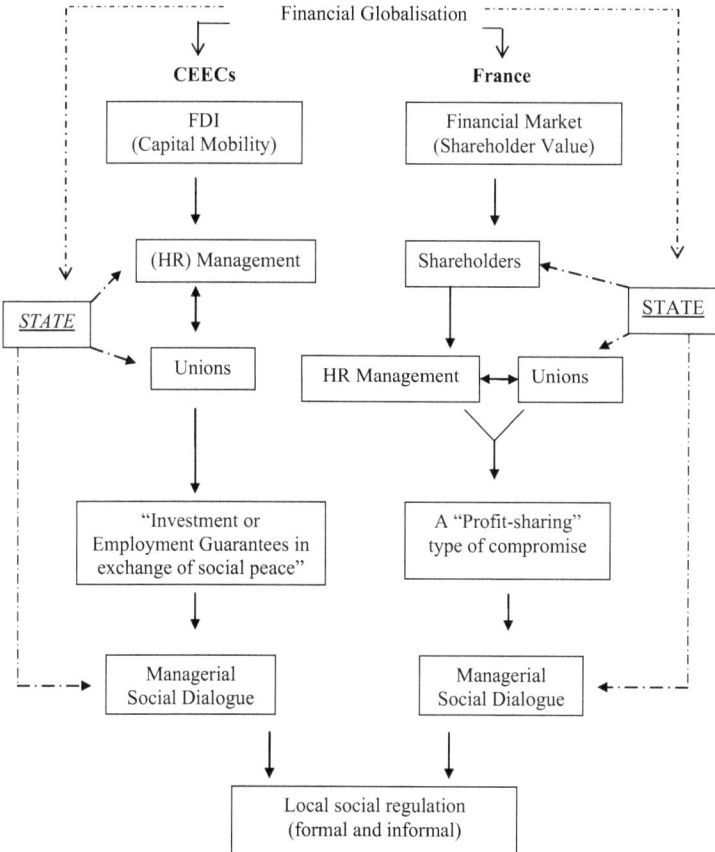

Flow Chart 10.2 The state and industrial relations within globalisation

It should be noted that the MSD expresses a particular socio-political balance within firms. Yet, it is not a substitute for social dialogue itself, especially concerning the legal and regulatory framework organizing such a dialogue, and hence Nation States which ultimately retain control over it. For example, in the sites set up in Eastern Europe, the State can be seen to play a key role in the face of MNCs vague desires over the preservation of employment. Similarly, MSD in France is not a management standard, valid once and for all. Indeed, the tensions resulting from the instabilities following the global financial and economic crisis (of 2007–2008) have not been without consequences, at the level of socio-political

---

– The emergence of new structures and new actors in the social dialogue, via the setting up of "world committees". At the local level, new actors in the social dialogue are also emerging (managers, collaborators, employees), who are competing with traditional actors (unionists and other personnel representatives) in the organization and management of new functions (mediation, coordination, communication) within firms' entrepreneurial activity itself.

equilibria, for the compromises reached within French firms. In fact, MSD has not come through this period of great instability unscathed, and should be the object of government attention. MSD cannot therefore be wholly disassociated from the institutional frameworks (legal, legislative and regulatory) which structure actors' games at the level of national systems and industrial relations (Amable 2005).

From this set of considerations, it follows that State action in the field of industrial relations may be apprehended at two levels. The first is linked to the way the State contributes to the shaping of socio-political compromises within the specific context of financial globalization and has incidentally participated to the putting into place of a "managerial social dialogue". The second level concerns the analysis of State responses to tensions caused by the fallout of the 2007 crisis in the field of industrial relations, and the lessons it provides from the point of view of institutional logics of reconstruction which govern the viability of this model. These are the two angles of analysis which are the focus of study here.

10.3 The Key Lessons of the Survey

Strictly speaking, the field survey does not explicitly look at the place and role of the State in the area of industrial relations. The intervention of the latter is seen more as a response to pressures from the environment in order to guarantee, or even put a little coherence into the game of social interactions at the local level, within the strategic decisions of the actors.[3] From this perspective, government action is meant to support or even cement specific socio-political compromises, that are locally situated and which may remain uncertain in a context of financial globalisation.

This presentation suggests that the place and role of the State should be viewed from a twofold perspective. The first sees it as a promoter of a *strategy to maintain or consolidate* socio-political equilibria forged locally. The second views the State as a negotiator striving to formulate a *strategy for updating and anticipating* industrial relations through the search for new institutional complementarities which may generate new socio-political compromises.[4]

---

[3] This approach is close, at least in spirit, to the propositions put forward by two major currents of thought in Industrial Relations Studies: the "strategic choice" current (Katz et al. 2008) which stress the strategic capacity of enterprises to stimulate a transformation dynamics in the field of industrial relations; and the "micro-policy" current of company strategy (Edwards et al. 2007) which emphasises power relations that run within multinationals, from parent companies to foreign subsidiaries.

[4] It should be noted that another perspective exists. In looking at the place and role of the State in the context of globalization, M. Lallement (2007, Ch. 17) identifies two levels of intervention: 1/the rise of (active) employment policies, grounded in bargaining that is as close as possible to the objectives and institutions of the EU (see the open method of coordination and the Lisbon Strategies I and II). 2/the development of aid policies that are increasingly targeted and differentiated, and based on local networks of employment intermediaries that are increasingly numerous and disparate (France's public employment agency (the ANPE), local missions, placement companies, training organizations).

```
                            CEECs
                              ▲
      ┌──────────────┐        │        ┌──────────────┐
      │ Consolidation│────────┼───────▶│ Anticipation │
      └──────────────┘        │        └──────────────┘
Employment/          ◀────────┼────────▶        Managerial Social
Social Dialogue               │                 Dialogue
      ┌──────────────┐        │        ┌──────────────┐
      │ Anticipation │◀───────┼────────│ Consolidation│
      └──────────────┘        │        └──────────────┘
                              ▼
                            France
```

Flow Chart 10.3 State strategy and forms of collective action

To complete this presentation, it should be noted that these strategies fall within a particular context, marked by before and after 2008, the year in which the real economy started to be affected by the global financial crisis. This episode revealed an astonishing dynamic in the reconstruction of industrial relations at the institutional level. While in the CEECs the epicentre of the institutionalisation process very rapidly shifted from a logic of social dialogue and employment guarantees to an institutional context favouring the emergence of a "managerial social dialogue", a shift in the opposite direction has occurred in France, where employment was very quickly placed at the heart of negotiations between the State and social partners (see Flow Chart 10.3).

10.3.1 Socio-Political Compromises and Consolidation Strategies: The State as an Actor in the Development of a (Managerial) Social Dialogue

Talking about a "consolidation" strategy suggests that State action only recognises or at best accompanies the game of the economic and financial forces weighing on national systems of industrial relations. Such an assumption is not without a link to a specific characteristic of globalisation, namely the competition between countries and geographical areas brought on by capital mobility. In the years from 1990 to 2007, governments thus gave greater weight to policies attracting investment with the aim of creating an environment favourable to the development of firms' activities. The result is a profound upheaval in the institutional framework and mode of governance of social relations, both in France and the CEECs.

In France: a strengthening of contracting policies in line with the formulation of a "profit-sharing" type of compromise
In France, legislative changes over the last 15 years have underpinned a profound process of restructuring collective bargaining laws. These changes are twofold.

Initiated by Minister of Labor, Martine Aubry, the Aubry I and II laws (voted in 1998 and 2000) on the 35-h week, a first set of adjustments affects the conditions of the social dialogue in companies, via the enactment of a number of important pieces of legislation:

- The programming law on social cohesion of the 18th January 2005 which obliges companies with more than 300 employees to negotiate arrangements for informing and consulting staff every 3 years, concerning company strategy and its likely effects on employment, and making it mandatory to implement measures for forecasting employment and skills needs.
- The law the 31st January 2007 on the modernisation of social dialogue, which stipulates in particular the obligation to consult social partners prior to any reform project.
- The law of the 20th August 2008 which allows standards to be inverted in branch-level agreements and which generalises mandating in firms with no unions as well as bargaining by personnel representatives.

These legislative provisions need to be reconciled with a series of measures voted in favour of profit-sharing, employee shareholding and employee savings plans. They have been progressively put into place over 50 years. But since the 2000s, it is possible to observe unprecedented processes of institutionalisation, with the creation of inter-company savings schemes (2001), collective retirement schemes (2003), and finally the law of December 2008 which modifies the regime for profit-sharing. These measures involve considerable sums of money.[5] They meet a management concern about creating a bond of trust between companies and employees by the search for a way of compensation which ensures better knowledge of the implication, the level of effort and the greater motivation of employees (CAS 2011). In substance, these measures strive to reinforce companies' "social performance" (CAS 2011), on the basis of greater participation by employees in firms' results. In exchange, these measures have the effect of considerably opening up the field contracting policy: directly by bargaining on a case-by-case basis and by individual subscriptions to different financial products; and indirectly by favouring the opening up of negotiations in various fields traditionally related to HR (training, time-saving, stress, restructuring).[6]

---

[5] €85 billion were involved in France, in 2009 (CAS 2011). "At the end of 2008, 58 % of 16 million employees were covered by at least one measure relating to profit-sharing, investment, or employee savings (...). For all measures taken together, the bonus ran to an average €2227 in 2008 (...). On average, 33 cents are paid for every euro contributed to the employee savings scheme [PEE] and €1 for every €1 paid to a collective retirement scheme [PERCO]" (Dares 2010).

[6] In the survey, the analysis of agreements reached between management and employees at PSA, as well as at Renault, provides an exemplary illustration of the enhancement of the social dialogue. A first wave of agreements was reached in the wake of the 35-h week laws and reinforced organizational flexibility ("flexibility agreements" at Renault or annualisation of working time at PSA).

The establishment of a compromise like "profit sharing" has reinforced the "established" field of social dialogue, at a more local level, where up until the 1980s relations had been more conflictual or informal. On the other hand, it opened up the way to instrumentalising legal and contractual regulation. In the face of increasingly-open and interpretable legal rules, firms have clearly had growing room for manoeuvre to adjust local social rules to the diversity of their industrial strategies.

Faced with this trend, unions have replied in a differentiated manner. On the one hand, they have expressed their resistance to engaging themselves alongside management to "co-manage" change and restructuring. On the other hand, they have fully played the game of social dialogue, by accepting or initiating the opening up of negotiations on subjects which could be considered as "non-strategic" or "secondary" (disability, diversity, skills and employment forecasting, etc.). In other words, for management, the construction of cooperative relations and the search for adhesion and trust are imperative in the application of strategic tenets concerning "permanent innovation" or organisational flexibility. For unions, their engagement in negotiation and the signature of agreements seems to constitute a means for re-conquering power and legitimacy which has been strongly challenged by the individualisation of employer/employee relations.

In the East: the assertion of an attractive institutional framework for FDI, though decentralised and weakly protective of employment.

The case of the CEECs highlights just as much the State's actions in mediating the game of social regulation within globalisation. In contrast to France, however, the context is very different. On the one hand, industrial relations in the East are part of a vast process of institutional compliance imposed by the adoption of the Community *acquis*. On the other hand, the dynamics of catch up, driven since the first years of transition by numerous privatisation programmes, and subsequently relayed by significant industrial restructuring, has been based largely on FDI inflows.[7]

In many countries, the minimal transposition of a certain number of Directives (on working time, on information and worker consultation, on the transfer of employees) has revealed the limited influence of the EU, which has not played the substitute role that could have been expected, *vis-à-vis* post-communist States. The latter are still influential but their legitimacy has been largely challenged. Similarly, the unions, which were widely disparaged under the former regime for managing their own interests, have had difficulties in finding their mark in tripartite bodies that are consultative, (in legislation and economic and employment policies, State budgets, etc.), or decision-making (in fixing minimum wages, the growth rates of wages, etc.). These bodies have been set up to ensure the definition and above all

---

[7] In 2008, FDI stock stood at 60 % of GDP in Hungary, 48 % in Slovakia, and 33 % in Rumania (OECD data).

the acceptance of reforms during the transition period. Lastly, the State, as the leading employer, has hardly withdrawn from the social dialogue, in a context of de-planning and the implementation of structural adjustment policies to the standards of the market economy.[8]

In this context, the investment guarantees offered by management of MNCs, the upgrading of outdated facilities for health and safety, as well as the outlook for improving living standards have acted as indicators for formulating an original socio-political compromise along the lines of "investment in exchange for social peace". Social guarantees have also played a non-negligible role in creating a climate of trust, be it guarantees offered by the State acting as the former owner (i.e. guaranteeing the gradual management of staff negotiated as part of buy-up contracts) or more "generous" redundancy programmes than those practiced by local firms, including outplacement measures for some. In general, MNCs have been very concerned about their social image, and have not hesitated in replicating programmes tested in their countries of origin. Unions, in turn, have accepted that restructuring plans lead to significant job cuts in exchange for spreading these out over a period of 3–5 years. Sometimes compulsory redundancies are even prohibited. Thus restructuring plans have stressed voluntary departures or else substantial financial compensation.

In fact, a well-oiled political scenario that usually unfolds is based neither on a Taylorist social compact, nor German co-management, but rather on a tripartite social dialogue which is the basis of an industrial relations system that is largely intermediated by the public authorities at the macro-level, and more generally "disintermediated" (Rugraff 2006) at company level. Within this dialogue there is a quasi absence of coordination between different levels of regulation (interprofessional, sector and company) and the extensive decentralisation of collective bargaining.

This particular context highlights clearly the features of the "managerial social dialogue" in Eastern Europe. State mediation, which is largely formal, has only extended local social regulation that draws heavily from patronage, haggling and the informal relations inherited from the planning epoch. This strategy of consolidation has contributed to the formation of a strategic equilibrium that has benefited MNCs continuously in the growth policy in Eastern Europe, especially by allowing them to break free from the reference to the social model of their parent companies. According to Bohle and Greskovits (2006), this strategy is also linked to the particular nature of the accumulation regime in the CEECs. Through FDI, it

---

[8] According to A. Vincent – for the CEECs in general – "the transition indicator defined by the EBRD reveals the extent of progress achieved with regard to very general criteria. While the score did not exceed 2.5 in 1991 – on a rating scale ranging from 1 to 4 – all grades since 2000 have stood at between 3 and 4, with the range tending to narrow in recent years" (Vincent 2010, p. 30). The transition indicator of the EBRD is based on an assessment of progress on privatization, enterprise restructuring, price liberalization of trade and the exchange regime, competition policy, banking sector reform, as well as the liberalization of interest rates, financial markets and non-bank institutions and lastly structural reforms defined more widely.

mobilises labour intensively, which is mostly unskilled and for the production of intermediate goods whose worth depends on international markets and not on income from local sales.

10.3.2 State Anticipation Strategies in the Crisis: The State as an Artisan of New Institutional Complementarities

The shock wave of the financial crisis in 2007 has been without precedent for the activity of companies in Europe.[9] The same holds for adjustments to the rules and strategies of the different actors in the game of social regulation. Two kinds of phenomena can be observed at this level: a refocusing of company management on employment management; and the strong implication of the State to support the "crisis compromise" of companies, especially in the auto sector (Point 2.1).

These developments raise questions about the meaning of the importance of the "return" of the State alongside unions and employers, in the field of industrial relations. In particular, the (relative) ebb of the financial and strategic logic of "sharing profits" (employee savings, profit-sharing) cannot but fail to raise the question of an evolution of the terms of compromise which underpinned the "managerial social model" during the boom years of global finance.

France-CEECs: the return of the minimal State in the game of short term social regulation, in the face of the crisis

Statistics from the European Restructuring Monitor of Eurofound (ERM) are used to get an idea of the scale of the fallout of the financial crisis which began in 2007. ERM identifies corporate restructuring and the number of jobs destroyed as a result (see the Fig. 10.1).

The ERM data show considerable job destruction throughout the EU: more than 200,000 in the 4th quarter 2008, 220,000 in 1st quarter 2009, and especially in the auto sector, textiles and construction. In the period running from the 1st quarter 2008 to the 1st quarter 2009, employment within the EU thus fell by 2.5 million. Given this situation, the overall reaction by companies has been to adjust levels of activity and staff, by using all the levers available (see the examples in the Table 10.1): shutdowns, layoffs of temporary workers, part-time unemployment, and above all the forced use of time savings accounts, requirements to take annual leave, and cuts in the working week.

Differences are emerging between East and West within the EU. In the new Member States, priority has been placed on short term adjustments and external

---

[9] Industrial output in the EU-27 fell by 17.6 % between February 2008 and February 2009, but the strongest contraction occurred in the auto industry (-41.2 % for vehicle output), which was far worse than for textiles (-30 %) and construction (-20 %) (Newson 2009).

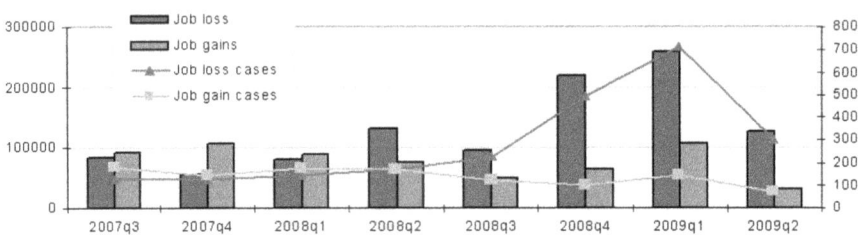

Fig. 10.1 ERM job losses and gains, 3rd quarter 2007–2nd quarter 2009. Note: The *left* vertical axis measures the number of job losses and job gains, the *right* axis the number of job loss/gain cases. Each case corresponds to one company or plant notice of losses or gains (Source: Eurofound 2009)

Table 10.1 Company-agreements and measures dealing with effects of the crisis

Issue/measure	Examples (instrument, country, company)
Flexible reduction of working time with **partial or full compensation** of losses in income, based on **statutory short-time working** or financed by public unemployment benefit funds	*GIGO*: Ordinary wages guarantee funds, applicable during 12 months (IT): Ilva, Powertrain, Fiat
	CIGS: Special wages guarantee funds, applicable for a period from 12 to 24 months (IT): Indesit, ThyssenKrupp, New Case Holland
	Temporary lay-offs (S): Volvo, Scania
	Short-time working (NL): DAF-Trucks
	Maintaining workers' net salaries through establishment of company 'crisis funds' at Renault (FR)
	Work-sharing (DK): Danfos, Grundfos
Internal restructuring and reorganization (mobility procedures solidarity contracts)	*Mobility procedures, internal transfer of workers* (IT): Indesit, Telecom Italia, Powertrain, Fiat
	Solidarity contracts (IT): Telecom Italia, Italtel
Training programmes	Restructuring agreement:
	Agreement on training and compensation during partial unemployment (FR): PSA
	Job-saving agreement: Eon (DE)

Source: Eurofound (2009)

flexibility. The fragility of the institutional framework in the East and more especially the deficit of legal and collective agreements' regulation in terms of measures to safeguard employment explain this dynamic adjustment. A certain *laisser-faire* in the game of social regulation has been encouraged by the absence of a law on part-time unemployment (Hungary and Bulgaria are exceptions); the near-absence of collective branch or company agreements regulating working time and making it more flexible; the under-development of vocational training (excluded in fact from regulation by bargaining agreements); the weak presence of unions in greenfield, MNC subsidiaries.

In France, and more generally in Western Europe, collective bargaining has been the principle means the social partners have used to define and implement such adjustments.[10] In as far as managements have been careful to preserve a "hard core" of permanent jobs and skilled labour, there has been a convergence of interests which should facilitate the implementation of a "crisis compromise", along the lines of the "solidarity fund" financed by all staff at Renault SA, or via the implementation of multi-annual time budgets at PSA, which draw on employees' time savings accounts. It should be noted that internal flexibility has been used even more massively in Germany, where managements have mobilised agreements signed on flexible working hours in order to obtain cuts in working time with no financial compensation (Daimler, Bosch): wage cuts have even run to between 10 % and 20 % (Eurofound 2009).

Of interest here is the way in which States have been implicated in supporting different agreements established at company and sector level (see the Table 10.2).

In Western Europe, this support essentially takes the form of tripartite agreements, whereas in the new Member States governments have put into place new and valid measures, usually without conditions. In two cases, however, the relative length of financial compensations provided is surprisingly short, compensations that are often adopted in the name of job preservation.

Far from being paradoxical, this minimal implication of the State, which is decisive in the short term, is not without links to the game of relations identified above within the framework of the "managerial social dialogue". In continuation of this model, it is possible to view the "return" of the State as a "tactical" response to the adjustment demands of the model in the face of the economic and financial crisis.

– In Western Europe, financial support from the State for agreements and other "crisis compromises" have had the effect of transforming profoundly the relationship between employees to labour law and collective bargaining. In France in particular, the entire institutional framework governing employees' free time (time savings accounts, the 35-h week legislation, time bands, etc.) put into place before the financial crisis has been "turned round" by management to make it an instrument for managing staff, and beyond this a level for organising the development of new ways of mobilising labour in the long term.

– In Eastern Europe, while the State has contented itself with implementing simple rules to ward off the dangers of wage deflation, these interventions have not at the same time altered the terms of the socio-political compromise, which is largely governed by FDI and foreign indebtedness. On this, the survey shows that neither the relative spreads between wages in subsidiaries and those of

---

[10] The auto sector is an exception, to a certain extent. In France, for example, employment in the sector fell by 7 %, between December 2007 and March 2009. It fell by 49.3 % for temporary employment, which initially represented 10.2 % of all staff (DGCIS 2009). Similarly, in Germany, where the sector accounts for 860,000 jobs directly, adjustment of temporary employment also played a dominant role.

Table 10.2 Selected public support short-time working and temporary lay-off schemes addressing the recession

	Name	New or adapted?	Eligibility	Type and extent of support	Duration
France	Partial unemployment/ technical unemployment	Adapted	In the case of short-time working, all employees, including part-time workers, temporary agency workers and those on fixed-term employment contracts, if their employer has a decrease in sales of at least 50 %. In the case of temporary lay-off, all employees	The employer pays up to 75 % of the hourly gross wage for the hours not worked hours at a minimum of €6.84 an hour; the State pays SMEs €3.84 and large companies €3.33 per hour/per worker In case of a company closure of more than 3 months, employees are entitled to unemployment benefits	Six consecutive weeks –in total, 800 h per employee per year or 1,000 h in the textiles, clothing and leather industry and automotive industry
Germany	Short-time working, short-time work allowance	Adapted	All employees, including temporary agency workers (under certain conditions) and workers on fixed-term employment contracts, if their employer faces a decrease in earnings of at least 10 %	The government pays up to 67 % of the difference between the normal wage and the lower wage, as well as 50 % of the social security contributions for the hours not worked (100 % in case of training)	Maximum 24 months (if started in 2009)
Hungary		New	All employees	80 % of the last wage, up to 150 % of the national minimum wage; 80 % of training costs if provided by the employer	6–12 months
Rumania		New	All employees	Employers and employees are exempted from paying social security contributions; workers' pay during a	Maximum 3 months

(continued)

Table 10.2 (continued)

Name	New or adapted?	Eligibility	Type and extent of support	Duration
			temporary suspension of business is free of income tax	
Slovenia	New	All employees	Employees on temporary leave are entitled to 85 % of their average wage over the last 3 months: 50 % is funded by the state, the remaining 35 % by the employer	

Source: Eurofound (2009)

domestic companies (which systematically favour the former), nor the payments in-kind policy (social works) by subsidiaries have been affected for the time being.

In other words, the 2007 crisis has above all acted to reveal a mode of governance of the employment relationship, which is based locally on a neo-corporatist anchoring of MSD, which State action is unable to modify without first having a negotiated legitimacy with respect to unions and management. From this point of view, the MSD may constitute as a "socio-institutional system" which is original and complementary to established forms of social dialogue at the national level, on a tripartite basis. In its role as an interface with the public authorities, the MSD has the facility of organising a system of flexible and adjustable industrial relations according to local management and employment conditions within companies.

The assertion of a "Porterian State" in search of new institutional complementarities

Under the effect of capital mobility and MNCs' FDI, the distinctions between national and foreign, between internal and external are blurring. The frontiers of national spaces no longer coincide with productive systems, so that in both Eastern and Western Europe the internationalisation of company strategies raises fears of an "instrumentalisation" of geographic areas by company group managements. In this context, the economic role of the State has to transform itself, mainly by ensuring conditions making geographic areas attractive.

Under these conditions, it is understandable that most EU States have implemented policies which go beyond anti-crisis packages which aim to minimise job losses, in the short term. For example, it is possible to observe that among the panoply of tools of State intervention in Eastern Europe, public aid granted has less impact on direct support for employment (in the short term) within a defensive or protectionist logic, than do measures aiming to ensure the upgrading of the auto industry. The latter includes, in particular, aid aimed at developing green technologies or at the modernisation of capital equipment (Delteil and Dieuaide 2011). Similarly, in France, the signing of a Car Pact in February 2009 with companies in the industry – reinforced by the implementation of a Strategic Investment Fund and a Social Investment Fund – meets the same preoccupations of enhancing productive potential in labour and capital, of the different firms in the sector.

It is with respect to these new priorities that it is important to understand the shift in State action in the field of industrial relations, following the crisis that began in 2007. Compared with the past, the aim is less to implement a tripartite institutional framework and put into place rules for decentralising the social dialogue, but rather to align jobs on qualifications and cost standards required by the dynamics and orientation of technical change imposed at the world level. In France in particular, this turnaround is partly occurring by a (partial) challenge to a profit-sharing type of compromise, in favour of a clear hardening of types of flexibility and the mobilisation of employees at work. In Eastern Europe, where the upturn has taken place far more rapidly, this new situation appears to have led to an extension of company bargaining, in particular concerning working time (in the auto sector in particular). In any case, it seems that MSD no longer seems to be a tool for managing social relations within companies, but seems to be more a strategic tool for regulating technological, industrial and sectoral changes.

This new positioning of MSD suggests that States are seeking to establish the bases for new "institutional complementarities" at the heart of the system of industrial relations. B. Amable notes that, "generally speaking institutional complementarity stems from the interdependence of institutional influences on agents' decision-making processes" (Amable 2005, p. 83). In this area, it is a little early to measure the consequences of actions by public authorities on actors' strategies, with policy in the last 2 years underlying the attempt by governments to reconcile two types of constraints (or time frames):

- That of the market, which requires bringing company activities into phase with the diversity of national economic conditions;
- That of innovation and technical progress, which needs individuals to enrol in long term apprenticeship and training programmes.

In fact, the scale of the crisis has revealed that if it is not the opportunity but the urgency of building a new socio-political compromise around a complete and sustainable model of flexisecurity.[11] There are numerous difficulties for moving

---

[11] For B. Amable (2005, p. 342), *"There is a space for training in the socio-political bloc, grounded in a series of compromises between major industrial employers and unions, by favouring a renewed continental model. This model allows for greater flexibility of employment in exchange for social protection extended to a more universal model..."*

forward in this direction. In particular, given economic nationalism, it will be necessary for State policies that attract business to be coordinated at the level of the EU, or even reinforced by the intervention of the Commission. However, experience in this field is not encouraging, as has been seen in the auto sector:
- The "crisis compromises" supporting the sector and employment have had to cope with the leanings of Community competition policy, which has led certain targeted aid measures to be annulled (in the new Member States), or which has prohibited the explicit and constraining nature of guarantees for keeping jobs within countries (the French case).
- In the East, the rapid return to restrictive fiscal policies, along with the demands by the international institutions, relayed by the EU and pushing for deregulation of the labour market are not without risk for the consolidation of a triptych based on "industrial policy, employment policy and industrial relations policy" which was born out of the crisis.

10.4 Conclusion

To sum up these ideas, two main lessons may be drawn from the survey:
- The process of transnationalisation and financialisation of companies has weighed strongly on the restructuring of the framework and practices of industrial relations. In the pre-crisis dynamics, the State tended to accompany this movement, by looking to stabilise the various socio-political compromises established to the benefit of companies, at an institutional level. The notion of a Managerial Social Dialogue expresses this particular, socio-political equilibrium at the local level.
- The second lesson relates to the re-dimensioning of the field of industrial relations which follows from the profound renovation of the institutional framework spurred on by State policies since the eruption of the crisis. In France, extrapolating the trends observed in the auto sector, an institutional conversion in the State's place and role towards a more strategic function serving industrial policy seems to be taking place. In Eastern Europe, though the goal of *laisser-faire* still seems to exist at the level of the organisation and functioning of national labour markets, the State has become more interventionist in industry.

The results need to be supported further, especially by field studies that will provide more detail about the conditions and methods under which social dialogue is conducted in firms. From a theoretical point of view, it underlines the necessity of moving towards a deepening of the frameworks of analysis mobilised in the field of industrial relations studies. The concepts of a Managerial Social Dialogue and a Porterian State could contribute to this.

References

Amable B (2005) Les cinq capitalismes: Diversité des systèmes économiques et sociaux dans la mondialisation. Ed. du Seuil, Paris

Bohle D, Greskovits B (2006) Capital, labor and the prospects of the European social model in the east. Center for European Studies Central and Eastern Europe working paper, no. 58. 33 p

Centre d'Analyse Stratégiques (2011) Participation des salariés et performance sociale : de nouveaux enjeux pour les entreprises françaises dans un contexte de sortie de crise. Notes d'analyse, no. 210, janvier

Contrepois S, Delteil V, Dieuaide P, Jefferys S (eds) (2011) Globalising employment relations? Multinational corporations and Central and Eastern Europe transitions. Palgrave Mac-Millan, Londres, 251 p

Dares (2010) Participation, intéressement, épargne salariale en 2008. Analyses, no. 071, Oct 2010

Delteil V, Dieuaide P (2011) French MNCs, managerial social dialogue, and the reconfiguration of industrial relations in Times of Crisis: the exemplary case of the automotive industry. In: Multinational companies, global value chains and social regulation, international conference. HEC, Montréal, 6–7 and 8 June

DGCIS (2009) La contraction de l'emploi de la fin 2008 s'accentue début 2009, Le Quatre pages de la Direction Générale de la Compétitivité de l'Industrie et des Services, no 4, juin

Dunlop JT (1993) Industrial relations systems. Harvard Business School, Boston

Edwards T, Colling T, Ferner A (2007) Conceptual approaches to the transfer of employment practices in MNC: an integrated approach. Hum Resour Manag J 17(3):201–217

Eurofound (2009) Restructuring in recession. ERM Report. 148 p

Katz H, Kochan T, Mc Kersie R (1986) The transformation of American industrial relations. Basic Books, New York

Katz HC, Kochan TA, Colvin A (2008) An introduction to collective bargaining industrial relations. Mc Graw-Hill International Edition, Boston

Lallement M (2007) Le travail, Une sociologie contemporaine. Gallimard, Paris

Lallement M, Mériaux O (2001) Tout n'est pas contractuel dans le contrat.... Relations professionnelles et actions publiques á l'heure de la refondation sociale, Année de la Régulation, n° 5, pp 171–210. http://webcom.upmf-grenoble.fr/regulation/Annee_regulation/AR5-2001-05LALLEMENT-MERIAUX.pdf

Michalet C-A (2007) Mondialisation, la grande rupture. Economica, Paris

Newson B (2009) Recession in the EU-27: length and depth of the downturn varies across activities and countries. Eurostat, Statistics in Focus, p 97. http://epp.eurostat.ec.europa.eu/cache/ITY_OFFPUB/KS-SF-09-097/EN/KS-SF-09-097-EN.PDF

Rugraff E (2006) Firmes multinationales et relations industrielles en Europe centrale. Relat Ind 61 (3):437–462

Vincent A (2010) PECO: la convergence à l'épreuve de la crise. Bulletin de conjoncture BNP-Paribas, janvier. http://economic-research.bnpparibas.com/Views/DisplayPublication.aspx?type=document&IdPdf=17652. Consulté le 1 Dec 2013

Part IV
Reshaping Industrial Relations and Labour Activism in Multinational Companies

11 Guangdong Economic Rebalancing and Its Implication for the Labor Market

Stéphane Cieniewski

Guangdong is now at a cross-road. Its ambitions to serve as a testing ground and to lead the way to the rebalancing and modernization of China's economy are high but international experiences show that public money is not a reliable yard stick of success. Public intervention cannot succeed without heeding market forces and in the case of Guangdong, those market forces are particularly strong: cost pressure is intense, final demand for the export-oriented industry is plummeting, legal environment is changing fast (environmental constraints, new labor laws, etc.) and financing constraints are tougher than ever, especially for private companies that account for most of the provincial output. Against that backdrop, advocating for more innovation and R&D and for better labor conditions and higher wages is not an easy task. On the other hand, providing state-of-the-art industrial parks and fiscal incentives may not work as well as before: as an example, the OECD calculates that only 8 of the 28 relocation parks earmarked by the double-relocation policy are within a 2-h drive of the strategic hub that gives access to export markets.

Since its early success in the 1980s, Guangdong has always relied on foreign capital and technical know-how to develop its economy. This remains truer than ever as the province aims at new specializations in high tech industries and high value added services. However this time a new issue is making the task even more complicated, i.e. the availability of skilled labor force. Considering that the average technical education of migrants is higher than the non-migrants average in Guangdong, the change of labor migration patterns within China is becoming a

---

Stéphane Cieniewski has over 12 years of experience as an economist covering emerging markets and most of all China. He is currently head of the economic department of the Consulate General of France in Hong Kong and Macau. This article was not written in his official capacity and therefore does not necessarily reflect the views or opinions of the French administration or the French government. Any view or opinions presented in this article are solely those of the author.

S. Cieniewski (✉)
Consulate General of France in Hong Kong and Macao, Hong Kong, PRC
e-mail: stephane.cieniewski@dgtresor.gouv.fr

headache for what was once an irresistible magnet for any would-be job-seeker in China. That is why Guangdong is at the forefront of the modernization of labor laws in China and that is why it is especially interesting to follow the latest development taking place there.

11.1 Guangdong or the Vanguard of China's Economic Development

11.1.1 Guangdong, Symbol and Limits of China's Economic Miracle

Since the start of the opening and reform era in 1979, the Guangdong province has always been in the vanguard of the Chinese economy. Thus it has lead the way in shaping the policies that aim to attract foreign capital and to develop export oriented manufacturing industry and became the symbol of the success of the Chinese model. At one point, its dominance over the Chinese industry seemed unchallengeable: for example in 1990, it accounted for 42 % of total Foreign Direct Investments (FDI) inflows dominant region and for 56 % of total exports in 1993. However, after having played for many years a leading role in the design and implementation of Chinese industrial and commercial policies, the Guangdong has started to lose its edge. Soon after China has entered the WTO in 2001, a new industrial core quickly emerged at the forefront, notably in the Yangtze River Delta (around Shanghai) and to a lesser extent in the Bohai Rim (around Beijing and Tianjin); whereas South China has become more and more constrained by its own deficiencies. The two graphs below indicate how Yangtze River Delta's economic weight has steadily increased over the past 15 years and is now overshadowing Guangdong: from 25 % to 50 % of China's incoming FDI and from 20 % to 40 % of China's exports (Figs. 11.1 and 11.2).

Indeed, after having enjoyed the benefits of catching-up for a long period of time, thanks to massive inflows of foreign capital and having dramatically improved its productivity through economies of scale, the Guangdong province began to realize that its development model was heavily unbalanced and that congestions costs had turned economies of scale into diseconomies. With the world economic crisis in 2008 also came the realization that this province's extreme exposure to world demand could also, at times, become a painful liability – Guangdong was indeed the most affected province by the slowdown of international trade, unable to mitigate the decline of exports' demand but domestic consumption. Of course, all of this did not prevent Guangdong from growing and remaining one of the most developed Chinese regions. However, it has clearly lost some of its clout to the benefit of the Yangtze River Delta (YRD), which has become the new poster child of China Inc. While Guangdong's share of national GDP increased from 7.1 % in 1990 to 12.5 % in 2007, YRD's jumped from 15.5 % to 22.7 % over the same period (see graph below). More importantly, YRD has replaced Guangdong as China's leader in attracting FDI, with Jiangsu province (which is part of YRD, along with Shanghai and Zhejiang province) alone

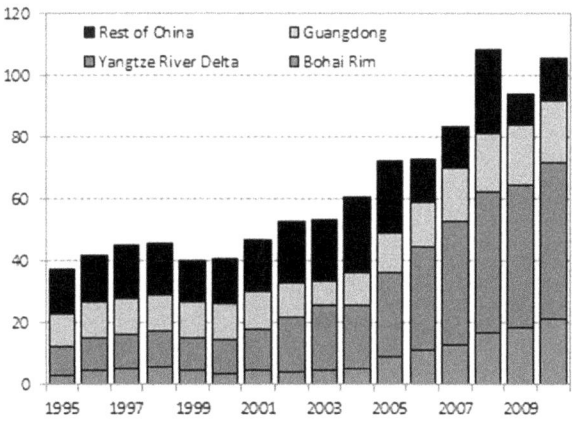

Fig. 11.1 FDI inflows in China (in RMB b.). * Bohai Rim = Beijing + Tianjian + Hebei/Yangtze River Delta = Shanghai + Zhejiang + Jiangsu

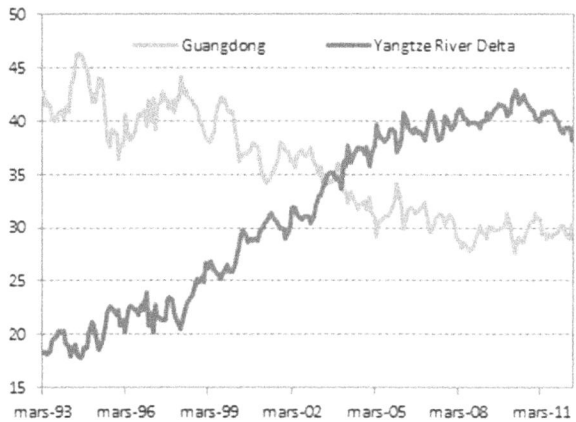

Fig. 11.2 Main exporting regions (as a % share of China's exports). (Source: CEIC)

outpacing Guangdong over the last few years. Likewise, with new foreign firms seeking to enter higher value-added and more capital-intensive markets, which prefer to invest in YRD, Guangdong's average productivity per capita was overtaken by YRD's. That is why in 2007, Guangdong was no longer the richest province of China but stood second to YRD, with an average GDP per capita of 33,000 CNY against 39,000 CNY for YRD (see Figs. 11.3 and 11.4 below).

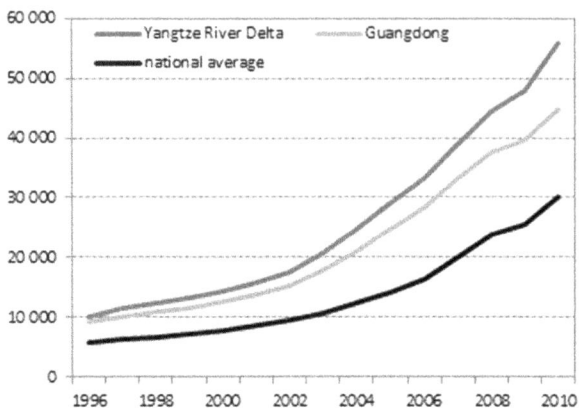

Fig. 11.3 GDP per capita (in CNY). * Bohai Rim = Beijing + Tianjin + Hebei/Yangzi River Delta = Shanghai + Zhejiang + Jiangsu

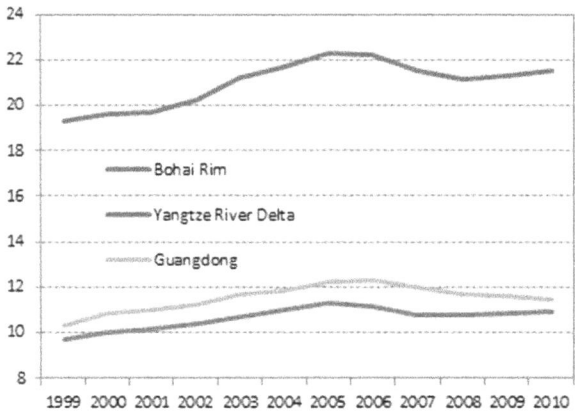

Fig. 11.4 Main economic regions (as a % share of national GDP). (Source: CEIC)

This declining influence under internal competition was somehow epitomized by the 11th Five Years Plan (FYP) 2006–2010, which did not even mention the Guangdong nor its more dynamic sub-region, the Pearl River Delta (PRD) among the national priorities in its chapter on "Promoting Balanced Regional Development". The contrast could not have been starker with the last visit of President HU Jintao, in 2003, when Guangdong was designated as the "leading pilot" in the national process of becoming a "xiaokang" society, i.e. a modern society in which economic advancement is not the sole focus of the society. By 2006, however, the biggest flaws of the Guangdong model had become apparent: most of the local production was related to low added value processing trade and most of the innovation and R&D were restricted to foreign multinationals (Huawei being the notable exception – being the largest applicant of patents worldwide ahead of

Philips, it accounts alone for more than half of provincial patents). Another obvious hurdle on the way to the "xiaokang" society is the extraordinary level of social inequalities within Guangdong itself. Indeed, with a Gini index of 0.4, Guangdong has one of the highest intra-provincial inequality rate among China's provinces, the Northern Region of Guangdong being one of the poorest districts of China whereas the Southern Region, i.e. the PRD of close proximity to Hong Kong SAR, is one of the richest.

11.1.2 An Official Ambitious Response: The Double Relocation Policy

By 2007, economic difficulties became serious and the implementation of the 11th FYP began to lose momentum. Hence the central government chose to make the PRD a national priority again through the "Outline for the Plan for the Reform and Development of the PRD region 2008–2020" (or "Outline for PRD"). The importance of this document cannot be overstressed since it is the first time in China's history that the State Council issued a sub-provincial regional development strategy. Of course it did not imply that decision making power of the Guangdong province itself was diminished. Quite the contrary: the Guangdong provincial government was given an explicit mandate for experimentation and reforms. Within the framework of the "Outline for PRD", Guangdong is expected to play the role of a "pilot region for further reforms" and "an experimental region for the pattern of scientific development". Like always in China, this strategy includes quantitative targets: per capita GDP should reach 80,000 CNY by 2012 and 135,000 CNY by 2020 (meaning a compounded annual growth rate of 19 % and 11 % respectively).

But the most important content hinges on more unusual objectives, especially for Guangdong. Indeed the strategy stressed the importance of introducing higher value-added industries, including modern services sectors (e.g. finance, logistics), advanced manufacturing sectors (e.g. automotive and petro-chemicals), high-tech sectors (e.g. electronic communications and biotech industries) while keeping the traditional sectors competitive (e.g. textile and footwear). According to the "Outline for PRD", such modern services and advanced manufacturing sectors should account for 60 % of service sector growth and 50 % of industrial sector growth respectively. By 2012, R&D expenses should reach 2.5 % of provincial GDP (compared with 1.41 % in 2008) and the total number of researchers should reach 280,000. From a social development perspective, specific targets have also been assigned: by 2020, the pension system is to cover 95 % of urban workers, 80 % of migrant workers and 60 % of rural residents.

How to achieve those ambitious objectives? An important part of the plan relies on the "Double Relocation" policy (DRP), whose double aim is to foster a more evenly spread economic development among Guangdong sub-region and, at the same time, facilitate the upgrading from low value-added to high-value added industries in the core sub-region, i.e. PRD. In other words, the Double Relocation

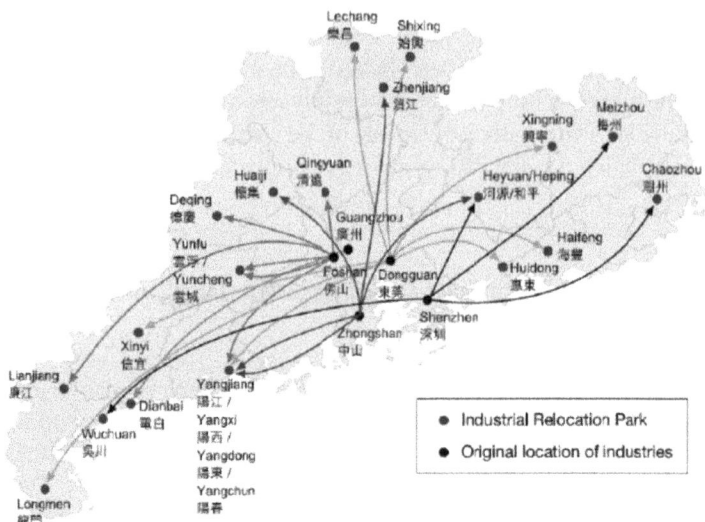

Fig. 11.5 Sending and receiving locations of "Double Relocation" policy (Source: Li and Fung (2008), in *OECD Territorial Review*, p.158)

policy is to kill two birds with one stone by: 1/moving the labor-intensive, resource-consuming and polluting industries from the central PRD to less developed areas, such as northern Guangdong, western and eastern PRD; 2/favoring the relocation of labor from agriculture to secondary and tertiary sectors and gather the skilled labor force in central PRD in other to support the emergence of higher value-added industries and services (Figs. 11.5).

As such, the "Double Relocation" Policy is a very ambitious effort, and the first of its kind in China, to directly address the issues frequently associated to the "Chinese Economic Model"; such as urban sprawling, environmental damage, social inequalities and more generally congestion costs derived from chaotic and uncontrolled development. Indeed the intended effects include a reduction of the demand for land resources, an easing of environmental pressures in the already industrialized areas as well as upgrading the quality of human resources (by delocalizing lower skilled people to lagging regions and attracting higher skilled laborers from other provinces). Some researchers have dubbed this plan as "emptying the nest for new birds" (Huang, quoted by OECD). On the ground, the main tool of the DRP is the creation of industrial parks in the lagging regions (for which RMB 40 b. of public investment has been earmarked over 2008–2012) and the promotion of education and skills training with a focus on migrant workers which are the backbone of the Guangdong industry.

The rapid development of the Guangdong automotive industry (which share in provincial industrial output grew from 1.8 % in 2000 to 4 % in 2008 thanks to the implantation of Japanese manufacturers such as Honda, Toyota and Nissan) proves that it is possible to develop new sustainable and competitive industries by providing the right incentives and creating a favorable ecosystem for those businesses. Shenzhen, the border city to Hong Kong Special Administrative Region (SAR) and the Guangdong district with the highest GDP per capita both in the province and in the whole of Mainland China, has already attracted notable investments from leading high-tech multinationals such as IBM, Siemens, Samsung and Hitachi. The city produces about 20 % of China's computers, 15 % of semiconductor integrated circuits and it ranks first in the sales of printers and liquid crystal displays. No matter how important it seems for the official blueprint to focus on local capacities and local innovation capabilities, the Guangdong authorities' attitude is shaped by this habit on relying on foreign input. For instance, the Guangdong Financial Innovation Service Zone has set the following targets for investment attraction over 2008–2012: 5 regional HQ of financial institutions, 20 financial institutions performing back office services, 8 manufacturers producing financial electronic equipment, etc.

11.1.3 Once Again, the Decisive Role of Hong Kong's Expertise and Support?

For obvious reasons, Chinese authorities expect Hong Kong to once again play a unique role, not only as a bridge to foreign capital and foreign markets (as it has successfully done so for the last 30 years) but as a bridge to foreign talent and foreign technology. Indeed, Hong Kong entrepreneurs have led the industrialization of the Guangdong province right from the start of the open door policy in the early 1980s, notably in low to middle-value consumer goods such as watches, consumer electronic goods, toys and other plastic products. Although their share in total exports has now begun to slightly decrease since the mid-2000s, foreign invested companies still account for around 60 % of Guangdong exports, higher than the national average of 50 %. Among those, Hong Kong invested companies alone are estimated to be around 60,000 and employ more than 10 million people.

However, the truth is that Hong Kong and PRD economies are relatively less integrated and that cross-borders flows of labor and intermediate goods are not as important as what could be suggested by the above figure. In order to increase the reach and the depth of foreign investors and especially Hong Kong investors in Guangdong, local authorities have therefore laid out a very ambitious plan of transport infrastructures build-up on the 2030 horizon. The focus is two-fold: 1/increasing the high-speed roads density all over the Guangdong province and partially close the gap between the outer districts whose networks is far behind those of the PRD region 2/setting up two rail transit systems, across the inner PRD and along a Guangzhou-Shenzhen-Hong Kong axis respectively. The idea is basically to increase the accessibility of the major industrial centers within the PRD region and especially to increase the accessibility to cheaper industrial locations and input markets for Hong Kong SAR. This plan is part of a wider MOU between Hong Kong SAR and Guangdong, which was signed in 2010 in Beijing, in front of the Vice-President XI Jinping and whose later inclusion in the 12th FYP

(2011–2015) clearly demonstrates how strategic it is for the economic rebalancing of China (which will probably be dubbed as the official motto of the incoming government).

Although Hong Kong's innovation has long been neglected and its R&D intensity is only one third of the rate of Singapore (0.81 % compared to 2.4 %), the SAR has unique advantages in attracting high quality researchers, including a pool of highly qualified scientists and top-ranked universities. Its ability to attract Chinese expatriates also provides considerable leverage for tapping highly qualified and internationally competitive talents. The Shenzhen – Hong Kong innovation circle is a clear demonstration of the benefits of such a partnership, in which Hong Kong provides the R&D capabilities and Guangdong provides the manufacturing base. For example, within this framework (which covers 24 co-operation projects), Dupont Apollo managed to set up its Thin Film Photovoltaic Business with the help of both governments. It sets up its R&D center in Hong Kong and its manufacturing facility in Shenzhen, thus planting the seed for a strong Solar Energy Research and Industrial Platform in the region.

11.2 Guangdong: Leading the Way for the Reform and Upgrading of China's Labor Market

11.2.1 The Unsustainable Labour Intensive Economic Model

Labor stands right at the center of China's economic model and therefore its reform is key to the rebalancing of the economy that Guangdong authorities are striving for. Indeed, without highly skilled and professionally trained labor force, how could it be possible to move up in the value chain? And without highly productive and highly paid employees, how could it be possible to enhance the domestic demand and thus correct the over-reliance on the export-oriented manufacturing. Part of the answer comes from the enhancement of labor supply through increased investment in education: this is already happening (spending on education increased in Guangdong from 11.7 % of total government expenditure in 1999 to 18.2 % in 2007) but with results still lagging behind. Contrary to Beijing and Shanghai, Guangdong is not particularly well-known for its emphasis on higher education and this translates still today in a ratio of 55 tertiary educated people per 1,000 inhabitants, much lower than the national average (62/1,000). That is why the OECD underlines that human capital is probably one of the most important challenges for Guangdong and that closing the gap with Beijing/Shanghai should be top priority.

Another way to address this issue is to attract larger number of migrant workers from other provinces, or at least migrants with more qualified skills (higher secondary/technical school). Everywhere in China, migrant workers are running the most dynamic components of the economy: they are estimated about 150 million in 2009, accounting for 40 % of urban employment, and even 80 % in construction and 68 % in manufacture. In Guangdong alone, they could be around 30 million by some estimates, i.e. roughly one quarter of total population. Although attracting qualified workers seems in theory easier than training them, the experience suggests that in a very fragmented and opaque labor market such as China, this is absolutely not the case. Indeed labor shortages have appeared in Guangdong since 2004 and with the brief exception of the impact of the global crisis which led to massive lay-offs in late 2008/early 2009, they have kept deteriorating. The fact that some regions such as the Yangtze River Delta have become more successful than Guangdong in attracting and keeping migrants demonstrates that this trend cannot be explained only by the demographic transition and involves on the contrary, a wide array of factors, deeply embedded in the so-called China model that epitomizes Guangdong. In other words, reforming Guangdong economy is inseparable from reforming its labor market.

First we need to understand that the living conditions and the status of migrant workers have far reaching implications that go well beyond the regulation of the labor market and reflect on the whole Chinese social and political structure. Thanks to what can be considered as extreme coercive measures (no right to strike, no workers' union outside of the realm of CCP and constraint of the freedom of movement by a kind of internal passport, the famous Hukou), there is no room for the matching of supply and demand of labor through market forces. What we have instead is a two-tiered society, in which the migrant worker originating from the rural areas (or Mingong for "farmer worker") is in some ways playing the role of immigrants or worse, illegal immigrants in the some other countries. This new class has grown at the same rhythm of Chinese economy, from two million people in 1978 to roughly 150 million in 2009 and accounts for most of the workforce in the export-oriented manufacturing sector which has made China such a powerful industrial nation.

De facto, migrant workers are treated as second class citizens and do not have access to the same opportunities : according to the 2005 census, about 90 % of them are working in the private sector, leaving the best paid jobs in administration and State-Owned-Enterprises (SOE) to local people, of which only 12 % work for the private sector. Although they are legally entitled to the same protection provided by the labor laws, various field studies have pointed to all kind of abuses that are invited by their precarious status, just like it would for illegal immigrants in any other country: 75 % do not have a proper employment contract and 80 % are paid below the minimum wage. According to official statistics themselves, 6 % of migrants are affected by wage arrears. Even after accounting for age and education (only 2 % of migrants have tertiary education), those wide inequalities in the access to white collar jobs cannot be fully explained without raising the issue of social discrimination. The new Labor Law, enacted in 2008, entitles migrants with new rights (such as the right to a labor contract and the interdiction of forced overtime) and new ways to lodge a protest against unfair and unlawful treatment. However, considering the mediocre track record of the previous labor law, it would be premature and over-optimistic to consider that legal reforms are enough to change deeply rooted habits and mentalities (Figs. 11.6 and 11.7).

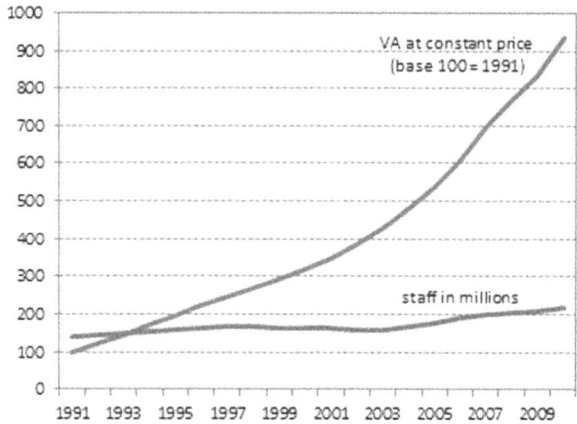

Fig. 11.6 Industrial output and employment in China

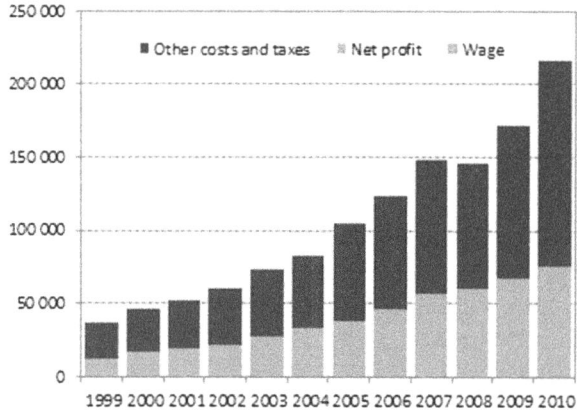

Fig. 11.7 Wages and profits in China's industry (in RMB per employee) (Source: CEIC – SE Hong Kong)

On the social front, such a fragmented labor market translates into record-breaking and persistent inequalities (the OECD estimates the Gini Index around 0.4 in 2007 against 0.22 in 1985). Even in Guangdong, the core of the China export-oriented manufacturing industry, where 40 % of total migrant population lives, income disparities between the PRD districts and the outer districts are as wide as nationwide between the richest and poorest provinces.

On the macroeconomic front, this two tiered society also illustrates the biased sharing of the national income in favor of capital and to the detriment of labor. According to the Chinese Academy of Social Sciences, migrant workers' wages have increased on average by 5–6 % per annum between 2000 and 2007, against 16 % on average in the SOEs alone. Considering that the nominal GDP has grown by 15 % per year over the same period of time, it means that only the most privileged class of employees, that is the resident urban population working for the public sector, can claim its fair share of the economic growth whereas the rest and especially the migrant workers receive much less than their contribution to productivity gains.

As demonstrated by the above graphs, those productivity gains have indeed been huge (roughly 500 % compounded growth in 20 years) but that the lion share has gone to the capital owners, as net profit. Indeed the industrial companies' total profit is currently 30 % higher than their total salary cost whereas it was 10 % smaller 10 years ago. Deutsche Bank thus estimates that industrial profits have grown by 28 % per year on average between 2000 and 2008 against 14 % for industrial wages. Of course the deficiencies of the labor market cannot alone explain why industrial profits have surged from 2 % to 12 % of China's GDP between 1998 and 2011. In fact profits are very unequally shared between on the one hand capital-intensive enterprises, generally state-owned and specialized in very profitable businesses such as commodities, energy and heavy equipment and on the other hand labor-intensive enterprises that are export-oriented and under intense pressure from international competition.

The implications of this unequal sharing of factor incomes between labor and capital cannot be overstressed. It goes far beyond issues of fairness or economic optimum and epitomizes all the excesses of China's economic model. As an example, the overreliance on exports and foreign exchange reserves is closely linked to the relative lack of private consumption, which does not follow from an excessive personal saving rate but from insufficient income. The graph below clearly shows how the households' income and consumption have declined almost along parallel lines over the last 10 years: the former from 55 % to 45 % of GDP and the later from 45 % to 35 % (Figs. 11.8 and 11.9).

The toughest question of all remains: Are income inequalities so bad that the average household does not even enjoy a steady increase of its real purchasing power? In other words, are the fruits of growth so unequally shared that a sensible part of the population does not benefit at all from the so-called China's economic miracle? The shortcomings of labor and income statistics are too serious and widely spread to enable an informed and reliable answer. To our knowledge, only two economists have managed to build credible estimates of the "true" labor and wages figures: Judith Banister of the US Bureau of Labor Statistics (but only for the year 2002) and Stephen Green of Standard Chartered, who has extrapolated her work to more recent years. Their estimate of urban salaries is both much lower than official figures (around 150 USD per month in 2006) and growing much more slowly (about 10 % nominal growth and 6–7 % real growth over 2003–2008). In theory, migrant workers should have enjoyed the slightly higher growth of the minimum wage, which is 10–13 % per year between 2003 and 2008 depending on provinces. However, field studies show that despite the acceleration of income growth since 2005 (first signs of labor shortages in the south), they have difficulties to keep up with the cost-of-living inflation (especially the food and housing components).

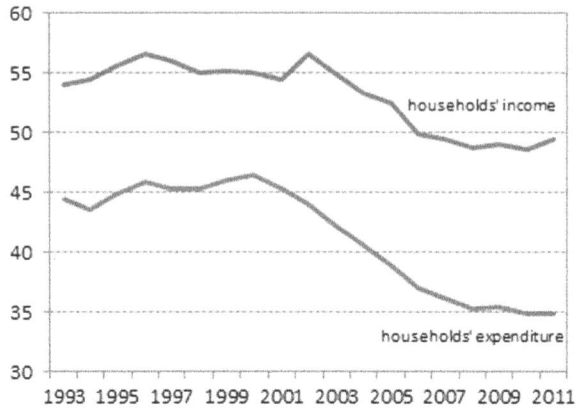

Fig. 11.8 Households' revenue in China (as a % share of GDP)

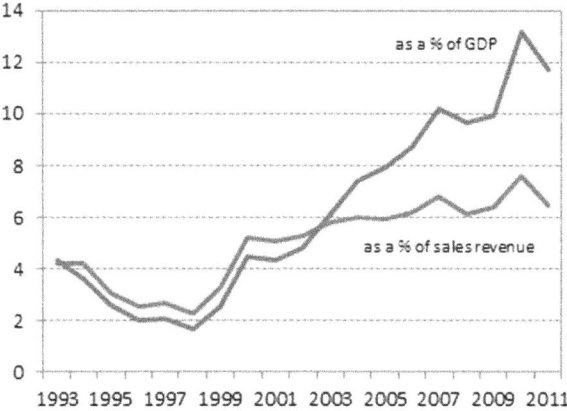

Fig. 11.9 Industrial enterprises total profit in China (Source: CEIC – SE Hong Kong)

11.2.2 Unbalances Lead to the Surge of Labor Conflicts

In any other country, all of the above should be more than enough to provoke skyrocketing labor disputes but there is more: the intensification of labor shortages and the coming of a new generation of workers (the so called 1980s generation) whose goals and psychology could not have been more different from their elders'.

Since 2004 labor shortages have become a recurring feature of China's main industrial centers, in the Yangtze River Delta and the Pearl River Delta. This at first unexpected phenomenon has provoked a dispute in academic circles about the extent of the demographic slowdown. As far as population census can be relied upon, there is no doubt that the working age population is still growing, although we are now very close to the inflexion point (see graph below). More relevant, however, is the breakdown between rural and urban population and the willingness of rural workers to migrate to the urban industrial centers. Indeed, as we have seen above, the Chinese labor market is very fragmented and cannot be understood with simple and crude tools such as demographics. Given the huge productivity gap between farming sector and non-agricultural business (from 1 to 6), Standard Chartered for example estimates that there remains a potential surplus of 50–85 million farmers out of a total of 200–235 million people, which according to their age structure and migration pattern could feed the current trend of rural exodus until 2013–2016 (Figs. 11.10 and 11.11).

Around this medium term trend, the market can go through short term upside or downside adjustments, as seen during the 2009 economic crisis (when migrants where packed in trains by the 100,000 s and then sent back home, sometimes under the supervision of the PLA) and more recently during the upturn of the manufacturing sector in 2010–2011 (with the comeback and intensification of the labor shortages) – see graph above. Overall, the fact remains that migrant labor supply is becoming scarcer and scarcer and that the ratio of jobs' supply to demand is now diverging above the one threshold.

On top of that, the new generation of young workers, the so called 1980s generation, features new inspirations and life ambitions : they wish to settle down in the city contrary to their elder which could accommodate living 10 years in promiscuous collective dormitories before returning to their village. This means they want more free time, more autonomy and are more sensitive to the cost of living (especially housing and food, their two main expenditures). As workers, it means they do not simply aim at the maximization of their income no matter the working conditions and the overtime they have to endure: a balance with the quality of life is becoming relevant whereas saving as much as possible and supporting the family back home is seen as a thing from the past (let us not forget those are single children, who are in fact supported by two parents and four grandparents). All of this make them more reluctant to move by several thousand kilometers and settle in the industrial clusters along the Eastern Coast (whose higher wages are mitigated by higher cost of living and greater distance from the family).

The 2009 crisis may have signaled a turning point in that regard: among the 70 million workers that went back home to celebrate the Chinese New Year 2009, only 80 % have then come back to work on Eastern Coast provinces. As a consequence, the weight of migrant workers in labor intensive industries has decreased by 8 % points between 2008 and 2009. Compared with the YRD, which enjoys a better reputation for labor conditions and career prospects, the PRD has paid the heaviest toll and lost 25 % of its migrant population in 2009 (against an average fall of 20 % for all the coastal provinces). Those rapid changes benefited from the massive 2009 stimulus plan which in the Western provinces led to massive spending in civil works and agricultural infrastructure. Hence the Ministry for Human Resources and Social Security reports that in 2009 the demand

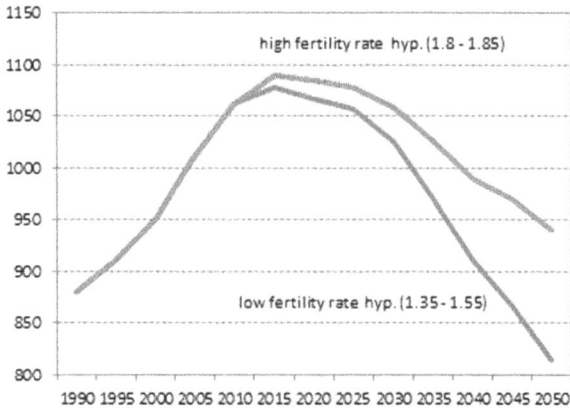

Fig. 11.10 Working age population in China (in millions) (Source: UNDP)

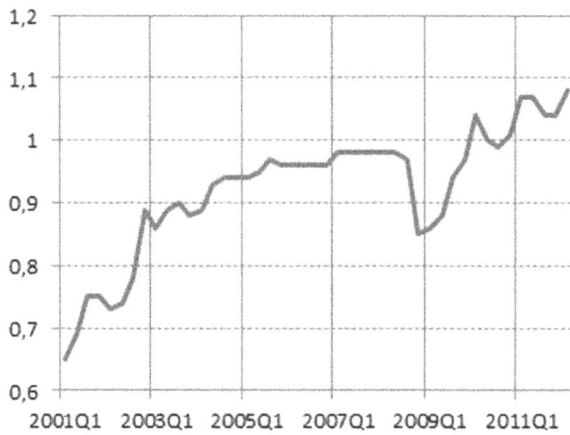

Fig. 11.11 Jobs supply/demand ratio in the main Chinese cities (Source: CEIC – Calculs: SE Hong Kong)

for labor increased by 16 % in Western provinces whereas it remained flat in the Eastern provinces. By the same token, the number of migrant workers in Central and Western provinces increased by 30 % between 2008 and 2009. In other words, the geography of rural migration is radically changing.

All of the above-mentioned factors (unequal sharing of the fruits of growth, apparition and intensification of labor shortages in the traditional manufacturing centers and generational change among migrant workers) are responsible for much more confrontational relations between employees and employers, as illustrated by the surge of labor disputes. To be fair, the central authorities may have themselves contributed and maybe even indirectly encouraged those conflicts when reforming the labor law and publicizing the new rights it granted the workers (such as a formal labor contract and the minimum wage). But a radical change came from the dramatic protest movements of the 2010 spring, such a string of suicides in Foxconn Guangdong factories or a collective strike movement, organized outside of and even against official workers' union, in Honda YRD factories. Actually the shock generated by those events was all the more reverberating across the whole country than, for the first time, newspapers were allowed to provide coverage and report those stories within China itself (at least for a couple of weeks, before the CCP decided a media blackout in late May 2010).

Although it has now become much more difficult to keep track of labor movements and strikes in Guangdong factories, there is no doubt that the increase of labor disputes is a structural trend which gives no sign of abating, all the more since the balance of power is now slowly but surely tilting in favor of labor against capital.

The latest and 4th edition of the China Labor Bulletin, edited by the eponym Hong Kong NGO and subtitled "Unity is Strength – The Workers' Movement in China 2009–2011" estimates that one third of mass protests (so called "mass incidents") are now related to labor disputes, whereas in the past most of them came from land disputes. The table below illustrates how labor disputes (as managed through formal channels such as arbitration and mediation committees) have more than doubled between 2007 and 2010, which signals both a problem of labor conditions and labor relations but also an increased self-awareness of the workers, which now do not hesitate to initiate legal actions and then go all the way through the possible appeals.

	Earliest available data	2007	2008	2009	2010
"mass incidents", of which:	**10,000** (1994)	n.a.	n.a.	**124,000**	**90,000**
Related to labor conditions (est.)	n.a.	n.a.	n.a.	n.a.	*30,000*
Labor disputes as treated but relevant institutions, of which:	n.a.	608,255	n.a.	1,236,748	1,287,400
Arbitration committees	47,951 (*1996*)	*350,182*	*693,000*	*684,000*	*602,600*
Mediation committees	31,747 (*1999*)	*258,073*		*552,748*	*684,800*

Source: China Labor Bulletin (from official statistics)

Although we lack reliable figures on strikes, the available statistics stemming from arbitration and mediation committees demonstrates that most actions are triggered by compensation issues: 52 % to be precise, of which 35 % relate to the regular wage and 22 % to contract termination. Such a level of dissatisfaction may surprise considering that the minimum wage has increased by 75 % in the main industrial clusters over 2006–2011 (i.e. around 12 % per year on average), which is no doubt higher than official price inflation whose compound growth is 20 % over the same period. The problem is that, once again, such an analysis does not reflect

the sometimes huge discrepancy between what is supposed to happen and what really happens on the ground:
- Public authorities themselves do not have a clear picture of what is exactly going on in the hundreds of thousands factories that populate China, partly because of the obsolescence of the statistical system and partly because of the open discrimination against migrant workers, which justifies the relative lack of data. Thus, according to a manager from the ACFTU quoted by CLB, 20 % of all workers have not received any pay increase over the past 5 years – in blatant contradiction with official data;
- The intensifying pressure on companies' margins since 2009 has also translated into intensifying pressure on the workers themselves. After having frozen for 1 year the minimum wage at its 2008 level in order to preserve the margins of their companies, the local authorities have been quick to acknowledge that the situation has dramatically reversed and they must now compete with each other not only by offering whole package of fiscal incentives but also by attracting sufficient migrant workers through highly publicized minimum wage increase (now twice a year in some provinces such as Guangdong, with an average annual growth rate exceeding 15 % in 2010 and 2011). Against that backdrop, firms had better to improve as much as possible the productivity of their workers: intensification of output rate, reduction of bonus and other advantages in kind, reduction of overtime (which are relatively better paid and thus more expensive for the employers), and even decrease of piecework pay (which is very widespread in some sector such as clothing industry).

Putting altogether this evidence, CLB doubts that for many workers the real purchasing power has seen any improvement at all over the last few years in spite of the impressive official minimum wage increases of more than 15 % per year.

11.2.3 New Local Experiments to Improve the Level Playing Field of China's Labor Market

There is no doubt that correcting the many biases of China's labor market and making it a more leveled playing field will take some time, even by China's standards of fast paced change. But although it may take a few more years and probably more tweaking of the current labor law in order to facilitate labor dispute resolutions and find a better wage-setting mechanism, new encouraging experimentations are already emerging to pave way for quicker solutions. Once again, Guangdong is leading the way as a testing ground, both out of necessity (it is the most affected province by labor shortages and margin deterioration) and out of political impetus (according to the 12th five-year plan, it has to lead the way of China's economy rebalancing).

Some of those reforms relate to the Hukou registration system: for example Guangdong is the first province to have relaxed its requirements for migrants to obtain permanent residency through quotas linked to a points system (various criteria such as age, education and wealth translate into a certain amount of points).

This system is still experimental but the quotas are supposed to be gradually increased up to very meaningful amounts.

Of equal if not greater importance are other vanguard reforms regarding collective negotiations within enterprises. Indeed the dramatic labor disputes of 2010 have not only demonstrated the dire condition of many workers, they have also seriously wounded the reputation of official unions, whose uselessness is becoming a liability for the CCP himself. If it wants to avoid the frightening perspective of workers' representation independent from the CCP and from its satellite unions, the CCP has to comeback in the middle of the game with new and innovative propositions. In Guangdong, this is already happening and CLB pays homage to the pragmatism and the positive role that some local authorities want to bring into the process, facilitating the dialog between employers and employees as much as possible within the constraint of maintaining at all cost the public order (which is indeed the red line which cannot be allowed to be crossed at any time and under any circumstances).

The ACFTU does not want to stay idle and has also brought some contributions to the debate. In August 2010, it proposed to increase the membership rate of union from 60 % to 90 % in 2 years. It also launched a pilot modernization program in a dozen of cities that could be extended in 2012 (direct election of union representatives by the employees, professionalization of permanent union staff, remuneration by a dedicated fund and not by the employer anymore).

Maybe the most interesting initiative of all, was the reform proposal of collective negotiation mechanisms, that the ACFTU aims at applying first to 60 % of the firms and in which official unions ought to play a more proactive role, meaning supporting the interests of their members and not simply helping the employers to keep public order. A couple of successful negotiations have thus helped the official unions to project a more positive image. In Wuhan, for example, 450,000 staff in hospitality sector has enjoyed a 30 % pay increase negotiated between unions and municipal authorities. In the Honda Nanhai factory, which was one of the epicenters of the 2010 strikers, ACFTU has also scored very big: the local union has been completely streamlined and reformed, its representatives directly elected by the workers and, cherry on the cake, it managed to get a 33 % pay increase in 2011 (on top of the +35 % pay increase that ended the 2010 strikes).

Conclusion

The 2010 labor disputes seem to have set in motion an irresistible trend of modernization of the labor conditions, the relationships in the workplace, and the public status of migrant workers. All of this goes well beyond pay increase figures and signals probably an irreversible trend in China's industrialization patterns. Of course, all the objectives set by Chinese authorities in that perspective may not be achieved and Guangdong's double relocation policy, for example, is still raising more doubts than hopes.

The upside, however, is that none of the parties involved can afford to fail, as the headwind from market, demographic, societal forces is simply blowing too strong : companies have to struggle to maintain their operational margins and that means upgrading their production and increasing labor productivity, local authorities understand they cannot rely on yesteryear's crude policy tools such as subsidized industrial parks and have to mobilize an entire array of factors in order to succeed (living conditions, public services, business environment, education, etc.), and finally workers are slowly but surely realizing that the choice is theirs and that they are able to vote with their feet (where to live, where to work) and directly participate in negotiation with employers (through the designation of representative and if needed through collective actions).

The latest initiatives of local Guangdong authorities seem nevertheless very interesting as they demonstrate the willingness of the CCP to accommodate to those changes instead of hopelessly trying to curb them. This is a change of attitude whose implications for China's and probably most of its trade partners cannot be understated.

12. New Social Conflicts in the Guangdong Province: Historical and Sociological Perspectives

Jean Ruffier

Over the past year, we saw a proliferation of disputes. Newspapers have even reported several conflicts in the Taiwanese and Japanese companies, which have resulted in very substantial increases in wages. The movement is so strong that more and more observers are discussing the possibility of a general strike in southern China.

Without being able to predict something unpredictable, we believe that conditions are gathered for a workers' spring in South China, with an explosive or creeping movement, which has already begun. We do think that it is just a beginning.

The Sino-French Centre of research on organizations, and Sociological Department of Sun Yatsen University in Canton, conducted observations on field and discussions with companies, unions, activists and authorities that we would like to report in this paper and which offer us a better picture of what is going to happen.

The chapter begins with by a discussion on the motivations of strikes. Then it will focus on the different actors interacting in social conflicts, trying to describe shortly their aims and strategies. All together everything seems set to prepare more strikes to come.

The era of low wages and obedient Chinese workers is about to end. If Guangdong, China biggest southern province – became the workshop of the world, this is due to several reasons but the main one is the existence of a labour force, obedient, and accepting without protest low wages and poor working conditions. Over the past 20 years, growth has been uninterrupted and wages have barely changed.[1] Chinese

---

[1] *To understand better Chinese industrial development, see:* R. Arvanitis et W. Zhao, "*Five Cases Studies of Private and Collective enterprises in Guangdong*", dans J.-F. Huchet et W. Wang (dir.), *Chinese Firms in the Era of Globalisation*, Beijing, China Development Publishing House, 2008; W.A. Byrd (dir.), *Chinese Industrial Firms under Reform*, Oxford, Oxford University Press, 1992; Y. Cao, Y. Qian et B.R. Weingast, "The Sale Goes on. Transforming Small enterprises in China", *Transition, février 1998, p. 5–7*; Y. Huang, *Capitalism with Chinese Characteristics*, Cambridge, Cambridge University Press, 2008; F. Navarro, "*L'avantage concurrentiel chinois – entre*

J. Ruffier (✉)
Centre franco-chinois de sociologie de recherche sur les organisations, Université Sun Yatsen à Canton, Chercheur CNRS, (中法组织研究中心, 中山大学,社会学系), Gyangzhou, China

IAE, Université Jean-Moulin Lyon3, Lyon, France
e-mail: jean.ruffier@univ-lyon3.fr

governmental statistics show that these wages would have rather decreased in proportion to the gross industrial product. But from 2011, up to now workers wages are sharply increasing.

12.1 Methodology and Data

In order to collect data for that paper, we used mostly field work of SUN Yatsen University Sino-French Research Centre on Organisations. That Centre exists from 2000 and has always been leaded by one French and one Chinese Directors. He mostly studies Delta Pearl River Factories, giving advises to Chinese and Foreign managers and to local industrial policy makers. That gives us access to workers, bosses and executive all over China. The study on labour conflicts was decided by the two directors and was helped by SUN Yatsen University Labour Studies Centre.

We too used labour statistics even if most are faked, they give us trends. We read newspapers even if they can report only on a conflict only if it is required by authorities. Because they are looking for foreign advises, we had the opportunity to discuss with Chinese unions. We participate a meeting between Shanghai union and Lyon unions helping both parts to understand the other part.

12.2 Why Do Workers Strike?

Mancur Olson is an American economist known for a theory of collective action, published in 1965. According to him, strike is primarily the result of a calculation: the workers think about what they might lose (unpaid hours, bosses or government retaliation) and what is at stake (wage increase) (Olson 1971). The seeking of these interests matches the mood of numerous Chinese workers. According to Olson, there is no action without coercion, because you earn more money if you let others strike for an increase but not to strike yourself to avoid losing your pay. The constraint requires a minimum of organization, and this explains why the strikes were so difficult to arrange in China until now: we know how the Chinese government violently crushed the very beginning of any rival organization of the Party.

In the first 30 years of the communist regime in China, being a worker meant to have a certain level of education and the privilege of working for the State. The reforms have substantially reduced the percentage of workers in State enterprises to the profit of private enterprises. These one have massively hired uneducated and poor young people coming from the countryside.

---

pratiques déloyales et avantages comparatifs", Perspectives chinoises, Hongkong, no 97, 2006, p. 13–29; H. Qin, Les leçons à tirer du miracle chinois, Lingdaozhe, Pékin; H. Qiu (éditeur), "Innovation régionale et développement d'entreprise", Pékin, Éditions des sciences économiques/ UNESCO), 2007; J. Ruffier, Faut-il avoir peur des usines chinoises ? Compétitivité et pérennité de l'atelier du monde, Paris, L'Harmattan, 2006, p. 186.

12.3   A New Generation of Workers

Thirty years after the industrial take-off, we face now the second generation of workers from rural areas. This second generation has a better education than the first one. It gets the experience of the first generation, and above all, it has known nothing but economic growth. The first generation of workers from rural areas had experienced civil wars and periods of starvation. The current generation knows what misery is, but it has rarely been confronted with starvation, and almost never to repression. This is a generation that believes in its future.

These workers have left villages that young people are fleeing or where there is unemployment. The average income of Chinese farmers is currently around 100 € per year, the one of the factory workers is ten times higher. The workers of rural origin have thus experienced a genuine social advancement.

Twenty years observation of Chinese factories gave us the opportunity to observe changes in the attitudes of these workers. It is impossible to describe the variety of views of the Chinese workers, but we can try out to sort some usual workers speeches when they refer to observed situations. The medias place great emphasis on working conditions that are often no worse than any other third world countries. These working conditions are indeed resented, but they are also seen as inavoidable. However, the work intensity increases. Twenty years ago, most plants that I observed were not enviable for their working conditions, but the work rhythm was not too hard.

There were many reasons for this: Firstly wages were so low that it did not require a significant amount of work. Perhaps the main reason is that it is not easy to make workers work hard.

Taylor has highlighted the need to mobilize a lot of intellectual work to achieve an increase of work productivity, and Chinese factories face a lack of organizers (Taylor 1911). So it is very gradually that work rates have increased. Working hours were lengthened due to a growing demand of work production. Employees and managers have also faced growing work intensity. Chinese employees did not mind working longer: the low intensity of their work and the improvement of their life quality justified it. In the last years of the twentieth century, the workers demanded more hours because they wanted to increase their income, work more to earn more was very fashionable at that time. This workalcoholism nourished a form of triumphant nationalism. During the years 2004–2006, we heard Chinese friends who mocked the supposed laziness of the West, which they said were more concerned with multiplying days off than developing their national economies. They told us that the Chinese economy would become more powerful because the Chinese themselves were not afraid to work and even willing to work hard for limited wages. We are no more listening this kind of speeches nowadays. The pace of work increased. It must also be said that you can work intensely for several years but not indefinitely. If you work too much, you eventually get exhausted, even if you are Chinese.

12.4 Work Less and Earn More

Today we hear many Chinese saying they want to work less. Workers are often more invested in their work in relation to the gains which result of it. They often make disillusioned observations: "We worked increasingly hard for years, and look who benefited of it – not we!". If these workers earn more than their parents, they are also in a more complicated world. Chinese workers' wages have not kept pace with China's economic growth. They remain third world countries wages in a region where GDP per capita is close to the one of eastern European countries. Making a living as a worker becomes a puzzle. Housing prices soared. While the majority of urban dwellers own their home, the workers realize they will not succeed. Getting married involves finding accommodation outside cheap dormitories. Raising a child in the city is often out of reach for a worker due to his financial income. Most of the time, they choose to let the grandparents raise their child in the countryside, or to postpone indefinitely the birth. And recently, food prices are also rising.

A few years ago, workers took their fate with fatalism, because they saw no way of improvement. But today they heard of wages rise in other plants as a result of strikes, and they feel they are underpaid. They have not experienced repression, are accustomed to changing business easily and they do not fear unemployment; therefore, they are not afraid to strike. It must be said that unlike their parents, these workers are usually issued from the one child policy, so they were used to get all the attention of their parents: they hardly bear frustration. If they do not strike very often, it is because most of them don't know how to organize it.

12.5 Employers Distraught Over Tensions

Facing their changing attitudes, private employers often seem clueless. Chinese private employers were accustomed to docile workers, but not loyal. They adapted to a high turnover especially since they had no trouble recruiting. Turnover appeared to be the best way to manage tensions. When recruiting new employees became more difficult, they only needed to slightly increase wages or improve housing conditions. In interviews with employers, unqualified workers appeared only very rarely as a major concern. Now, those same bosses are faced with people who openly discuss wages and this is new for them. They appeal to authority, the Confucian virtues of obedience and show toughness in dealing with the workers. These employers have little opportunity to discuss in depth with colleagues. Chinese employers are not allowed to organize themselves in association. No surprise that they are coping badly with social troubles in their factories.

The communist government has sufficient knowledge of the thinking of Karl Marx to understand that if China becomes a capitalist country, capitalists should take the power. The authorities do everything they can to delay the time for this Marxist prophesies to become true. As a result, the Chinese bosses have little places to debate together on common strategies, and no real way to express themselves collectively. There are official employers' organizations, but they are run entirely by Communist Party. The only ones who can speak for the employers are employers' organizations in Hong Kong or foreign trade chambers.

Western business leaders are also taken aback by this attitude change of the workers. Unlike most of their Chinese counterparts, they usually set up a minimum of Human Relation management, and they try to have good relations with their employees. As a result, they know better and the staff generally knows who is likely to trigger unrest.

But they felt they were able to maintain social peace in anticipating the claims. Their workers usually look satisfied with the situation and hardly do not even complained of wages or working conditions. Yet here, in the last few months, they realize that increases in wages or benefits granted, was not enough to calm the discussions in the workshops. They feel like giving gifts to people who in return tell them that they should give them more. This situation is new for them in China.

Of course, foreign bosses expected to have to raise wages. They were rather surprised not to have to do it earlier. In terms of wages, Western employers visions differ, depending on whether their activity is directed towards the Chinese market or not. If they are in China to take advantage of low cost and industrial facilities, they are reluctant to increase wages and they tend to take the minimum wage as base salary. If they target the Chinese market, the fact that a larger part of their national wealth is redistributed hinted that growth of the Chinese market which should make their business profitable and that they often wait for years. Those who target the Chinese market have generally more long-term policies and favour more their workforce. Moreover, it is in these foreign companies facing the Chinese market that most of Chinese employees want to work.

Facing workers who are not afraid of conflict, authorities are much more divided on the issue of social risk. Chinese political power is not a model of democracy. The methods of nomination are by appointment from top to the bottom.

12.6 A Power Less Monolithic Than We Think

The power is much less monolithic than were those of Eastern Europe when it was socialist. The visions, strategies and situations of the central government are very different from those of municipal authorities or provincial powers.

The personality of the party cadres is also important. Joining the Party is an opportunity not offered to everyone. It often requires a lot of effort. But the motivations of the candidates strongly varied: some wish to defend the ideological and legal options, while others seek personal enrichment. The authorities in China are traversed by heated debates on policy implementation. This particularly appears in the management of labour disputes.

The central government intervenes rarely in these conflicts. If it does, it's always a disavowal of local authorities and often brutal. His main concern is to protect its power, and that's for this purpose it will consider whether to intervene.

The government has always opposed violently to the creation of autonomous militant organizations.

12.7 China Is a "Cryptocracy"

Chinese government does not deny the growing number of social conflicts. Even if only few conflict statistics are given, not always reliable, for 2 years, the authorities have noted increasing number of conflicts and announced they expected other major conflicts. A way to say they are ready to cope with social unrest. We know very little about the central government. China remains essentially a "cryptocracy". The main leaders remain in the shadow and give very few information on the internal conflicts among them. Most of the time, we have seen two leaders, one who seemed to embody the opening, while the other opted for continuity, just as two puppets pulled by the strings.

China has a form of power with few equivalents elsewhere or in the past. This is not a personal power but an oligarchy or government of a few. It is a small group of leaders, consisting initially of survivors of the long march, which took the power in 1949. This small group formed a small private company that reproduces within the last 60 years and retains the reins of power. Foreign observers generally agree to say that a collective takes key decisions.

12.8 An Oligarchy of Exceptional Longevity

This group holds firmly the reins of a Communist Party composed of hundreds of thousands of people. The oligarchy solves the problem of transmitting power from one generation to another. The same people who are responsible for errors in the initial planning, thus the crimes of the Cultural Revolution, are now those who run the so-called policy of "market socialism" or opening. This explains the longevity of the regime.

We can have a better idea of the power of this oligarchy when it is said that 98 % of Chinese billionaires are related to persons who hold or have held ministerial positions. The relative strength of the group over one person is a leader did too visible mistakes; the group of people has already a plan to correct the effects of these mistakes and suggest alternative solutions.

Chinese leaders are not smarter than the leaders of other countries, but their system is more "forgiving", by correcting errors made by their leaders. And the duration of the group is potentially infinite. The central government does not work for posterity, like a potentate who knows he will die; it does not work to prove its results in sight of the next election, since there are not real elections. The government has the ability and interest to project its country in the long term. Due to the large opacity of the central government, it is very difficult to predict how they would react to a major social crisis.

Generally, municipal authority is responsible to intervene in labour disputes. They are the one who manage Chinese's daily life. They manage social rights, which vary considerably from one city to another. The minimum wage is generally set by city. The union appears to be a municipal authority. Municipal authorities are the first on the front line in case of complaints. Of course, they are sensitive to the pressure from the central government, but their action is intended to show that they control the situation. It happened that municipalities should bear the last wages of employees in case of bankruptcy of the contractor. Like all cities, they wish to accommodate more businesses and get more taxes. This means that in conflicts, they are rather sensitive to the arguments of employers rather than those of workers. Thus, cities can send the police, or mobilize the union to end a conflict.

12.9 Guangdong, Laboratory of Social Experimentation

Guangdong Province got from Central Government the mission and ambition to have an advanced economic development and political openness. It is a roadmap already old, but updated recently. In its program, the province has to take the form of a developed country and abandon the attributes of the third world. They want to move towards high technology industries with creation of high value added economic activities. It is also the province that does the most research and development; the province files the most patents and receives most of foreign investment.

Province's number one, the party secretary, regularly takes avant-garde positions. He pushed for social laws that will be more stringent than anywhere else. This should complicate the life of struggling industries whose strategy is based mainly on the exploitation of low-cost labour. Province's number two, the governor of the province, appears more concerned with social harmony. He wants to avoid the tensions that will inevitably arise if a new production model let people aside. This balance between two heads is rather classical. But it may give the impression of a hesitant power, which does not facilitate the task of those who have to manage conflict. The province has taken leading positions in the representation of employees.

Employees currently have no real way of representation because of the violent repression of any organization supposed to compete with the Communist Party. This situation makes it particularly difficult to manage conflict, companies having to guess why there is a conflict without being able to meet representatives of the people involved in the conflict. However, in 2010, the Party Secretary of the province has repeatedly stressed the need to directly elect representatives of employees. He even proposed a law for that purpose, but decided to delay it because of opposition from employers' organization in Hong Kong. The reluctance of the authorities is especially noticeable when you look closely at union leaders. Union officials in Guangdong are quite divided on the role of unions and the strategy to pursue in a conflict. In the Chinese constitution, the union is primarily a propaganda organ of the Party turned to the employees. Most of their actions consist in various campaigns for social education. The union does not represent the employees, they defends them in seeking what can improve the workers situation.

12.10 Unions Seek to Reduce Social Tensions

Over the past year, unions got a new mission by the central government: to help reduce social tensions. The first consequence is to increase union presence in firms. In fact, the union is present mainly in state enterprises and joint ventures. Currently, unions seek to enter the 100 % foreign companies. These one usually disagree with unions' intrusion as they fear more bureaucracy adds to the running of the company, increases of social costs, with limited things done to reduce tensions in the workplace. The union is virtually absent from Chinese private firms. During a strike, the union does not hesitate to take the initiative to fire striking employees, or hire non-strikers. This can disrupt the workshops, while creating resentment against the company. It is not uncommon that the union is sending militias to bit the strikers.

12.11 Sometimes, the Union Stands by the Workers' Side

The union is driven by many debates. We personally participated in meetings of Chinese and French trade unionists where the first asked the second advices in understanding employees. We also found that in Guangdong, the internal debate could go further. There is a centrist trend that considers that in any dispute, the union's role is to be located halfway between employers and employees to find as quickly as possible solution to the conflict. There are other Cantonese unionists who feel that they should stand firmly on the side of workers against the bosses. This position is easier to hold when the boss is a foreigner. Thus, in Guangdong, we saw a union involved in a factory on strike electing delegates from the workshops, which were responsible for negotiating the exit of the conflict. This conflict resulted in an important and rapid increase in wages.

All conflicts are not won by workers. Sometimes, especially in the case of Chinese private employers, workers get nothing.

12.12 Activists, Uncontrolled Actors of the Social Fight

We cannot conclude this overview of actors of these conflicts without speaking about the activists. There are activists working condition beyond the union and fighting for the betterment of workers. Some are related to training or giving advice NGO. They are often students who decide to spend some of their time to help workers. Their action is essentially to inform workers on their rights and which institutions may help workers in cases of abuse. These people are courageous in the sense that their NGO may be an embryo of labour organization, thus running a real risk. At the same time, the authorities sometimes recognize the usefulness of their actions, which generally stay within a legal framework. Thus, the union can require an employer to provide training to their employees about their rights.

There are other activists more determined to defend the rights of workers, including by organizing strikes. These activists are more difficult to meet because the authorities hunt them. They are no less active. Thus, we have heard people claiming they entered big companies to strike. Once the strike is over, these activists tend to disappear in the wild. Their action is not very difficult because their speeches are quite close to the views of a majority of workers. Basically, they explain to other workers that they are exploited and that their situation can be improved by struggling. And most importantly, they give the start of the conflict. This was the case of a multinational where militants had managed to persuade many workers to strike. Together, they decided which day and hour the strike should begin. In due course, nobody dared to strike. An activist then cut the power in his workshop. The workers alerted their colleagues by SMS in other workshops, and the strike began that way. Later, the strike was in other plants of the same company. It lasted several weeks and ended with large increases in wages but also layoffs and the departure of all militants and some strikers.

12.13 We Have Not Reached the Peak of the Conflicts

This panorama of actors, determination and fearlessness of the workers on one hand, the employers' confusion and indecision of the authorities on the other hand, all this suggests that these conflicts will multiply. Some activists and intellectuals even imagine they will take the form of a general strike starting from local conflicts spreading. So we strongly suggest the peak of the conflicts is yet to come. Wage could increase more without harms for economic development or enterprise wealth. All these elements make me suppose that wages will rise rapidly in South China.

As we have seen, this will not affect much the presence of foreign firms. Certainly, it will become less attractive to move to China to benefit from low wages, but those who are there already will think twice before moving elsewhere, while a new purchasing power is emerging. The workers' spring in South China is going on...

References

Olson M (1971) The logic of collective action: public goods and the theory of groups, 1st edn. 1965, 2nd edn. 1971. Harvard University Press, Cambridge, MA

Taylor FW (1911) Principles of scientific management. Harper brothers, New York/London

13 The Dynamics and Dilemma of Workplace Trade Union Reform in China: The Case of Honda Workers' Strike

Chris King-Chi Chan and Elaine Sio-Ieng Hui

13.1 Introduction

Based on an intensive case study of the Chinese Honda workers' strike in May 2010 and its further development in 2011, this article explores the potential of and barriers to workplace trade union reform in a new socio-economic and policy context. The authors suggest that a new generation of relatively well-educated Chinese migrant workers (see Pun and Lu 2010) has developed a higher level of consciousness of associational rights through their participation in collective struggles. This has put political pressure on the All China Federation of Trade Unions (ACFTU) to promote effective trade unionism and create a vital foundation for exercising democratic union representation in the workplace. The main barrier to effective workplace unionism, however, is the lack of external support for workers' unionisation efforts. On the one hand, the local trade unions at the town and district/county level are supposed to provide organisational support to workers under the Trade Union Law, but they fail to comply with their legal responsibility because of their bureaucratic nature and structural integration into the patron-client relationship between the local state and the global capital. On the other hand, support for workers from civil society is handicapped by the party state's opposition to independent labour organising. This dilemma has forced the higher trade union

---

This paper has been previously published in the *Journal of Industrial Relations* 54(5), 653–668 under Chris King-Chi Chan and Elaine Sio-leng Huithe title "The dynamics and dilemma of workplace trade union reform in China: the case of the Honda workers."

C.K.-C. Chan (✉)
Department of Applied Social Studies, City University of Hong Kong, Tat Chee Avenue, Kowloon, Hong Kong
e-mail: kccchan@cityu.edu.hk

E.S.-I. Hui
Department of Political Science, The University of Kassel, Nora-Platiel-Str. 1, 34109 Kassel, Germany

federation to intervene directly in workplace trade union reform and promoted state-led wage bargaining. Data for this paper is based on interviews with 40 Honda workers, supplemented by information obtained from a systematic review of internet materials, media information, trade union documents, NGO reports and interviews with labour organisation personnel.

13.2 Chinese Trade Unionism in Transition

Much as in other state socialist countries, the All China Federation of Trade Unions (ACFTU) has a double institutional identity: as a state instrument under the leadership of the Chinese Communist Party (CCP) and as a labour organisation nominally representing the interests of workers (Chen 2003). However, it has experienced difficulties serving the latter function in the reform era. On the one hand, owing to the privatisation of a large number of state-owned enterprises (SOEs), the share of SOE workers in urban employment has dropped significantly; this has led to a steep membership loss for the ACFTU (Chiu and Frenkel 2000; Cooke 2005; Lee 2007) . On the other hand, workers generally do not trust trade unions on the grounds that many trade union officials at the enterprise level are typically not elected, but appointed. Furthermore, the ACFTU officials and the CCP cadres closely overlap (Taylor and Li 2007). Workers believe that trade unions always side with the management and the government during labour disputes and thus cannot help them to solve their problems (see Taylor and Li 2007). For these reasons, since 1998 the ACFTU has started to actively establish union branches in the private sector, especially in foreign invested enterprises (FIEs).

The unionisation campaign has been further strengthened since 2006 after a rising number of strikes in South China, some of them demanding the establishment or reform of workplace trade unions (C. Chan 2010). Official statistics on strike are absent in China, as workers or unions are not granted the right to strike. Nevertheless, it is clear that an increasing number of labour disputes and workers' protests, which often bypass the official trade unions, have emerged in China in the past decade (Chan and Pun 2009; Chen 2010; A. Chan 2011). The number of labour disputes handled by the labour dispute arbitration committees at all levels in China has jumped dramatically, from 120,191 cases in 1999 to 693,465 cases in 2008 (China Labour Statistical Yearbooks various years). In addition, the total number of mass incidents – an official term for popular protests – jumped from 10,000 in 1994 to 87,000 in 2005 (CLB 2009).

In 2004, a government report found that labour laws were not well respected by FIEs in China. Following that, the ACFTU blacklisted some FIEs to try to encourage them to establish trade unions. In March 2006, President Hu Jintao commented on a report entitled '*A Situational Analysis of the Factors of Instability in FIEs in China's Coastal Area, and Some Proposed Countermeasures*'. He issued an order to: 'Do a better job of building Party organisations and trade unions in foreign-invested enterprises' (CLB 2006). Since then, the ACFTU has dramatically increased its efforts to unionise FIEs, paying particular attention to Fortune 500 companies (A. Chan 2005). By the end of 2008, most of the Fortune 500 companies in China had agreed to set up trade unions[1] (Christian Science Monitor 2008). As a consequence, the number of the ACFTU's enterprise affiliates has increased, from 1,324,000 in 2006 to 1,845,000 in 2009 (ACFTU 2007).

A top-down approach has been used in the unionisation campaign in most instances. Usually, the local branch of the ACFTU, with assistance from the party committee at the same level, puts direct pressure on the factory management to set up a trade union. However, there is no sign that the ACFTU will take the initiative to mobilise its workplace members, confront management with collective negotiations backed by strikes or apply other forms of collective action, as their Western counterparts do. The unionization campaign by the ACFTU in Wal-Mart's Fujian store was the only one case commented as bottom-up approach by Anita Chan (2006).[2] On the contrary, studies suggest that the emerging pattern of independent worker activism and its pressure on the party state, more than the legal and institutional framework, have significantly underpinned and determined the development of trade unionism (C. Chan 2010; Chen 2010; Clarke and Pringle 2009; Howell 2008a). We should therefore explore the possibility of self-mobilisation of rank-and-file workers to put into practice the collective negotiations and democratic framework guaranteed by the law. In the next section, we analyse the new development of workplace trade union reform in FIEs by examining the Honda strike.

13.3 Strikes and Trade Union Reform: The Honda Case

The strike staged by workers at Honda Auto Parts Manufacturing Ltd. (CHAM) in Foshan in the Pearl River Delta from 17 May 2010 attracted both nationwide and international attention (including the *New York Times* (Martin 2010), which wrongly interpreted it as a case of workers asking for an 'independent trade union'). Honda has opened four branches in China since the 1990s (Hagiwara and Lin 2010). CHAM is one such branch, producing transmissions. It is solely owned by Honda and was set up in 2007. Since its establishment, all workers in CHAM have been recruited from a small number of technical schools (*jixiao*) through an internship system. Normally, final-year students at the technical schools have to do a 1-year internship in an industrial organisation. After the students graduate, CHAM offers the interns formal employment status. At the time of the strike, workers told us that about 80 % of CHAM's workers were interns and only 20 % were formal employees.

---

[1] In the top-down approach of union-building, usually it is the management who takes an initiative to establish a trade union requested by the higher level trade union or local government.

[2] However, after the trade unions were established, the ACFTU does not continually to mobilize workers in the wage negotiation (CLB 2008). It has forced Gao Hai Tao, one of the Wal-Mart store trade union Chairs, to resign as a protest.

CHAM's workers have relatively more bargaining power than workers in other low-skilled export-oriented industries. First, the production of transmissions is of the utmost importance to car making and car companies usually consider politically stable and strike-free countries to be the most suitable places for this purpose (Martin 2010). Therefore, CHAM's workers could not easily be replaced by newcomers, at least not quickly. Second, like many Japanese automotive companies, Honda in China has adopted the just-in-time and zero inventory systems, which means they only keep a minimal amount of stock. CHAM's workers' strike definitely upset the supply of transmissions that is supposed to flow smoothly under normal circumstances. Third, CHAM mainly produces transmissions which are then sent to other branches for the making and assembly of cars. This means that the disruption of the supply of transmissions by CHAM had serious chain effects on car production in other Honda automotive factories in China. As a matter of fact, three other Honda factories were forced to halt production, leading to a daily loss of 240 million yuan (Jingji guanca bao 2010).

13.3.1 The Development of the Strike

The strike involved about 1,800 workers and lasted for 17 days. It was initiated by workers from the transmission assembly division, but quickly spread to and was supported by workers from other departments. Workers listed 108 demands at the meeting convened by the management after the strike but two of them in particular were retained consistently: (i) a wage increase of 800 yuan for all workers and (ii) a democratic reform of trade unions (*minzhu gaixuan gonghui*), as the existing trade unions barely represent their interests. The enterprise at first was reluctant to hold any negotiations with workers. Instead, it resorted to intimidation, firing two activists (who in fact had already resigned before the strike), pushing student interns to sign a document undertaking that they would not lead, organise or participate in any strikes (Takungpao 2010a) and mobilising their teachers from the technical schools to persuade the workers to return to work. Despite the company's threats, however, the strike continued. The company did come up with two proposals concerning a wage increase, but the workers turned them down since they were still far below their wage demand of 800 yuan.

Workers told us that, throughout the strike, the enterprise trade union was not on their side, but instead backed the management. One worker noted that:

> The chairman of the trade union tried to talk workers into resuming their work. And he maintained close communication with the CEO of the company during his first meeting with workers' representatives on 24 May. He is deputy head of the Business Management Department (*shiye guanli bu*).[3]

---

[3] Interview with workers on 30th May 2010.

In his own blog, a worker representative involved in the strike wrote that:

> It is frustrating that many enterprise trade unions fail to represent workers; instead, they are on the side of companies. The enterprise's interest, rather than that of the workers, is their principal concern.

The failure of the workplace trade union to provide representation was further manifested by the physical confrontation between a crowd of people claimed to be 'trade union members' and strikers on 31 May. That morning, many workers resumed work after meeting with the CEO of CHAM, the local government representative, the CEO of Guangqi Honda Automobile (who is also a member of the national People's Congress) and the student interns' teachers. However, about 40 workers refused to work and gathered together in the factory grounds. Workers told us that the company management and the riot police stationed outside the factory witnessed how the strikers were beaten up by about 200 people mobilised by both the town- and district-level trade union (*Shishan* town and *Nanhai* district), but they did nothing to intervene. A few of the strikers were hurt and sent to hospital. Official sources did not declare where the 200 'trade unionists' had come from, but one reliable source said that they were mobilised by the local government. They wore yellow caps and carried a 'trade union membership card' (*gonghui huiyuan zheng*), according to workers.

This incident served as a turning point, after which the company and trade unions came under even greater pressure and sought to resolve the dispute by means of a stronger initiative. The factory-wide strike continued and on 1 June hundreds of workers gathered near the factory gate. Zeng Qing Hong, the CEO of Guangqi Honda Automobile, went to talk to the strikers, asked them to elect their own representatives and promised to negotiate with them 3 days later. In the presence of Zeng, some strikers elected about 16 representatives. Later, at 5 p.m. the same day, Nanhai District Federation of Trade Unions (NDFTU) and Shishan Town Federation of Trade Unions (STFTU) issued a letter of apology to all CHAM's workers, but hinting at the faults of workers who continued to insist on striking. It said:

> Yesterday, the trade unions took part in the conciliation meeting between workers and management at CHAM. Since some workers refused to perform their duties, the factory's production has been seriously affected. During our communication with about 40 workers, verbal conflicts arose due to misunderstandings; some workers were emotionally unstable and had a physical confrontation with trade union members ... having learnt about this incident, some workers think the trade unions are biased in favour of the company ... we would like to express our apologies about a number of things that workers find hard to accept ... the trade unions coming out to exhort those workers (who refuse to work) are in fact protecting the rights of the majority of workers; this is what trade unions should do. (Caixin net 2 June 2010)[4]

---

[4] Our translation. The apology letter issued by the trade unions were first published by the Caixin Net on 2 June 2010 at http://policy.caing.com/2010-06-02/100149369.html, with the title 'An open letter from the Nanhai district trade unions and Sishan county trade unions to CHAM workers' (Caixin Net 2010). However, this was later removed from the website, probably due to government censorship.

Endeavouring to gain wider public support and calling for stronger solidarity among workers, workers' representatives issued an open letter to all CHAM workers and the public on 3 June, reiterating their demands: (i) a wage increase of 800 yuan, (ii) a seniority premium, (iii) a better promotion system and (iv) democratic reform of the enterprise trade union. This letter manifested the workers' strong class consciousness. The open letter declares:

> We urge the company to start serious negotiations with us and to accede to our reasonable requests. It earns over 1,000 million yuan every year and this is the fruit of our hard work ... CHAM workers should remain united and be aware of the divisive tactics of the management ... our struggle is not only for the sake of the 1,800 workers in CHAM; it is also for the wider interest of workers in our country. We want to be an exemplary case of workers safeguarding their rights.[5]

Although the Chinese migrant workers have not a mature 'class consciousness' compared with some workers in the democratic capitalism, the Honda workers' voices reflected in this statement does serve as a significant evidence to the growing level of class consciousness.[6] At the request of worker representatives, Zeng held a pre-negotiation meeting with them in the afternoon of 3 June. The same evening, the company initiated a democratic election in all departments and altogether 30 representatives were elected. The same day, with outside help, workers' representatives were able to get in touch with a prominent labour law professor – Chang Kai – at Remin University, Beijing, who later agreed to be their advisor.

On 4 June, the newly elected workers' representatives, representatives of the company, the labour bureau, the local government, the workers' legal advisor, the chairman of the enterprise trade union and Zeng attended the negotiations. At the end, both parties reached an agreement raising workers' wages from 1,544 yuan to 2,044 yuan – a 32.4 % increase – and intern students' wages from about 900 yuan to around 1,500 yuan (an increase of 70 %). The company refused to discuss the workers' demand to democratically reform the enterprise trade union, arguing that it should not intervene in matters concerning workers' associations.

13.3.2 The Uniqueness of the Honda Case

The coordination and persistence of the workers in this strike, the nature of their demands and the impact of the strike go well beyond previous instances of strike action (Lee 2007; C. Chan 2010; A. Chan 2011). This can be explained by two major factors. First, CHAM's workers have a stronger sense of injustice and are better organised. In their early twenties and some even teenagers, they belong to the 'new generation of migrant workers' (*xin sheng nong ming gong*) (see ACFTU

---

[5] This letter had been widely circulated during the strike by Internet media, *Caixin Net*, and a number of independent websites including Chinese Workers Research Network that will be elaborated below.

[6] See also Chan (2012a) for elaboration.

2010a; Pun and Lu 2010).[7] Comparing them with their parents' generation, they are less tolerant of unfairness and have made greater efforts to advance their rights. Although their wages were higher than the legal minimum wage, one thing they found extremely unfair was that the wage gap between the Japanese staff and student interns at the company was enormous. 'The salary of the Japanese manager is as high as 50,000 yuan. It is 500 times bigger than ours!', one student intern complained to us. This triggered their strike to demand higher wages. Also, they are relatively well educated. Almost all of them are graduates of technical school.[8] This is in strong contrast to workers in other low-skilled industries who have usually completed only junior secondary school or have even lower qualifications. The fact that quite a lot of CHAM's workers are former students at technical school means they have a strong network; this definitely made it easier for them to mobilise each other to join the strike. Furthermore, familiarity with electronic communication technologies, such as mobile phone text messaging, instant messaging using the Internet and blogs, is an important attribute of these young and educated migrant workers (Qiu 2009). QQ, a commonly used instant messaging system in China, is a key instrument of communication and mobilisation among workers. They have set up a number of QQ groups in which workers discuss their strategies of struggle. Workers can access these groups even with their mobile phones; this makes it not only financially affordable, but can also speed up communication. This internet activism laid an important foundation for effective mobilisation during the strike and coordination among workers.

The second factor contributing to the distinctiveness of the strike is the strong external support from local and international civil society. Recalling the negotiations on 4 June, one worker representative wrote in his blog that:

> Being able to get in touch with and have Professor Chang Kai as our advisor is very encouraging; I am very thankful for his help ... without his assistance, we would have played a more passive role in the negotiations, since we have limited abilities.

Also, apart from the support from Professor Chang, over 70 local and overseas scholars, signed a joint petition to support the workers' demands. It said:

> Living on meagre wages and struggling to survive, workers are forced to strike so that they could live with dignity ... let us unite and put pressure on the company. We should tell Honda to stop suppressing and dividing workers and to accede to the workers' reasonable demands.

This petition was issued a day before the negotiations and to some extent represented pressure from civil society on the company and the local government. More importantly, it strengthened workers' morale and confidence. One worker said: 'it is hard to believe we have so much support from so many professors'.

---

[7] According to a report by ACFTU (2010a), to begin with, migrant workers started work in cities at an average age of 26.

[8] Only the best junior secondary school or very good high school graduates can be admitted to study in a *jixiao* or technical school, but admission standards have declined due to the expansion of higher education in China since the mid-1990s.

Alongside these, the Chinese Workers Research Network (CWRN; *Zhongguo Gongren Yanjiu Wang*), a website that reports news on labour issues, launched by a few young mainland intellectuals and registered in Beijing, covered the CHAM workers' strike in detail. Furthermore, many Hong Kong labour NGOs and trade unions showed their support by protesting against Honda in Hong Kong. They kept updating the international community with news of the strike and a global signature campaign to solicit international support was initiated by Globalization Monitor, a Hong Kong NGO focusing on the negative impacts of globalisation on labour in China.

Shortly after the strike was over, the government started to strengthen its control over the media reports on strikes and the civil society actors who supported the Honda workers. For example, the CWRN faced retribution and was ordered to be closed down by the State Council Information Office of PEOPLE'S REPUBLIC OF CHINA for 'having covered articles with bad intention without authorization' (*weijing xuke kandeng buliang daoxiang de wenzhang*) on 8 June 2010.[9]

In short, the uniqueness of the Honda strike when compared with many other cases lies in workers' better organizing strategy and a higher level of interventions of civil society actors during the final stage of the strike. This kind of civil society actors' intervention in the direct support of strikers is uncommon in China (see Chan 2012b). As elaborated, different levels of state pressure were imposed on most of the civil society actors involved in the strike, including the close-down of the CWRN website and the detention of some labour activists supporting the strikers. Although it is not its strategy to totally clamp down on intellectual activism on labour rights issues, there is no sign that the Chinese authoritarian state tolerates independent social actors' efforts in radicalizing workers overtly during large-scale strikes, like the case of Honda. This, however, has not completely ruled out the possibility of hidden support lent to workers, which usually takes a more subtle and covert form when compared to that received by the Honda strikers.

Wage Negotiation and Trade Union Reform as Concessions?

The strike had forced the party-state to take the issue of workplace trade union reform more seriously than any time before. Shortly after the CHAM workers' strike, Wangyang, the Chinese Communist Party secretary of the Guangdong province, emphasized that when handling collective labour grievances, workplace trade unions should position themselves as workers' representatives and help safeguard workers' rights according to legal regulations (Yangchengwanbao 2010). Besides, the vice president of the Guangdong Provincial Federation of Trade Unions (GDFTU), Mr. Kong Xiang Hong, confirmed that the democratization of Chinese trade unions would be sped up so that members could elect their own president in the near future. He also announced that a pilot scheme of democratic election of workplace trade unions and the relevant training would be

---

[9] Information from CWRN.

carried out in 10 factories, including the Honda factory in Foshan (Takungpao 2010c).

Although CHAM workers' pressure was immense enough to push forward some changes in the company, a once and for all democratic trade union reform was still far-fetched given the relatively feeble power of labour vis-a-vis the capital and the state at the moment. Trade union elections organized from the department level to the factory level took place in CHAM from September to November 2010 with the GDFTU's active intervention. However, the GDFTU delegates ruled out the call of workers' representatives to remove the existing trade union president who was on the side of the management during the strike, as they thought he should be given 'a chance to correct himself' (*gaizheng de jihui*). Moreover, by manipulating the candidateship and isolating active workers' representatives who had close contact with the civil society during the strike, most union committee members elected are from the managerial or supervisory level. While the union Chair remains unchanged, two Deputy Chairs were elected in February 2011. According to workers, one of them is a department head while the other is the deputy-head. CHAM's trade union election in the wake of the strike demonstrates that the party-state, along with the Japanese management, is still determined and inclined to manipulate workplace class organizations even though it is under some bottom-up pressure from workers. However, in exchange for their grip on working class organizations, the state and the capital have to pacify workers by wringing material concessions in the form of significant wage increase. From 25 February to 1 March 2011, almost a year after the strike, wage negotiation took place between the trade union and the management in CHAM. The plant union demanded a wage rise of RMB880 for production line workers in 2011, a 46.1 % increase according to the management. Rejecting the trade union's demand, the management proposed a 27.7 % increase of RMB531, saying that the union's demand was too aggressive. In the end, both parties agreed to a pay rise of RMB611 (Southern Metropolitan Daily 2011). Mr. Kong Xianghong, who has been deeply involving in the Honda workplace issues in the capacity of the Vice President of the GDFTU after the strike in 2010, played a key role in driving both parties to reach the final agreement.

As can be seen, CHAM workers' increasingly sophisticated organizing strategy and growing class consciousness have enabled them to negotiate a higher wage level. Without compromising its grip on workers' freedom of association, the party-state in return has to concede to workers' strong demand by pressuring the global capital to raise its wage standard. In the next section, we will discuss the impact of the CHAM strike on the industrial relations in the industry and national levels.

13.4 The Impact of the Honda Strike

13.4.1 Impact in the Automobile Industry

Against the background of economic revival, labour shortage, rising marketplace bargaining power and confidence of workers, the knock-on effect of the CHAM workers' strike on the car industry and other industries was remarkable. According to a *Guangzhou* Federation of Trade Union official,[10] strikes took place from 20 June to early July in four automobile spare factories in the *Nansha* district of the Guangzhou city. One of them occurred in a Honda supplier factory. Workers wrote in a 'letter to promote strike' (*ba gong changyi shu*):

> Colleagues, watch around us, Foxconn, Honda in Foshan, Toyota in Tianjin, [we] believe that the result is good as long as we can unite till the last moment...

Their demands included a wage increase of 800 yuan and democratic trade union reform, which highly resembled to that of the CHAM workers in Foshan. On 25 June, 4 days after the strike started, a written agreement was reached between representatives of the workers and the management. Workers' monthly wages were to increase by 550 yuan (400 yuan of basic wage and 150 of subsidy) and a bonus equivalent to 4 months of salary was granted. Almost at the same time, workers from another Honda supplier factory in Zhongshan, a city next to Foshan, also staged a strike requesting similar wage increase and enterprise trade union reform. It was also reported that workers from a Hyundai supplier factory in Beijing launched a strike to demand higher wages. Adding to this, workers from two Toyota factories in Tianjin, Atsumitec Co (a supplier to Honda) and Ormon (a supplier to Honda, Ford and BWM), followed the example of their counterparts and went on strike in June (Washington Post 2010). The linkage of these strike cases is confirmed by that fact that a leader of the Zhongshan Honda supplier strike had contacted worker representatives in the Foshan factory and tried to seek their advice.[11]

13.4.2 Impact on Wider Labour Relations

After the wave of strikes around the country in May to June 2010 led by CHAM workers (Asian Weekly 2010), the reform of trade unions on the basis of the existing legal framework and the establishment of a better collective consultation system in the workplace have seemingly come to the top of the agenda for the ACFTU and the government. Commenting on the CHAM workers' strike, the Xinhua agency, the official press agency, emphasised that it is a matter of great urgency to push forward collective wage consultation in enterprises in order to

---

[10] Interview on 12 August 2010.
[11] Information from the Honda workers.

further safeguard workers' legal rights and promote harmonious labour relations (Takungpao 2010b). On 5 June, the ACFTU issued a document entitled *'Reinforcing the building of workplace trade unions and giving them full play'* (ACFTU 2010b), which advocates the election of workplace trade union representatives in accordance with the law and the role of workplace trade unions in ensuring effective implementation of the Labour Code, trade union law and the labour contract law in enterprises. It also emphasises workers' right to information, participation, expression and monitoring in workplace trade unions. This was also the context in which Wangyang, the CCP Guangdong general secretary, and Kong Xiang Hong, the GDFTU deputy Chair made the speech that urged for workplace trade union democratization we mentioned earlier (Yangchengwanbao 2010; Takungpao 2010c). In August 2010, a source from the ACFTU suggested that the GDFTU experienced an unprecedented level of pressure due to the Honda strike and Foxconn suicides.

In this circumstance, the central and local governments have sought to introduce a legal framework for workplace collective consultation. The Guangdong provincial government debated the second draft of the Regulations on the Democratic Management of Enterprises in August 2010 after a suspension of almost 2 years, while the Shenzhen Collective Consultation Ordinance (amended draft) that had also been suspended since the world economic crisis was under public consultation at around the same period (Hong Kong Commercial Daily 2010). Alongside this, at least 13 provinces have issued documents in the name of the CCP branch committee or the local governments to promote collective wage consultation (China News Net 2010).

Although the introduction of workplace collective consultation system has seemingly come to top of the government's agenda, in reality it is undetermined and its attempt to build up a collective interest based legal framework had been halted by the capital pressure. It is reported that many overseas business chambers were strongly against the legislation on collective negotiation. In Hong Kong, over 40 business associations have published their petition in newspapers while some of their representatives have paid official visit to the Guangdong government to reflect their concern (Singtao News 2010). As a consequence, the Regulations on the Democratic Management of Enterprises and the Shenzhen Collective Consultation Ordinance have been put off (Wenweipao 2010).

Conclusion

As has been elaborated, CHAM workers have consistently demanded the reformation and re-election of the enterprise trade union committees during and shortly after their strike. This reflects an advancement of their consciousness of associational rights. Driven by the workers' pressure, direct elections were held at least at the departmental level and a number of strike leaders were elected as shop-floor union representatives. This is clearly the achievement of workers' collective struggles which sought to enhance their associational rights within a highly constraining political environment. Although the CHAM workplace trade union remains under the leadership of the ACFTU and its president remains in position, the state and the ACFTU have made a partial compromise on the associational rights issue because of workers' huge pressure.

Based on the analysis of this important case as well as its further development and its wider impact, we conclude that the bottom-up pressure from workers and the external support to workplace trade union are two important conditions for the promotion of effective trade union reform and collective bargaining in China's workplaces. The first condition shapes the dynamics of the current trade union reform, as the ACFTU and the party-state feel increasing pressure imposed by the new generation of migrant workers who have rising consciousness and organising skills. The second condition puts the ACFTU and the party-state in a dilemma when handling workplace trade union democratization, due to their opposition to civil society's intervention with workplace organising. These two points will be elaborated below.

First, the bottom-up pressure from workers' strikes is essential although not a sufficient condition for effective workplace trade union and sustainable wage negotiation. In a sharp contrast to the top-down mobilisation strategy to reform the workplace trade union by having direct union elections in some pilot companies (Howell 2008a), the pressure imposed on the enterprise and the lower-level trade union organisation by CHAM's workers was bottom-up in nature. Although the enterprise trade union and the trade unions at the town and district level were on the side of management, workers at CHAM stood up to them and took the lead throughout the strike and during their negotiations with employers. Their demands for a wage increase and democratic trade union reform were clearly articulated. Although collective contracts are common, wage negotiation was very rare in China, especially in FIEs (Clarke et al. 2004). The wage negotiation in CHAM is a breakthrough in terms of its process and outcome. Neither the union election nor the wage bargaining undertaken in CHAM is fully democratic in the Western sense. Instead, both of the election and bargaining are monitored by the higher level trade union, the agency of the party-state. However, as the main concern for Chinese workers at this stage is wages and working conditions, and their political consciousness is still very weak, if there is any, the state-led intervention is enough to pacify workers as soon as their wage demands are satisfied.

In her study of trade union elections in China, Howell (2008a, p. 863) concluded that '[a]ny significant move forward with direct elections is only likely to happen when there is a shift in the political context, either because of regime crisis or because of political liberalization'. Echoing Howell (2008a), we took the view that without more significant political change it is hard to imagine the proliferation of independent and democratic trade unions in China.[12] However, an extension of union elections and wage negotiation is also possible due to

---

[12] In Taiwan, South Korea and Indonesia, previously authoritarian regimes with a similar trade union structure to China, democratic workplace trade unionism also failed to proliferate until political democratisation took place: 1987 in South Korea and Taiwan, and 1989 in Indonesia.

pressure from workers' unrest even without a political crisis. In other words, while *democratic and independent* (from both management and the party-state) trade union is unlikely to occur without a significant political change, *effective* workplace trade unionism in terms of its capacity to negotiate a better wage and working condition with the support from the party-state is still possible.

Second, external support is another condition for effective workplace trade unionism in China, as A. Chan (2009) suggested. External support is especially important for Chinese migrant workers, given that most of them – and in fact also their parents – do not have the experience of collective association. However, the question of external support is also one that causes dilemmas and barriers for workplace trade union reform in China. Institutionally, external support should come from the local union centre, the only legitimate source of support under the current trade union regulations. Article 1 of the Trade Union Law declares it a duty of trade unions 'to protect the exercise by workers of autonomous self-organisation and association in trade unions so that they may undertake collective action, including the designation of representatives of their own choosing to negotiate working conditions'. But in practical terms, the bureaucratisation of local union centres and their traditional and institutional subordination to local government impede their possible leverage in implementing union policy from above and supporting efforts to exercise union power from below (Clarke and Pringle 2009; Chen 2010). From the CHAM case, we can see from STFTU's apology that they did not recognise that it is in principle wrong to persuade strikers to go back to work; they apologised only due to political pressure. While the GDFTU can intervene in trade union election in CHAM and other factories in the pilot scheme, it is impossible for the provincial trade union to organise trade union elections and participate in wage negotiation for hundred thousands of factories in the province. Opposition from overseas capital also impeded the leverage of the GDFTU and its subordinate branches to promote collective bargaining in workplace, as the local government and thus the local trade union centres still have to bend toward the global capital's interests under a patron-client relationship.

In practical terms, civil society groups are also able to provide support to workers striving for real trade unions, especially in South China where labour NGOs are prevalent (Howell 2008b). However, although the support from the civil society to workers is not illegal and in fact organising strategies have been accumulated by NGOs in the past two decades and can be transferred to workers, the party state is sceptical about the promotion of independent workplace organising and shows its capacity to constrain such activism. Reform of trade unions in China will continue to be a process full of dynamics and dilemmas for the foreseeable future.

Funding This paper is partially supported by a start-up grant provided by City University of Hong Kong.

References

ACFTU (2007) A brief introduction of the All-China Federation of Trade Unions. All China Federation of Trade Unions (AFCTU), Beijing. http://www.acftu.org.cn/template/10002/file.jsp?cid=63&aid=156

ACFTU (2010a) A report on the new generation of peasant workers [Guanyu xinshendai nongmingong wenti de yanjiu baogao]. All China Federation of Trade Unions (AFCTU), Beijing [in Chinese]. http://www.acftu.org/template/10004/file.jsp?cid=222&aid=83614

ACFTU (2010b) Further strengthen the building of workplace trade unions and give them full play [jinyibu jiaqiang qiye gonghui jianshe chongfen fahui qiye gonghuii zouyong]. All China Federation of Trade Unions (AFCTU), Beijing [in Chinese]. http://www.acftu.org/template/10004/file.jsp?cid=222&aid=83564

Asian Weekly [Yazhou zhoukan] (Hong Kong magazine) (27 June 2010) Vol. 24, issue 25. http://www.yzzk.com/cfm/Content_Archive.cfm?Channel=ae&Path=2376481752/25ae2b.cfm

Caixin Net (2010) An open letter from the Nanhai district trade unions and Sishan county trade unions to CHAM workers, 2 June. http://policy.caing.com/2010-06-02/100149369.html (Note: This open letter was originally posted on the internet by Caixin Net. It has now been removed, but can still be found in other blogs which indicate the source as Caixin Net, e.g. http://bbs1.people.com.cn/postDetail.do?view=2&pageNo= 1&treeView = 0&id = 100136168&boardId = 1)

Chan A (2005) Recent trends in Chinese labour issues – signs of change. China Perspect 57:2–12

Chan A (2006) Organising Wal-Mart: the Chinese trade unions at a crossroads. Japan Focus, 8 Sep 2006

Chan A (2009) Challenges and possibilities for democratic grassroots union elections in China: a case study of two factory-level elections and their aftermath. Labor Stud J 34(3):293–317

Chan CKC (2010) The challenge of labour in China: strikes and the changing labour regime in global factories. Routledge, New York/London

Chan A (2011) Strikes in China's export industries in comparative perspective. China J 65:27–51

Chan CKC (2012a) Class or citizenship? Debating workplace conflict in China. J Contemp Asia 42(2):308–328

Chan CKC (2012b) Community-based organizations for migrant workers' rights: the emergence of labour NGOs in China. Community Dev J (in press)

Chan CKC, Pun N (2009) The making of a new working class? A study of collective actions of migrant workers in South China. China Q 197:287–303

Chen F (2003) Between the state and labour: the conflict of Chinese trade unions double identity in market reform. China Q 178(Dec.):1006–1028

Chen F (2010) Trade unions and the quadripartite interactions in strike settlement in China. China Q 201:104–124

China Labour Statistical Yearbook (Zhongguo Laodong Jingji Tongji Nianjian) (various years). China Statistical Publishing House, Beijing [in Chinese]

China News Net (9 June 2010) http://www.chinanews.com/cj/cj-gncj/news/2010/06-09/2331521.shtml

Chiu SWK, Frenkel SJ (2000) Globalization and industrial relations and human resources change in China. ILO Regional Office for Asia and the Pacific, Bangkok

Christian Science Monitor (2008) Unions in China still feeble, but gaining a foothold, 29 Sept. http://www.csmonitor.com/World/Asia-Pacific/2008/0929/p01s02-woap.html

Clarke S, Pringle T (2009) Can party-led trade unions represent their members? Post-Commun Econ 21(1):85–101

Clarke S, Lee CH, Li Q (2004) Collective consultation and industrial relations in China. Br J Ind Relations 42(2):235–254

CLB (2006) Wal-Mart unionisation drive ordered by Hu Jintao in march – a total of 17 union branches now set up. China Labour Bulletin (CLB), Hong Kong. http://www.clb.org.hk/en/node/39060

CLB (2008) Union chair resigns over the imposition of collective contracts at Wal-Mart. China Labour Bulletin (CLB), Hong Kong. http://www.clb.org.hk/en/node/100310

CLB (2009) The observer: China fears riots will spread as boom goes sour. China Labour Bulletin (CLB), Hong Kong. http://www.clb.org.hk/en/node/100376

Cooke FL (2005) HRM, work and employment in China. Routledge, London

Hagiwara Y, Lin L (2010) Honda rises after most workers end strike in China (Update 3). Bloomberg Business Week 14 June 2010. http://www.businessweek.com/news/2010-06-14/honda-rises-after-most-workers-end-strike-in-china-update3-.html. Accessed 30 Apr 2011; note: the report has now been removed by Bloomberg

Hong Kong Commercial Daily (30 Sept 2010) http://www.hkcd.com.hk/content/2010-09/30/content_2606047.htm

Howell JA (2008a) All-China Federation of trades unions beyond reform? The slow march of direct elections. China Q 196:845–863

Howell JA (2008b) NGOs, civil society and migrants in China. In: Murphy R (ed) Labour migration and social development in contemporary China. Routledge, London, pp 171–194

Jingji guanca bao (Chinese newspaper) (28 May 2010) http://www.eeo.com.cn/industry/real_estate/2010/05/28/171178.shtml

Lee CK (2007) Against the law: labor protests in China's rustbelt and sunbelt. University of California Press, Berkeley

Martin J (2010) China: Honda workers' strike – the beginning of a new labour movement? New York Times, 11 June 2010

Pun N, Lu HL (2010) Unfinished proletarianization: self, anger and class action of the second generation of peasant-workers in reform China. Mod China 36:493–519

Qiu JL (2009) Working-class network society: communication technology and the information have-less in urban China. MIT Press, London

Singtao News (Hong Kong Newspaper) (27 Sept 2010) http://news.singtao.ca/calgary/2010-09-27/china1285574889d2754336.html

Southern Metropolitan Daily (2011) 2 March, P. a17. http://gcontent.oeeee.com/7/1b/71bfbe458113bbc3/Blog/b4f/433268.html

Takungpao (2010a) 1 June, p. A14. 'bentian bubagong chenluoshu neng jieque jifeng?' (Can 'not-to-strike' agreement letter solve the Honda dispute?)

Takungpao (2010b) 2 June, p. A14 'guanmei ping bentian bi gongren chenluo "bubagong"'. (The Chinese official media criticizes Honda for forcing workers undertaking not to strike.)

Takungpao (2010c) 14 June, p. A16. 'Nanhai bentian yi minxuan gonghui zhuxi.' (Nanhai Honda plans to hold democratic election of trade union president)

Taylor B, Li Q (2007) Is ACFTU a union and does it matter? J Ind Relation 49:701–715

Washington Post (2010), Honda Supplier Atsumitec's China Plant Suffers Strike. http://www.washigntonpost.com/wp-dyn/content/article/2010/07/15/AR2010071500247.html. Accessed 20 Nov 2011

Wenweipao (Hong Kong Newspaper) (18 Sept 2010) http://trans.wenweipo.com/gb/paper.wenweipo.com/2010/09/18/FI1009180018.htm

Yangchengwanbao (Hong Kong Newspaper) (13 June 2010) http://news.xinhuanet.com/local/2010-06/13/c_12219411.htm

Domestic Labor Regulation and Foreign Business Influence: The Case of the Guangdong "Transnational Capitalism"

14

Violaine Delteil

The interplay between transnational business dynamics and Chinese labor politics has given rise to lively debate and a stimulating literature in the past decade. It echoes the broader "hot button" issue of international and foreign influence on Chinese domestic politics that has punctuated China's gradual integration into the world economy since the inception of the 1978 Chinese Open Door policy. Somewhat tainted by nationalism, the debate among economists and policy analysts became more animated after China joined the World Trade Organization (WTO) in 2001 and later, when China was called on to comply with international standards and rules.

Many discussions raised in particular on the potential impacts of Foreign Direct Investment (FDI) on which China is heavily reliant compared to other emerging economies. Some analysts voiced concern that foreign capital could "swallow up" the domestic economy (Zhang 1997) and endanger workers' rights (Chan 2001), echoing earlier concerns about the disruptive effects of globalization on labor and social standards (Tilly 1995). Others expressed greater confidence in the capacity of the State-led Chinese regime to "tame" international and foreign influence and harness FDI to help China catch up and global integration while using its unprecedented economic success as a new source of legitimacy for the contested authoritarian political regime (Guthrie 1999).

Together with the dramatic increase in inequality, the spread of labor unrest throughout the 2000s provided evidence of the imbalanced nature of China's

---

The empirical part of this article, presented in Sect. 14.4, is based on a research project the author joined in 2011, led by Dr. Chris King-Chi Chan at City University of Hong Kong and with Elaine Sio-ieng Hui. The outcomes of the interviews have been firstly analysed in a report submitted to the project funder (Hui and Chan 2012). The author thanks both researchers for sharing with her the outcomes of the interviews made by them with Asian organizations.

V. Delteil (✉)
Université Sorbonne Nouvelle, Paris, France
e-mail: viodelteil@hotmail.com

economic transformation, exacerbated by FDI liberalization and labor deregulation (Chan CK 2009; Chan 2012). Responding to the spread of social discontent and strikes against foreign-owned as well as state-owned companies, the Chinese party-state initiated the review of the National Labor Law (1994) that introduced a framework based on individual rights at the expense of collective rights, including the right to organize, strike, and bargain collectively (Feng 2003). The law was largely dictated by concerns related to attractiveness to FDI in response to lobbying by foreign investors (Gallagher 2005; Wilson 2009). Part of the broader goal of promoting a "harmonious society," the government's ambition was to shore up worker's rights by reducing job insecurity and establishing new mechanisms for channelling workers' grievances.

Beginning in 2007, "the year of social legislation" (Zhu 2007), three new labor laws were enacted: the Employment Promotion Law, the Labor Dispute Mediation and Arbitration Law, followed in 2008 by the Labor Contract Law, which emerged after an unexpectedly long and difficult drafting process. The process of developing the law was turbulent to a large extent due to the active and highly visible participation of large overseas business organizations in the consultation process. Statements by the American and European Chambers of Commerce, who were officially invited to comment publicly on successive drafts of the labor laws clearly revealed – and the Chinese media emphasized – the contradictory interests of foreign businesses and Chinese workers' rights.

Exemplified by the Labor Contract Law, foreign business opposition to workers' rights found new expression in the laws proposed by the Chinese government and the All China Federation of Trade Unions (ACFTU) to promote collective bargaining. The purpose of the proposed laws was to pacify workers, who had became radicalized in 2010 during the Honda strike and similar cases against the backdrop of recurrent labor shortages, by addressing their most urgent demand to add elements of collective rights to the existing labor regulatory framework (Hui and Chan 2012).[1] Shortly after the Honda strike, 13 provinces released documents in the name of the Chinese Communist Party committee or local governments to promote collective wage consultation. The governments of Guangdong province and the Shenzhen Municipality were deeply concerned and responded in August, 2010 by opening discussion on the Regulations on the Democratic Management of Enterprises (hereafter called "Democratic Management Regulations") and the Shenzhen Collective Consultation Ordinance (hereafter called "Collective Consultation Ordinance").

The discussion that follows is organized into six sections. Section 14.1 presents the focus and methods of our empirical survey. Section 14.2 presents briefly some elements of the "Transnational Institutionalist approach" (Nölke 2011) as a stimulating framework for investigating foreign business influence on domestic institutional changes and politics. It also discusses selected academic works that

---

[1] A total of two million workers were needed in the Pearl River Delta in early 2010, and some factories were forced to halt production due to a labor shortage (Hui and Chan 2012).

followed a similar analytical ambition for analysing the dynamics of transnational business influence Chinese labor practices and regulations. Section 14.3 presents and discusses the results of the survey dedicated to the influence of Foreign Chambers of Commerce on the ongoing making up process of collective bargaining laws in Guangdong Province. Section 14.4 broadens the analysis to discuss the dynamics that reshape business-labor-state relationships in the Guangdong "transnational capitalism". The conclusion includes preliminary perspectives on future comparative analysis of "transnational capitalisms."

14.1 Survey's Focus and Methodology

The empirical study is based on a regionally-based analysis grounded in Guangdong Province. The choice of a sub-national analysis reflects Chinese "decentralized state-led capitalism," which structures the devolution of authority to local governments and allows room to manoeuvre for the negotiation and adaptation of national laws at the local level. It is also consistent with the growing tendency of FDI (especially operating in high value-added segments) to deal directly with regional or local authorities in adapting to the "local business system" and other sub-national institutions that could be decisive in terms of competitive advantage (Kristensen and Zeitlin 2005; Almond 2011).

The choice of the Guangdong Province also arises from its status as a pilot laboratory for China, both in terms and business and labor regulations. After receiving an explicit mandate for "experimentation and reforms" in the 80s, Guangdong Province rapidly rose to become the largest export-led manufacturing region in China and the fourth exporting region in the world (after Singapore, Hong Kong, and Luxembourg), with an industry accounting for 40 % of Chinese exports in 2009. While widely integrating the world value chain, Guangdong progressively shifted production away from light industrial goods such as apparel and toys to become China's leader in high-tech industrial manufacturing such as automobiles, electronic communications, and biotechnology products.[2]

Boosted by tax reductions and distribution of fees for export companies by local authorities, this export-fuelled economic model has largely been supported by FDI, which represented 9.6 % of local GDP for the 1992–2006 period, ranking second in China after Hainan Province and well above rates in other countries.[3] The FDI/GDP ratio dropped slightly to 7 % in 2009, reflecting a reorientation towards the domestic capital and market (Sheng 2009).

---

[2] According to official targets for 2012, R&D expenses will account for 2.5 % of regional GDP, the number of researchers will reach 280,000, some 100 state laboratories for engineering innovation and research and development will established and 3–5 industrial clusters powered by high-tech industries will enter into operation. Social targets such as pension and health-care systems are also considered.

[3] For the period 1980–2006, average FDI/GDP share was only 0.43 % for India, and 1.07 % for the United States (Sheng 2009).

As regards the distribution of FDI by country of origin, Asian countries have a significant lead (74.5 % of total FDI in Guangdong for the period 1979–2010), with a heavy presence of Hong-Kong capital (61.5 %), far ahead of European and North America capital (3.4 % each). The distribution is slightly different according to more recent 2010 data related to our investigation, showing most FDI coming from Asia (73.4 %), with Hong-Kong again dominant (63.7 %) in comparison to Japan (2.5 %), Singapore (2.3 %) and Taiwan (1.2 %), while European FDI represented 3.9 % with France well ahead (2.6 %), and North American investment at only 2 %, with 1.3 % from the United States.[4]

The Guangdong region's status as an economic pilot resulted in particular tensions in terms of labor regulation. Famous for its sweatshops exploiting migrant workers with second-class citizenship rights, the export-led manufacturing industry experienced large-scale labor unrest and activism compared to the rest of the country. Social conflicts tended to concentrate on multinational companies for both economic and political reasons (Chan 2009), with the reputational effect of foreign brands often serving as a highly effective weapon for workers. Taken together, those peculiarities largely explain why Guangdong and Shenzhen became prime movers in the design of labor-management mechanisms involving consultation and collective bargaining, as mentioned earlier.

The second focus of the analysis bears on "organized foreign business" (Foreign Chambers of Commerce and other overseas business associations), complementing previous studies that have investigated either the "macro power of foreign business" (the systemic pressure of FDI stock) or the "individual power of foreign business" (i.e., multinationals). We then interrogate the "intermediate" power of foreign business through the lobbying of public authorities. The assumption that foreign business is becoming increasingly organized and is indeed under pressure to do so is no accident, but is triggered by the new selectiveness of Chinese FDI policies. Rebalancing the foreign business/public official powers to the benefit of the later, selective FDI policy will force foreign businesses to build coalitions as a new form of leverage to defend their interests.[5]

Questions that have motivated our empirical investigations in Guangdong Province include (1) the lobbying strategies of foreign business organizations to influence public officials on labor regulation; (2) the kinds of coalitions that can be observed among business forces; and (3) the extent to which political organizations are able to channel business interests. The particularly high representation of foreign business organizations, foreign consultancy agencies and foreign political agencies (consulate, embassies, etc.) in the region is no coincidence.

The survey was conducted between April and July, 2011 and entailed a series of interviews of 27 representatives of 25 business chambers, foreign embassies and

---

[4] Source: Guangdong Statistical Yearbook 2011, p. 498.

[5] The selectiveness of FDI has been supported by a gradual reduction in tax-related preferential policies. For example, foreign invested export- and tech-oriented companies' income taxes increased from 15 % to 25 % under the 2008 Enterprise Income Tax Law.

consulates, 1 labor expert from ILO, 9 labor and legal scholars, 2 trade unions and government officials, as well as 1 attorney. As far as business chambers are concerned, we investigated regional as well as national business chambers in order to explore the extent to which their positions either complemented or opposed each other. Documents produced by the business chambers, trade unions, governments and think tanks were also systematically reviewed.

14.2 Foreign Business Influence on Chinese Labor Politics: Using a "Transnational Institutionalist Approach"

The acceleration of the globalization process during the past two decades has undoubtedly complicated the understanding of the interplay between foreign business and domestic politics, pressuring the International Political Economy (IPE)[6] to be renovated. Unsurprisingly, the mainstream approach of International Relations or IPE gradually lost ground because its state-centered analysis, focused on government preferences and inter-governmental negotiations, was unable to offer an endogenous explanation of domestic institutional changes. Opposing this "top-down" approach, in the late 1990s a firm-centered conception of IPE became a new "magnet" for examining the way in which multinational companies, through their growing cross-border productive networks, acted as vehicle of rules and practices from "home country" to "host countries." Based on monographic surveys, a large literature discusses the transfer, local adaptation or "hybridization" of firm models from headquarters to foreign subsidiaries. Dominated by "Global Value Chain" or "Global Production Network" approaches, most studies focused their discussions on technology, know-how, and management models of the MNCs, neglecting industrial relations and labor-management relations as pointed by Collings (2008, p. 8). Initially directed to Western multinationals operating in North America and Europe (Almond and Ferner 2006; Meardi et al. 2009; contrepois et al. 2011), this "bottom-up" IPE approach has been increasingly used for discussing Chinese dynamics triggered by a rapid, massive influx of FDI. More evidently in that case, the discussion on the transfer/adaptation of business models (primarily for the automotive industry), has largely ignored counterpart effects on labor and industrial relations.

Complementing the "top-down" and "bottom-up" IPE approaches, and more promising for analysing the complex interaction between foreign and domestic actors in the reshaping of labor-business relationships, is the "Transnational institutionalist approach of International Political Economy" proposed by Nolke (2011). Of particular interest are the two main analytical proposals: (1) A "multi-level analysis" of the globalization dynamics, with a emphasis on the sub-regional, sub-national, and sub-local dimensions of cross-border interconnections that lead to

---

[6] As defined by Nolke (2011), IPE "may be understood as the study of the interplay of policies/politics/polities and economic patterns in a cross-border perspective" (p. 2).

the penetration of global or transnational concerns into local features.[7] This multi-level approach allows for investigation of how rules and practices from different levels are diffused simultaneously among various spaces and levels. It helps to shed light on the complex interplay through which transnational rules spread to sub-national or national levels as well, via various pathways (including international or bilateral agreements, cooperation and expertise, lobbying, economic pressure) and more or less significantly according to the "filtering" role of domestic institutions. (2) A "multi-actor" orientation that allows exploration of the interconnections between a variegated group of actors beyond classical business, labor, and state officials actors, including new transnational private actors and institutions (including NGOs, international business consultants and experts). This framework helps highlight the development of a form of "transnational private governance" (Graz and Nölke 2008).

As regards the impact of FDI on domestic institutions, this approach invites to take into consideration three distinctive business powers: firstly, the anonymous "systemic power of foreign business" (Bohle and Greskovitz 2009) that derives from FDI location arbitrage and tends to pressure host institutions to adapt to business needs; secondly, the infused power of MNC's common rules and practices, which can alter the performance of the existing host institutions; and finally, the bargaining power of individual MNCs or organized business associations with public officials and labor representatives, which can influence alterations in local, regional or national institutions.

Interesting echoes to the programmatic research agenda proposed by Nolke (2011) could be found in the recent comprehensive analysis that Gallagher (2005) and Wilson (2009) dedicated to the exploration of the interplay between foreign and domestic interests in shaping Chinese economic and labor reforms as presented and discussed below. Similarly, both authors assume that foreign business influence largely channelled by FDI played a determining role in helping China to upgrade its economic model and comply with international standards, but the authors also argue that this influence was largely mediated by domestic actors, particularly reformers.[8] The Open Door policy that translated into a 'FDI liberal policy' was indeed highly instrumental for Chinese reformers and managers of state owned enterprises (SOEs) "as a source of new competition for the state sector, as a laboratory for sensitive labor reforms and as an ideological justification for deeper

---

[7] As noted by Nolke (2011), this approach can correct two of the major shortcomings of Varieties of Capitalism (VoC) approach : its focus on the national dimensions of the globalization and treatment of national economic systems "as closed containers and does not reflect their embeddedness within transnational economic regulations or within the institutions of global value chains" (p. 2); its exclusion of the role of labor forces in influencing institutional changes, considered as driven exclusively by business interests.

[8] Explicitly for Wilson, and implicitly for Gallagher's contribution, the "path dependency" approach is mobilized as offering an endogenous explanation of institutional changes, shedding light on the resistance of domestic institutions to external influences, the inheritance of economic models and routes experimented.

reform" (Gallagher 2005, p. 9).[9] Economic reforms then spread gradually from foreign companies to SOEs firms, nourishing the demands of the latter for a "level playing field" as foreign units in order to correct unfair competition rules,[10] and gradually from the Special Economic Zones (the first recipients of FDI) to coastal and later backward regions, in a process that causes competitive FDI local policies to become widespread.[11] Labor reforms towards increasing flexibility and contractual employment rules appeared to support 'FDI liberal policy' in complementing the attractiveness of the Chinese market. The autonomy to hire and fire workers and raise wages to attract and retain skilled workers was initially given only to foreign companies and joint ventures, but these powers progressively spread throughout economy, gradually replacing the state-mediated labor relations ("iron rice-bowl") with a model of contractual employment relations that was generalized with the 1994 National Labor Law. Following an initially low resistance of labor actors to new increases in job insecurity, that was undermined by the segmentation of labor policies (largely triggered by foreign companies) and nationalist rhetoric, growing tensions over time in the "labor-state relationships" were conducive to the creation of new contractual obligations in the employment relationship and new mechanisms for resolving labor disputes. Given more emphasis on individual rights and equal representation, "the employment relationship as a contractual obligation can be a powerful motivator of 'rightful resistance" as quoted by the author and illustrated by the very recent past (Gallagher 2005, p. 158).

Less attentive to labor-business contradictions, Wilson's analytical framework is nevertheless of particular interest for its apprehension of the way by which the micro "institutional sub-regimes" of labor relations proper to foreign companies – and in particular the US model of pay-for-performance and flexible-contracts – progressively spread throughout the economy through a series of channels involving domestic and foreign actors at and across micro, meso, and macro levels. Wilson ascribes particular importance to the role of foreign lawyers, consultants, and other business experts at the meso level, where they carry the institutional logics of the international community to the top and the bottom of the Chinese regime, i.e., to "policy communities" and "local policy communities" (p. 39). As far as labor rules and practices are concerned, foreign human resource consultants "have been instrumental in introducing new cognitive scripts in the form of industrial relations institutions to Chinese companies" (p. 150) and in spreading information about the practices and rules used in foreign companies (such as salary

---

[9] It echoes the more general Guthrie's (1999) view that the slogan "getting on track with international practices (jiegui guoji)" added force and legitimacy to socially difficult reforms.

[10] Given to the competition pressure a key role for introducing institutional changes, Gallagher's thesis differs from Guthrie's one (1999) who emphasizes on the organizational learning role of JV to diffuse international and foreign models into domestic firms.

[11] Since 1994, preferential local policies were extended to all provinces. As noted by the author "thousand of local governments set up development zones in a mad dash to court foreign investors, announced tax and land-use fee breaks, and offered foreign investors access to low-cost labor" (Gallagher 2005, p. 42).

surveys, compensation schemes, and hiring methods) to domestic firms and State officials. Curiously enough, and despite a large group of interviews of representatives of foreign business organizations (mainly US and Japanese ones in Shanghai) by the author, Wilson provides little empirical evidence of the "bargaining process" of those organizations with public officials.

More precisely related to our own concern, Gallagher and Dong (2011) focused on the role of "organized foreign business" in the process of drafting 2007 labor laws. As underscored by the authors, the inclusion of the three main foreign business organizations in the consultative process gave rise to lively debate that was widely reported by the media and focused on two issues: the new official pathway to a role in domestic politics for foreign business interests; the contents of the messages from foreign organizations that "focused their criticisms on the folly of raising standards even higher while continuing to ignore the pernicious problems of lack of implementation and enforcement" (p. 20). Opposition to increased workers' rights and labor standards related to the following items: restrictions on fixed-term contracts, work rules and firm decision-making, trade union rights and responsibilities, use of labor subcontracting, and restrictions on layoffs; specific comments were also released for the high-skill/high-pay workforce in order to reduce the employers' duties and costs. Threatening to leave China and relocate to areas with lower labor standards was a rhetorical weapon employed by this official lobby that complemented direct pressure exerted by some big MNCs as Wall-Mart, Google, and General Electric and widely echoed by the press.

In terms of the influence of foreign business, three primary consequences have been noted by Gallagher and Dong (2011): First, the active role of the comments of foreign Chambers of Commerce in orienting and fuelling the domestic debate on specific issues, including how to enforce labor laws and balance social protection with labor market flexibility, and the best foreign model to follow for labor regulation; second, the convergence of American and European Chamber criticisms of pro-labor legislation, which ultimately diverged when the European Trade Union Confederation successfully applied pressure to soften the European Chamber position; and third, the relatively low direct influence of foreign business organizations in shaping the Labor Contract Law, if measured by the final version, which retained most of the new protective clauses. This conclusion is shared by Karindi (2008) but contrasts slightly with that of Chinese labor advocacy groups like Global Labor Strategies (2007), who lamented the "undue influence" of foreign business organizations over central authorities (through formal and informal lobbying), as compared to domestic business and labor organizations.

14.3 Foreign Business Strategies Confront Collective Bargaining Legislation

As emphasized above, foreign business is not a single front but instead a constellation of nationally-based business interests that are differentiated by a number features: size (percentage of national FDI within total FDI located in the region), position in the global productive chain (from low to high value-added activities) and related labor bargaining power (from low to high-skilled workers), model of industrial relations from the home country, degree of institutional unity among national investors, cultural proximity between home and host countries, and finally investor's abilities to enter into alliances and commitments with economic and political actors or organizations (Whitley 2005; Morgan 2009).

For that reason, the "Democratic Management Regulations" and the "Collective Consultation Ordinance" are not expected to have an identical effect on every business segment. Both laws will undoubtedly exert greater impact on labor-intensive factories that hire mostly unskilled or semi-skilled workers under conditions close to or even below the legal requirement because they do not possess much bargaining power due to low "labor market power" and low "labor organizational power". By reinforcing their bargaining power in the workplace, collective bargaining legislation is expected to boost upward wage pressure in such low-end factories. Conversely, capital-intensive activities that rely on skilled and managerial employees will be much less affected because they offer wages well above the legal standards and have skilled workers who benefit from a stronger bargaining power, which is increasing as a consequence of a skilled-labor shortage (Hui and Chan 2012).

As stressed below, the position of investors in the value channel (which is closely related to the nationality of FDI) appears to be a key factor in differentiation. But deeper analysis focusing on actors' strategies allow us to identify other determinant factors referring to cultural and political patterns. The following sections describe the strategies of the foreign business associations of the United States, Europe (further divided into the European Union and other European countries), and East Asia (Hong Kong, Japan, South-Korea and Taiwan).

14.3.1 The Informal Struggle of the American Chamber in Favor of Deregulation

Two U.S. business chambers in China were interviewed: the American Chamber of Commerce in the People's Republic of China (AmCham China), located in Beijing and representing 2,600 members in over 1,200 companies, and the American Chamber of Commerce in South China (AmCham South China), located in Guangzhou, with over 1,800 members (Hui and Chan 2012).

AmCham China
AmCham China expressed no official objections to the Collective Consultation Ordinance and the Democratic Management Regulations, which was in stark contrast to the chamber's open opposition in 2008 and its efforts influence the drafting of the Labor Contract Law through a multi-action lobbying effort and that was recalled by the chamber President in interviews. Their strategies included distributing of a white paper to a broad range of institutions such as governmental departments, media, think-tanks, and academics; meeting with government

officials, collaborating with the Development Research Center (a think–tank that reports to the State Council); establishing close working relations with the EU Chamber; and seeking support from the US consulate involved in the U.S.-China Joint Commission on Commerce and Trade and Strategic Economic Dialogue.[12]

The absence of apparent concern and lobbying by the American Chamber regarding collective bargaining measures might appear surprising in view of the statement voiced by its President that the laws run counter to the prevailing U.S. model of industrial relations and the preference of "U. S. companies based in China to manage labor relations themselves" and their view that "having workers' representatives on the board is problematic".

It is less surprising if we remember first that members of AmCham China are from the Northern and Central parts of China and are thus not affected by the new legislation; second, that around 75 % of AmCham China's membership is not directly engaged in labor-intensive manufacturing: by subcontracting intensively the low-end activities to Taiwanese, Hong Kong, and local Chinese suppliers, and by concentrating on assembly, marketing, and sales, they primarily transfer competitive pressure to Asian producers (Hui and Chan 2012). Third, and directly related to U.S. investor's economic specialization as to the new strategic issues negotiated at the WTO, the chamber is above all eager to lobby on such issues as intellectual property rights, market access, and transparency but seldom on investment incentives, as revealed by the interview and recent Chamber position papers.

AmCham South China

In contrast to the position of AmCham, the AmCham South China has clearly expressed opposition to the Collective Consultation Ordinance and Democratic Management Regulations. As its President revealed during our interview, this position seems to be strongly related to the direct and indirect interests of U.S. investors in the region, who are far more engaged in manufacturing and labor-intensive production. To express its reservations, AmCham South China resorted to a multi-channel lobbying effort that included submitting a position paper to the two respective local governments (which is not publicly accessible); private discussions with the government and the Mayor of Dongguan city; the mediation of the Dongguan City Association of Enterprises with Foreign Investment (of which the organization's president has been vice-president for 5 years),[13] which has weekly meetings with the Mayor's office and monthly meetings with the

---

[12] Interesting enough, as stressed by the president of the AmCham, the White paper was distributed to large segments of the society, whereas it was reserved for the government 10 years ago.

[13] The Dongguan City Association of Enterprises with Foreign Investment is a local non-profit social group approved by State authorities and registered with the industry and commerce administration departments. Similar associations exist in other cities in Guangdong Province (Hui and Chan 2012).

Mayor (Hui and Chan 2012).[14] Lobbying relies mainly on informal relationships with public officials, using the principle of the "mutual benefit of the businesses and Chinese government, as the sole way to have a chance to influence the latter,"[15] and also on strong cooperation and alliances with other foreign investment associations. According to the interviewee, this strategy is certain to be decisive in determining the fate of the two proposed ordinances.

Interesting enough, the posture of the regional chamber was reversed at the time of the debate on the Labor Contract Law. Unlike its national-level counterpart, AmCham South China was rather supportive (or neutral) at the time, because it was expected that the law would help promote peaceful workplace labor relations and reduce the high incidence of social conflict in the Guangdong Region. The fact that the Labor Contract Law could reinforce the role of trade unions was not considered as detrimental for business, because U.S. companies tend to "support trade unions that are independent from other factories and do not form industrial coalitions. Trade unions in China are not like the AFL-CIO model, they have direct communication with management and could act as vehicle to allow employer to better hear the voice of employees" according to the interviewee.

Finally, it is worth noting that the collective bargaining law, while having become a real concern for the AmCham South China, has progressively been replaced by other more strategic or pressing issues in the relationships with local or/and national authorities: the protection of intellectual property rights, the reversal of the discrimination of foreign firms vis-à-vis domestic firms in terms of rules and taxes observance; the reversal of the obligation for expatriate workers to contribute to public pension systems; improved access to skilled labor in a context of a growing labor shortage; and finally, the access to international schools for the children of expatriate families.

14.3.2 European Business Under New Moral Pressure?

In China, European firms can be represented at two levels: their national business chambers and the European Union Chamber of Commerce in China (EUCCC). As an organization officially invited to express its views on the consultation process, the latter places more emphasis on policy advocacy and the lobbying of government officials, while the former deals more with supporting its own members, solving their particular issues, and promoting the business networking, in cooperation with consular officials. The following section first describes the interests and actions of

---

[14] Our interlocutor is also vice-chair of the Guangdong China Council for the Promotion of International Trade (CCPIT), and a board member of the Shenzhen International Chamber of Commerce (Hui and Chan 2012).

[15] An example was provided by the interviewee: he tried to convince Chinese public officials to pursue the issue of Intellectual Property Rights by pointing out that most IPR cases in the courts are actually filed by a Chinese firm against another Chinese firm.

the EU Chamber before identifying a set of distinctive positions hold by national business chambers.

The Cautious Position of the EU Chamber

The EUCCC represents over 1,600 member companies. Its headquarters are in Beijing, with branches in eight other cities, including Chengdu, Chongqing, Nanjing, Guangzhou, Shenzhen, Shanghai, Shenyang and Tianjin. Interviews conducted at the EUCCC in Beijing, Guangzhou, and Shenzhen all indicate that no official position regarding the Collective Consultation Ordinance and Democratic Management Regulations has been formulated.

The silence of the EUCCC at national and regional level contrasts strongly with its initial open opposition to the Labor Contract Law. The principal explanations offered by interviewees again referred to the economic specialization of EU companies. As mentioned by our interlocutors, EU business is even more focused on high value-added activities and will therefore be only marginally affected by collective bargaining laws. A second explanation, frequently referred to in interviews with European business representatives, relates to the fact that European companies are far more accustomed to collective bargaining than American firms. Persistent differences between the views of European interviewees support the assertion that national models of industrial relations are not neutral in terms of their positions on new labor laws. Finally, another, more implicit reason for the tacit acceptance of the collective bargaining law by EU business could be to avoid the previous volley of criticisms expressed by vigilant EU pro-labor institutions (such as the ETUC) and their potentially detrimental effect on the reputation of EU businesses.

Finally, the interviews conducted at the EUCCC in Guangzhou and Shenzhen revealed the initiative taken by the Chamber in 2011 to organize seminars for members on how to manage collective bargaining, showing that tacit acceptance does not imply indifference, but could on the contrary appear critical for the organisations and their members (Hui and Chan 2012).

The Diversity of National Business Chambers Mirrors the Variety of Economic and Social Models

Among European businesses in the Guangdong Area, the France is the most present in terms of FDI/GDP (2.6 % for France, and 3.9 % for all the EU) and is the most organized in terms of the mediation of business chambers and consultations. All of the officials who were interviewed, from the French Chamber of Commerce in Guangdong and Beijing, the French Embassy in Beijing, and the French Consulate in Guangdong, revealed a low level of concern about the legislation of Collective Consultation Ordinance and Democratic Management Regulations that amounted to a neutral position. The principal explanation offered by interviewees suggests that French companies are accustomed to collective bargaining and that most see wage pressures as manageable, particularly given the steady upgrading of economic activities that incorporate increased innovation and less unskilled labor. The same explanation was also offered by the representatives of the German Chambers during interviews in Shenzhen and Hong-Kong. Although largely in agreement with his French and German counter-parts, the president of the Benelux Chamber expressed greater concern regarding the new laws, which he sees as giving more power to workers in determining wages, to the detriment of small- and medium-sized businesses. Because of it highly marginal share in the business, the Benelux chamber could only hope that its position would be channelled by the EU chamber.

Contrasting with this neutral stance of "continental" business chambers, which were generally consistent with their national economic and social models, two other positions have being identified inside the archipelago of the European national business.

The first could be termed an actively pro-labor influence and is represented by the Swedish embassy. In contrast with the minuscule regional presence of Swedish business, too small to benefit from influential representation, either in Beijing or the regions, the Swedish embassy expressed strong support for the legislation, as underscored by its representative, who emphasized that "the labor market in China is strange and volatile, laws do not ensure a functional labor market, and collective bargaining is a means to stabilize the labor market". (Hui and Chan 2012). As it delegated officers to work on issues related to labor rights and labor market regulations with the central government, it also mandated expert intervention on collective bargaining issues. This pro-active stance was explained by our interlocutor by the powerful influence of Swedish trade unions on the Swedish government's structure and foreign policy. This resulted in close cooperation between the Swedish Embassy and trade unions for promoting the Swedish model of industrial relations model in China. This promotion goes largely through bilateral cooperation with the government and the ACFTU. For instance, it is supported through the organization of workshops, monitored jointly with the Chinese Ministry of Commerce, that are provided to provincial government officials on Corporate Social Responsibility and that covered collective bargaining (Hui and Chan 2012). As revealed by our interviewee, additional seminars may be introduced on collective bargaining for trade unions and government officials, a unique case that contrasts with the far more moderate governmental strategies of the other European Members (Hui and Chan 2012).[16]

As opposed to the pro-labor stance of Swedish officials, the more anti-labor position of the UK business representatives was clearly expressed by the President of the UK Business Chamber in Hong Kong. This stance could be tied to the fact that the law largely contradicts the Anglo-Saxon model of industrial relations, but it also seems more related to the close historical relationships between UK and HK businesses, in both HK and in the Guangdong Province. Recalling its initial opposition stance to the two legislations, our interlocutor suggested that lobbying

---

[16] Bilateral cooperation on social issues is not the monopoly of Sweden. French and German governments in particular have been cooperating with Chinese public authorities at national and local levels, in the topic of the redesign of pension systems in Beijing, Shanghai, while the EU has more recently been involved in helping China manage the transferability of pension rights between provinces.

activities were left to HK business and political organizations, seen as more powerfully influential with mainland public authorities. Similarly, the British Business Chamber in Guangdong, which has the particularity of also representing non-UK members (particularly from HK) and of being quite distant from the EU Chamber (as shown by its website), was largely mute on the issue, which leads us to suggest that it was largely relying on powerful HK businesses to curb the provisions of the law.

14.3.3 East Asian Business Pressure Against Pro-Labor Regulation

As previously mentioned, Hong Kong exerts particular economic influence in Guangdong Province that is further reinforced by the political channels that it enjoys in Mainland China and by the geographical, cultural, and linguistic proximity of the two regions. The relevance of the lobbying actions and arguments of HK business organizations, contrasting with U.S., EU or other Asian organizations, confirms the very singular position and influence of HK business.

The Hong Kong Coalition Against Collective Bargaining Laws

HK businesses expressed a massive opposition to collective bargaining legislations. It is above all related to the perceived economic threat represented by pro-labor legislation in terms of labor cost increases, because 80 % of the HK capital invested in Guangdong Province is concentrated in export-led manufactory industry and in the labor-intensive service industry. As consistently expressed by HK and UK business and think-tank representatives interviewed in HK, 20 % of HK industry may be forced to close, although this figure should be treated with caution, as a possible tactic to exert influence.[17]

Opposition to the laws can also be traced to the HK tradition of a "free-market economy" that makes HK employers strangers to collective bargaining and to the notion of employee participation (Hui and Chan 2012). This cultural factor should not be neglected and furthermore should be seen in a broader perspective in which HK is more generally seeking to influence Chinese business legislation.[18]

A careful analysis of the lobbying operations of the four largest HK business associations shows that opposition extends beyond the question of labor costs to include precise considerations of industrial relations. Through two position papers, the Hong Kong General Chamber of Commerce (HKGCC) that represents 4,000 corporate members, most in the service industry, openly opposes the position of worker-directors who would be involved in the supervising companies and

---

[17] It is estimated that 10 % of the 60,000–70,000 Hong Kong-run factories in the Pearl River Delta have closed their plants in 2008 due to increased labor costs.

[18] The interview conducted with one representative from the Bauhinia Foundation (an influential "free trade" HK think-tank) revealed the attempt of HK for exporting its commercial law inherited from the commonwealth law (arbitration process, commercial dispute, etc.) in a Mainland China more attracted by the "Continental Law".

decision-making. Their primary concern is with preserving confidential businesses information, but they also insist that these laws "will not only deepen labor-management conflict, but also create difficult business environment for enterprises and obstruct their development; in the long run, it will also affect the country's economic development and peoples' living standard" (Hui and Chan 2012). In its position paper, the Federation of Hong Kong Industries (FHKI), which has about 3,000 members, most involved in manufacturing, underscores the risks posed by the two laws to "industrial harmony," which would give rise to labor-management conflicts, and to the danger that it "might even lead to a return to the situation of everybody eating from the same 'big pot of rice' as in the state-socialist period" (Hui and Chan 2012). Because of their obvious free-market orientation, they furthermore argue that wages should be determined by the market rather than through collective bargaining (Hui and Chan 2012).

The Chinese General Chamber of Commerce (CGCC) is also explicitly opposed to the legislation, pointing out the risk that collective bargaining could be engaged in a company at the request of only one-third of its employees (Hui and Chan 2012). The CGCC suggests that the laws should limit "the frequency of collective bargaining that employees can initiate and to raise the quorum to 50 %". It therefore suggests that workers only be represented by state-recognized trade unions during collective bargaining, which means the ACFTU and its affiliates.

As pointed out by Hui and Chan (2012), the Chinese Manufacturers' Associations of Hong Kong (CMA) website does not show a position paper on the two laws, but the organization was highly active in organizing seminars on collective bargaining among its members and was involved in numerous joint actions with the other three chambers.

By contrast with their Western counter-parts, HK business associations displayed much clearer-cut criticisms and proposals on the subject of the two labor laws. They also showed far more active and multi-directional lobbying strategies that targeted Hong Kong, Guangdong, and the Central government. At the level of Hong Kong, in order to first strengthen the legitimacy of their opposition and solicit the support of their members, the four chambers had held joint consultations to assess the reactions of businesses to the two laws (Hui and Chan 2012). Second, the chambers released their own position papers as well as a joint position paper, which was submitted to the Hong Kong and Guangdong governments. The FHKI representative revealed that after taking their comments into consideration, Hong Kong government submitted its own position paper to the Ministry of Commerce in China that broadly reflected the interests of Hong Kong businesses (Hui and Chan 2012). Third, the chambers appealed to key Hong Kong politicians with symbolic, if not important, positions in the Chinese government to influence the Guangdong and central governments (Hui and Chan 2012).

The survey also yielded information about additional tools used by the chambers to support their lobbying efforts with the Guangdong government. One issue that interviewees revealed was the expected negative economic impact of the laws for the Province, which would lead to large-scale withdrawal of investment and business closures, which in the end would weaken the region's competitiveness

(Hui and Chan 2012). This argument is convincing if one considers that the independent fiscal status of local government reinforces their reliance on investors and economic growth for accessing fiscal resources. Other tools deployed by the four largest chambers included, as quoted by Hui and Chan (2012): (1) the Hong Kong Business Community Joint Conference (consisting of over 40 business associations) and its published petition in two Hong Kong newspapers on September 16, 2010; (2) the submission of lobbying letters by Hong Kong politicians to the Mayor of Guangdong Province, the Secretary of the Guangdong Committee of the Communist Party of China, and the Legality Committee of the Guangdong Provincial People's Congress; (3) the attempt of the four chambers to lobby the provincial government face-to-face, meeting officials from the Ministry of the Human Resources and the Social Security of Guangdong Province, for example. The interviewee from the HKGCC stated that in some instances, officials from the Guangdong government travelled to Hong Kong to hold discussions with its members; (4) direct lobbying of the Central government by delegations of HK business chambers sent to Beijing, with the political channel of HK legislative councillors complementing this strategy.

Highlighting the successful lobbying of the Hong Kong business, interviewees' comments are consistent in reporting that the proposed legislations have been postponed, perhaps only temporarily due to the objections of business organizations, their political alliances, and coalitions with other influential East-Asian Business Organizations.

Ambivalent Pressure from Taiwan and Japan

Representing a far smaller proportion of foreign business than their HK counterpart, Japanese and Taiwanese businesses (respectively 2.5 % and 1.2 % of total FDI for the region) have, however, played a significant role in the success of the Guangdong economy since the beginning. Unsurprisingly, they have ardently defended their own interests in the Guangdong Province and have exploited local connections to lobby local authorities. Because they are primarily specialized in the production of electronic components and low-end products, they have not completely shared the viewpoints of the coalition of HK businesses, however.

Japanese businesses have consistently opposed collective bargaining laws, as expressed to us by the representative from the Japanese government-supported External Trade Organization in Hong Kong (Hui and Chan 2012). Opposition to the legislation is first related to the risk of increases in labor costs and labor disputes, against the backdrop of the Honda strike that erupted in the province in 2010 and spread labor discontent. Japanese scepticism refers also to the power that the legislation will give to outsiders –hired trade union presidents and government officials with no knowledge of the companies involved— to influence the bargaining process (Hui and Chan 2012). The organization voiced its concern to the Guangdong provincial government through meeting and opinion paper. It has also exchanged information with the Hong Kong business associations on the issue but has not initiated joint lobbying efforts because of distinctive concerns over the legislations. While the HK associations oppose including worker representatives on boards of directors, the Japanese association is more concerned about the bargaining process, which it believes has not been clearly enough defined by the laws (Hui and Chan 2012).

In terms of Taiwan Business, it is worth noting that Taiwanese firms were unable to reach consensus over the laws, which were supported by larger firms while smaller ones were more sensitive to the risk of labor cost increases (Hui and Chan 2012). Local Taiwanese business associations, instead of being very powerful in economic terms in some localities, like in Dongguan, Guangzhou, and Shenzhen,[19] proved unable to convert their bargaining power and use their privileged access to political channels of influence to voice their concern. Some initiatives have been launched, however, as illustrated by the Taiwan Merchant Association Dongguan lobby, which meets with the government every month, and has regular contact with the Vice-Mayor regarding important matters (Hui and Chan 2012). In particular, it took advantage of the 3 month joint meeting held at the municipal level to discuss the Collective Consultation Ordinance and Democratic Management Regulation (Hui and Chan 2012). Despite this influence, our informants indicated[20] that the Taiwanese association has not being able to go farther than submitting a very general official position on the collective bargaining law, focusing instead on the major concern of Taiwanese enterprises during the global economic downturn, a reference to their transformation from export-oriented businesses to more domestically-oriented firms (Hui and Chan 2012).

14.4 Labor-Business-State Relationships and the Interplay of Domestic and Transnational Forces

The previous section was dedicated to an overall perspective on foreign business interests and strategies. This section proposes to broaden the discussion on the interactions between foreign and domestic actors that participate in the reshaping of labor-business-state relationships. We focus here on three principal issues that relate to the bargaining powers and strategies of labor, business and State: (1) the extent of overlap or opposition between domestic and foreign business interests; (2) the extent to which domestic labor forces can count on transnational labor or societal organizations such as international trade unions and NGOs to exert pressure on Business or State decisions; and (3) the extent to which the State mediates between the interests of antagonistic labor and business or domestic and foreign interests.

---

[19] Informants noted that Taiwanese investment altogether contributes over 51 % of GDP in Dongguan and 15 % of GDP in Guangzhou.

[20] Interviewees were representatives of the Shanghai and Guangzhou office of the Taiwan World Trade Center, a Taiwanese government-supported agency focusing on economic affairs in China, and the Taiwan Merchant Association Dongguan.

First, and as far as business is concerned, it is worth noting that domestic businesses have not been silent on the subject of the two laws and have often wielded considerable influence over local authorities' decisions. As was revealed by some of the scholars interviewed by Hui and Chan (2012), state-owned enterprises have been among the strongest opposing voices within the party-state. Two different channels were used to voice their concerns: (1) the official channel of the State-owned Assets Supervision and Administration Commission of the State Council (SASAC), which supervises and manages state-owned enterprises on behalf of the state (Hui and Chan 2012); and (2) informal relationships between SOE managers and local and central public officials. Echoing Zhu and Warner's (2004) assertion that "due to the political system in China, internal pressure is rather cautious, even surreptitious, compared with external pressure that is more open and direct." (p. 6). Domestic private business voiced its reservations far more informally. Compensating for its lack of access to official political channels or representation, domestic private business has instead used its client-patron relationships with local officials. More interesting in terms of this study, they have also relied on foreign business, particularly East-Asian firms, as relays for expressing a shared interest in protecting low value-added activities. This foreign-domestic alliance is particularly significant for Hong Kong and Guangdong local businesses due to powerful, intricate webs of economic and cultural relationships. Finally, in consideration of the role of foreign forces in the episode of the successful postponement of the idea of direct foreign influence should be considered with caution. Our research supports the assumption that these changes were not driven by foreign forces, but that they can, however, provide significant leverage for domestic interests.

If business forces do not represent a single block but a more variegated group of distinctive interests, the same can be said of public authorities in China, as illuminated by the distinctive views of the Guangdong government on one side and of the Party-State and Central government on the other. While the Party-State decided to push both laws back into discussion in 2010 in a bid to address the new wave of labor protests that sparked by the Honda workers' strike, Guangdong Province ultimately opted to postpone the legislative process on collective bargaining, under strong pressure from business in the midst of the global financial crisis. However, as the wave of strikes began to fade in late 2010 and the economic downturn deepened, central and local governments converged in considering the negative socio-political impact of the Collective bargaining laws stronger than its positive effects (Hui and Chan 2012). Finally, implementation of both laws has been halted in the face of a convergence of interest among foreign and local capital, the local government, and the party-state (Hui and Chan 2012).

As pointed out earlier, labor forces have also not been made their presence felt. Labor protests were decisive in persuading public authorities at the Central level to introduce plant-level collective bargaining mechanisms in many Chinese provinces. In Guangdong Province, the bargaining power of labor was fuelled by the process of economic growth. Transnational productive networks, just-in-time production, and skilled employees have together made businesses more vulnerable to unstable labor-management relationships and to the threat of labor unrest. The looming risk of labor shortages also played in favor of the increasing power of labor. This rebalancing should not be overestimated, however, if we keep in mind the short-term effects of the economic downturn on job destruction, the highly gradual process of economic upgrading, and, more importantly, the endogenous limits of the labor force in terms of its ability to organize, represent workers, and defend their interests. On that domestic concern, it is worth noting the ambivalent role of the Party-State strategy, which promotes on the one hand collective bargaining and cautiously paves the way for direct employee representation, while on the other hand maintaining the All China Federation of Trade Unions (ACFTU) as the only channel for expressing labor concerns.

Labor forces could hardly place all of their hopes on the ACFTU, which is under the supervision of the Party-State, while at the plant level it is typically controlled by management.[21] To consolidate its power, the labor camp would have then to prove itself capable of building reliable internal alliances in civil society through NGOs or academic labor specialists, as well as external alliances with foreign labor representatives and organizations. This double leverage remains to be created, however, in view of the relative lack of feedback pro-labor forces to the two laws, both by the labor NGO, whose reaction was far more limited in scale than for the Labor Contract Law, and by Western and especially European pro-labor forces. Because transnational labor solidarity within multinationals is still in its infancy, especially in terms of integrating the interests of the workers working at the far end of the global productive chains into a Western-style trade union agenda and because international political pressure appears to have little influence in encouraging upgrades in China's labor standards, one could speculate that labor improvements will largely depend on internal forces. More precisely, it will depend on labor's domestic capacity to pressure public authorities to better mediate their interests in the face of overall business forces. If the two collective bargaining laws are ultimately enacted, they will undoubtedly offer new opportunities for the labor camp to gradually dismantle the official trade union's monopoly, with unpredictable effects on the political arena. For the time being, the resolution of several labor disputes highlights a new focus on the issue of collective bargaining after the protests. There is also an impressive "*bricolage*" under way, against the background of a lack of legislation that could establish a system of peaceful conflict resolution at firm level. This was exemplified in late 2011 by the introduction of a face-to-face mechanism for management-labor negotiations at the Citizen Watch factory in Shenzhen and a tripartite talk involving employees, employers, and local government officials by the Tesco supermarket in the Zhejiang city of Jinhua (Guangdong Province).[22]

---

[21] For discussions of the identity of Chinese trade unions, see in particular Feng (2003), Taylor and Liqi (2007).

[22] See, China Labor Bulletin, "The development of collective bargaining in China – two case studies", 26 January 2012, http://www.clb.org.hk/en/node/101233.

Conclusion

Widening our perspective to a comparative analysis of "transnational capitalism," the study offers clear justification for distinguishing Guangdong Province as a separate case from the South American or Eastern European ones, which have been depicted as "peripheral" or "dependant capitalism" (King 2007; Nölke and Vliegenthart 2009). Differences between the Chinese type and others do not rely as much on quantitative terms (as the FDI/GDP or the Export/GDP ratios) or the qualitatively high level of interconnection within global production chains. Instead, differences are more related to the role of public authorities in arbitrating labor and business interests as well as foreign and domestic business concerns. There is no question that Chinese public authorities are far more active in controlling labor and business actors and in filtering and mediating their respective claims and pressures. The discovery through the interviews that foreign businesses in Guangdong Province organized themselves early on into Foreign Chambers of Commerce or Business Associations to voice their interests to face powerful domestic authorities is consistent with the specific state-led feature. This contrasts with Central and Eastern Europe, where foreign businesses have gained individually greater bargaining power with respect to local authorities and more extensive political channels, primarily through the EU, to influence the alteration of host countries' institutions in a way favorable to multinational activities (Contrepois et al. 2011). It can further be speculated that "state-led decentralized transnational capitalism" that describes the Guangdong Area will continue to diverge in the following years from the European "market-led dependant transnational capitalisms," as a double consequence of the Chinese economic dynamism and upgrading and of Central and Eastern European difficulties in coping with external shocks they are highly exposed.

Analytically speaking, this comparative ambition will benefit from combining the Comparative Political Economy with the Institutionalist Transnational Approach, as advocated by Nölke (2011). It will allow to precise the distinctive modalities of articulation between national and transnational forces but also to better capture the endogenous dimension of the domestic institutional changes in transnational capitalisms. It will then transcend some of the weaknesses of the Variety of Capitalism or Public Choice approaches, which focus on formal political institutions or election rules as the main vehicle of institutional changes.

References

Almond (2011) Multinationals strategies and labor regulations: Europe and Asian perspectives. Hong Kong Baptist University. Mimeo, Hong-Kong, 14–15 June

Almond P, Ferner A (eds) (2006) American multinationals in Europe. Oxford University Press, Oxford

Bohle D, Greskovits B (2009) Varieties of capitalism and capitalism "tout court". Arch Eur Sociol 50(3):355–386

Chan A (2001) Workers under assault: the exploitation of labor in a globalizing economy. M. E. Sharpe, New York

Chan CK (2009) Strikes and changing workplace relations in a Chinese global factory. Ind Relations J 40(1):60–77

Chan CK (2012) Class or citizenship? Debating workplace conflict in China. J Contemp Asia 42(2):308–327

Collings D (2008) Multinational corporations and industrial relations research: a road less travelled. Int J Manage Rev 10(2):173–193

Contrepois S, Delteil V, Dieuaide P, Jefferys S (eds) (2011) Globalising employment relations. Palgrave Macmillan, London

Feng C (2003) Between the state and labor: the conflict of Chinese trade unions' double identity in market reform. China Q 176:1006–1028

Gallagher ME (2005) Contagious capitalism China Quarterly, globalization and the politics of labor in China. Princeton University Press, Princeton

Gallagher ME, Dong B (2011) Legislating harmony: labor law reform in contemporary China. In: Kurubill S, Gallagher ME, Lee CK (eds) From iron rice-bowl to informalization: markets, state and workers in a changing China. Cornell University Press, Ithaca/London, pp 36–60

Global Labor Strategies (2007) Undue influence: corporations gain ground in battle over China's new labor law—but human rights and labor advocates are pushing back, March. http://laborstrategies.blogs.com

Graz J-C, Nölke A (2008) Transnational private governance and its limits. Routledge, London

Guthrie D (1999) Dragon in a three-piece suit: the emergence of capitalism in China. Princeton University Press, Princeton

Guangdong Statistical Yearbook (2011) China Statistics Press

Hui E, Chan CK (2012) The role of foreign chambers of commerce and government agencies in shaping labour legislations in China: a case study on the Shenzhen collective consultation ordinance and the Guangdong regulations on democratic management of enterprises, FNV report. http://www.fnvmondiaal.nl/media/pdf/352260/1135148

Karindi L (2008) The making of China's new labor contract law. China Analysis 66, November. www.chinapolitik.de

King L (2007) Central European capitalism in comparative perspective. In: Hancké R, Thatcher M, Rhodes M (eds) Beyond varieties of capitalism: conflict, contradictions, and complementarities in the European economy. Oxford University Press, Oxford, pp 307–327

Kristensen P, Zeitlin J (2005) Local players in global games. Oxford University Press, Oxford

Meardi G, Marginson P, Fichter M, Frybes M, Stanojevic M, Toth A (2009) Varieties of multinationals: adapting employment practices in Central Eastern Europe. Ind Relations 48 (3):489–511

Morgan G (2009) Globalization, multinationals and institutional diversity. Econ Soc 38 (4):580–605

Nölke A (2011) Transnational economic order and national economic institutions – comparative capitalism meets international political economy. Max Plank working paper 11/3

Nölke A, Vliegenthart A (2009) Enlarging the varieties of capitalism: the emergence of dependent market economies in East Central Europe? World Polit 61(4):670–702

Sheng Y (2009) How globalized are the Chinese provinces?. EAI Background Brief no 423. http://www.eai.nus.edu.sg/BB423.pdf

Taylor B, Li q (2007) Is the ACFTU a union and does it matter? J Ind Relations 49:701–715

Tilly C (1995) Globalization threatens labor's rights. Int Lab Work Class Hist (47):1–23

Whitley R (2005) How national are business systems? The role of states and complementary institutions in standardizing systems of coordination and control at the national level. In: Morgan G, Whitley R, Moen E (eds) Changing capitalisms? Internationalisation, institutional change and systems of economic organization. Oxford University Press, New York, pp 190–231

Wilson S (2009) Remade in China: Foreign investors and institutional change in China. Oxford University Press, Oxford, p 290
Zhang H (1997) Will foreign capital swallow up China: where should national industry go? (Waizi Nengfou unbing Zhongguo: Minzuqiye ying xiang hechuqu). Qiye Guanli Chuban She, Beijing
Zhu Z (2007) Legislation to focus on social issues. China Daily (12 March 2007), online: China Daily. http://www.chinadaily.com.cn/china/2007-03/12/content_824812.htm
Zhu Y, Warner M (2004) Changing patterns of human resource management in contemporary China: WTO accession and enterprise responses. Ind Relations J 35(4):311–328

GPSR Compliance

The European Union's (EU) General Product Safety Regulation (GPSR) is a set of rules that requires consumer products to be safe and our obligations to ensure this.

If you have any concerns about our products, you can contact us on

ProductSafety@springernature.com

In case Publisher is established outside the EU, the EU authorized representative is:

Springer Nature Customer Service Center GmbH
Europaplatz 3
69115 Heidelberg, Germany

www.ingramcontent.com/pod-product-compliance
Ingram Content Group UK Ltd.
Pitfield, Milton Keynes, MK11 3LW, UK
UKHW022131220326
11407UKWH00003B/24